EST
2009

Neoclassical Tattoo Flash

Neoclassical Tattoo Flash

+ STIZZO +

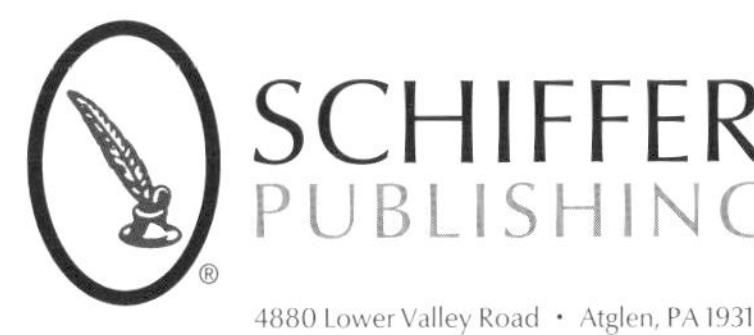

4880 Lower Valley Road • Atglen, PA 19310

Other Schiffer Books by the Author:

Italian Tattoo Flash: The Best of Times Collection, Stizzo, Max Brain & Silvio Pellico, ISBN 978-0-7643-4626-2

Other Schiffer Books on Related Subjects:

Classic Flash in Five Bold Colors, Jeromey "Tilt" McCulloch, ISBN 978-0-7643-3165-7

The New Old School: Exploring the Modern Renaissance of Old School & Neo-Traditional Tattooing, Jakob Schultz, Photography by Peter Booker Nielsen, ISBN 978-0-7643-4936-2

The Cut-Ups: Tattoo Flash from the Third Mind, Brian Kelly, ISBN 978-0-7643-6285-9

Library of Congress Control Number: 2021942410

Designed by Christopher Bower
Cover design by Justin Watkinson
Type set in CornerStoreJF/Myriad Pro

ISBN: 978-0-7643-6397-9
Printed in India

Published by Schiffer Publishing, Ltd.
4880 Lower Valley Road
Atglen, PA 19310
Phone: (610) 593-1777; Fax: (610) 593-2002
Email: Info@schifferbooks.com
Web: www.schifferbooks.com

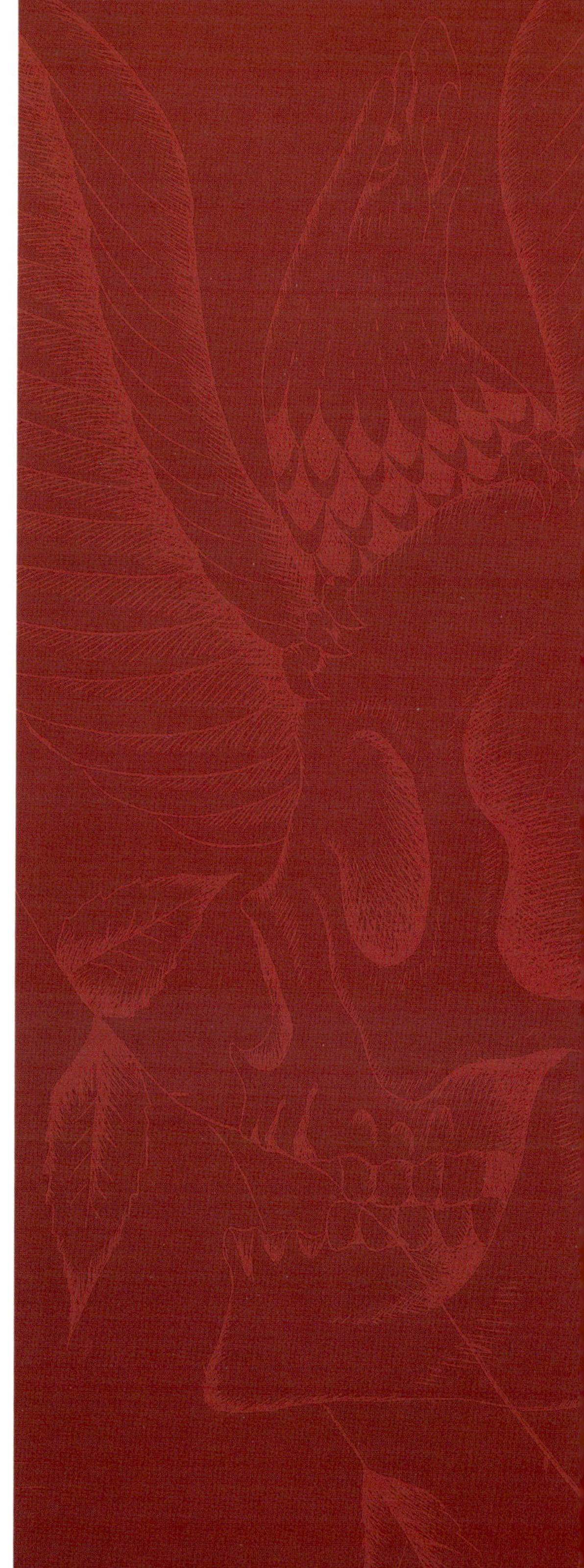

Foreword

All through the years, I've revolutionized and reinvented my work many times because of a constant and incessant dissatisfaction I carry with me, but which I'm grateful for.

Even from a single figure or illustration, it is possible to draw inspiration and implement a reinterpretation—for instance, getting closer to Italian art history, which is completely separate from tattoo art.

To see a sculpture or a painting and immediately imagine how to reinterpret it on paper, respecting the traditional tattoo's criteria: this is what I do, and what I'd like to share with you.

Also, I hope you can realize how important it is to preserve the handicraft of real drawing on paper and to perpetuate the poetry of graphite that lightly touches the paper, or of the brush immersed in colors.

Studying the subject, the shading technique, and, finally, the sense of color, which primarily highlights a tattoo artist's personality, is essential to me.

The experience that tattoo artists of the past left us is a treasure to be fully taken advantage of.

This book is a collection of the best flash I have made over the last few years, selected by me according to my personal taste.

As you will discover, the subjects are very often interpreted in different ways: bold or fine lines or a combination of both, water or dry-brush shading, and some with lettering. After all, it depends on my mood and inspiration in conjunction with each drawing.

There is no minimum amount of time to dedicate to drawing during the year, but there is infinite fun and poetry. That's the way it is to me, at least.

—Stizzo

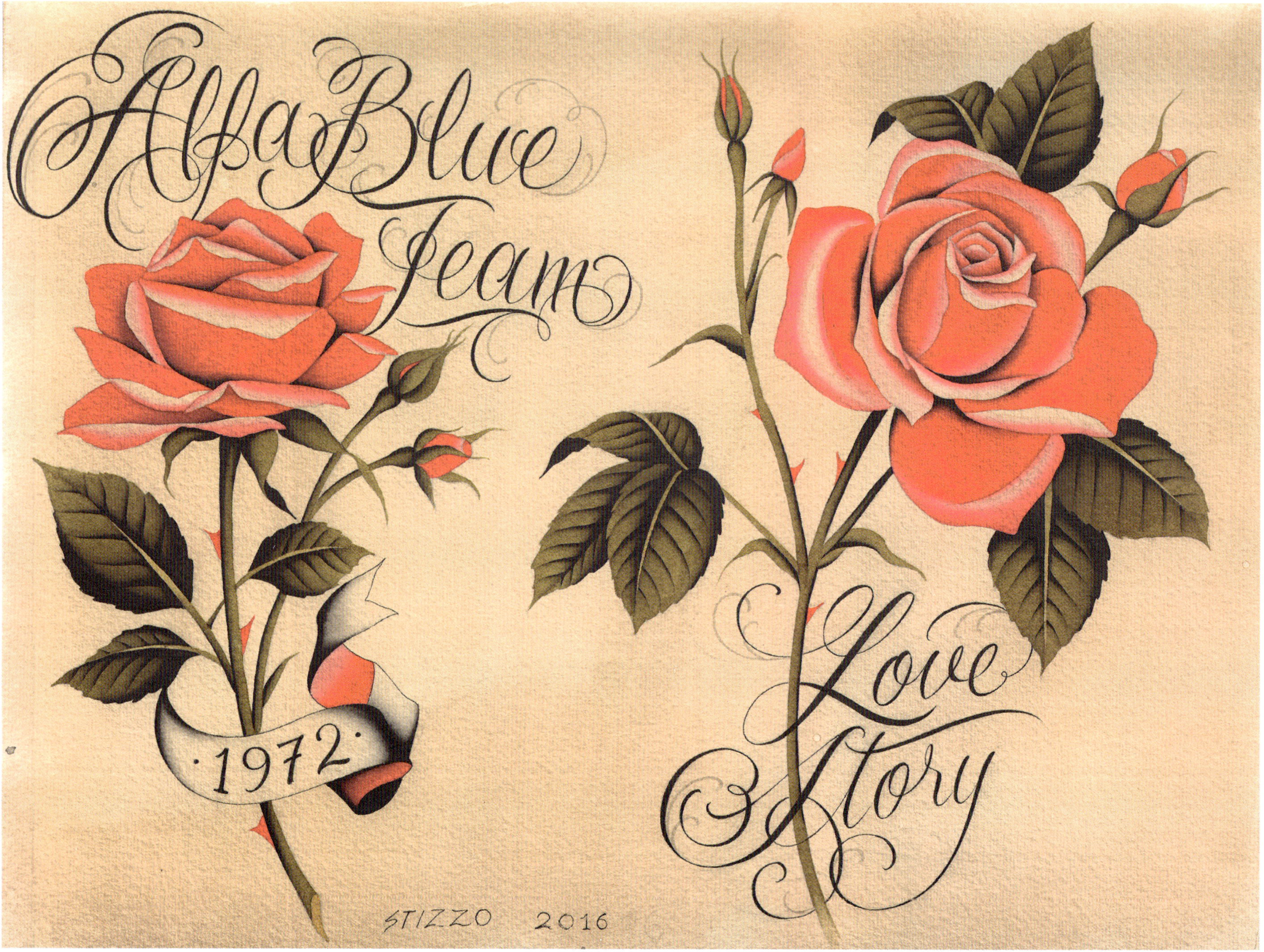

Alfa Blue Team

1972

Love Story

STIZZO 2016

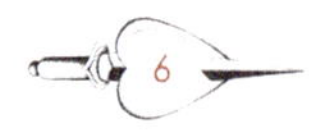

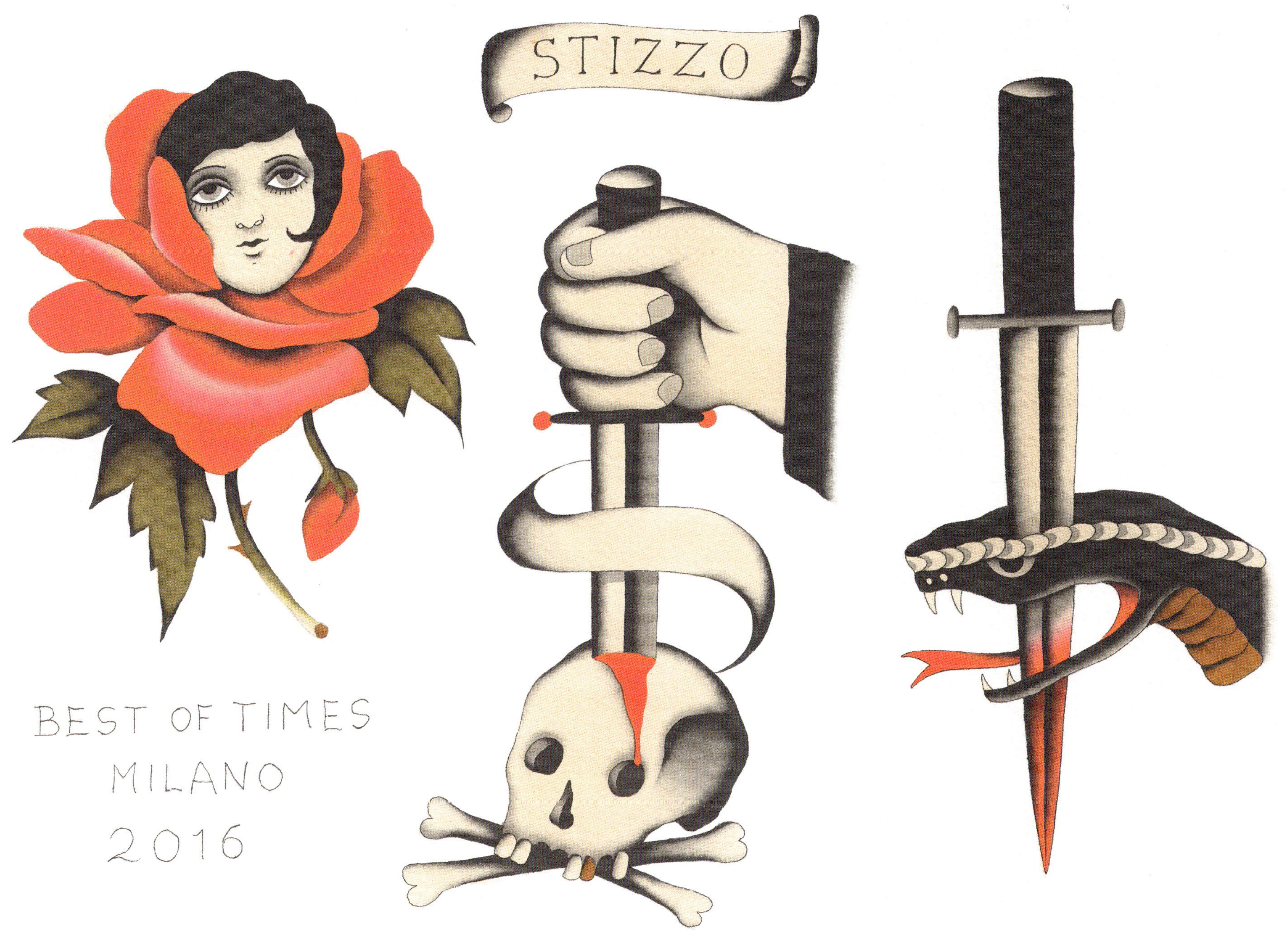
STIZZO
BEST OF TIMES
MILANO
2016

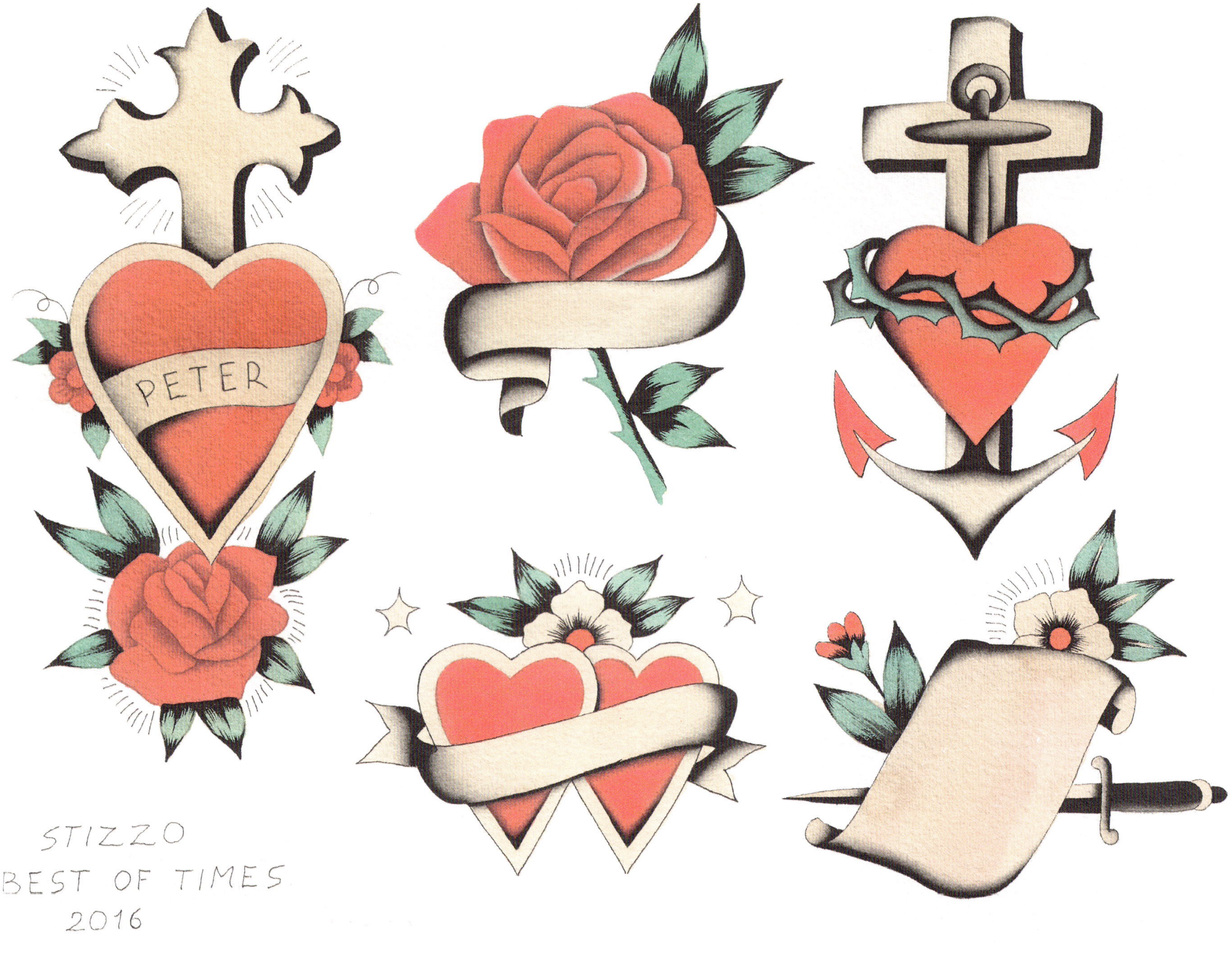

PETER

STIZZO
BEST OF TIMES
2016

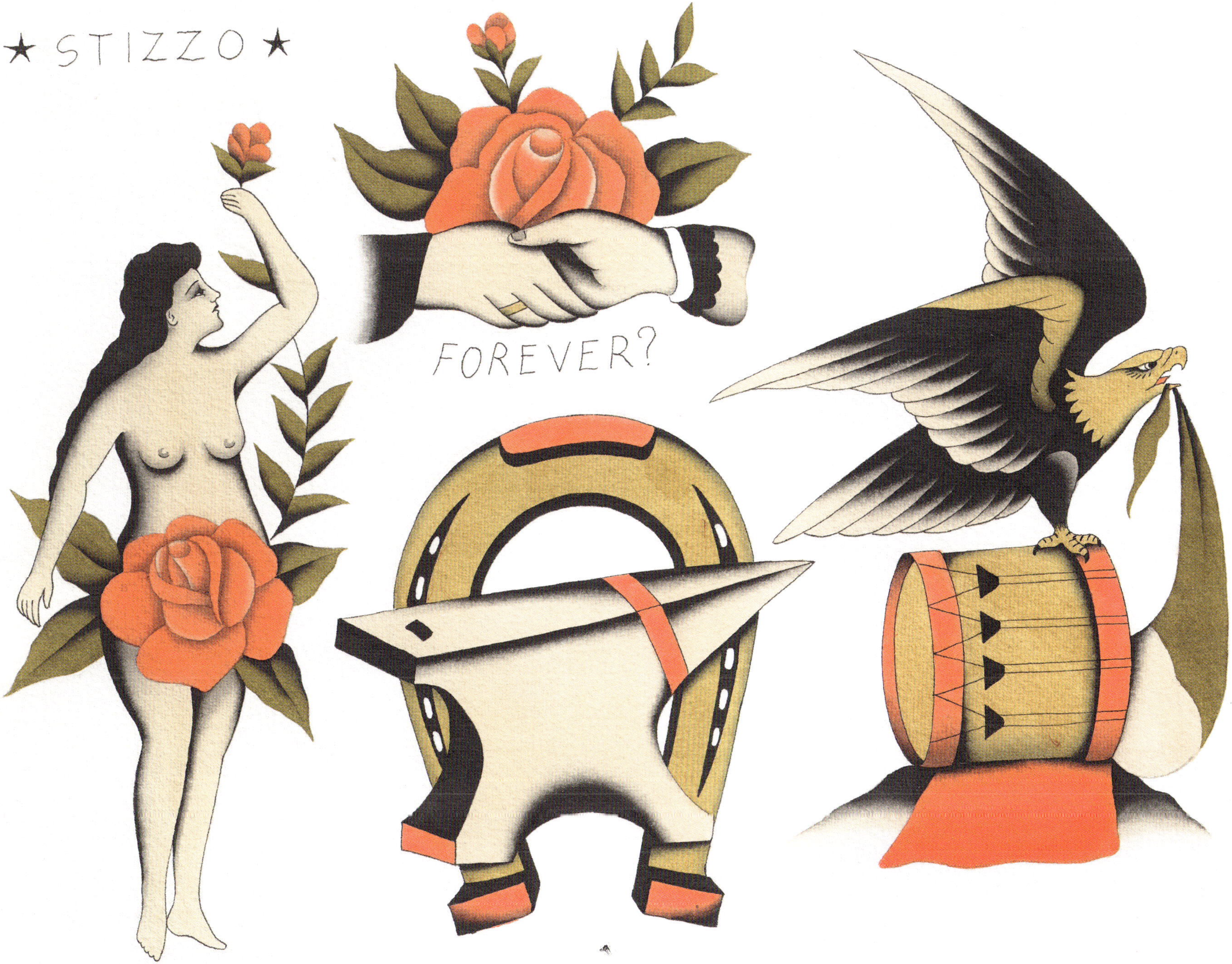

★ STIZZO ★

FOREVER?

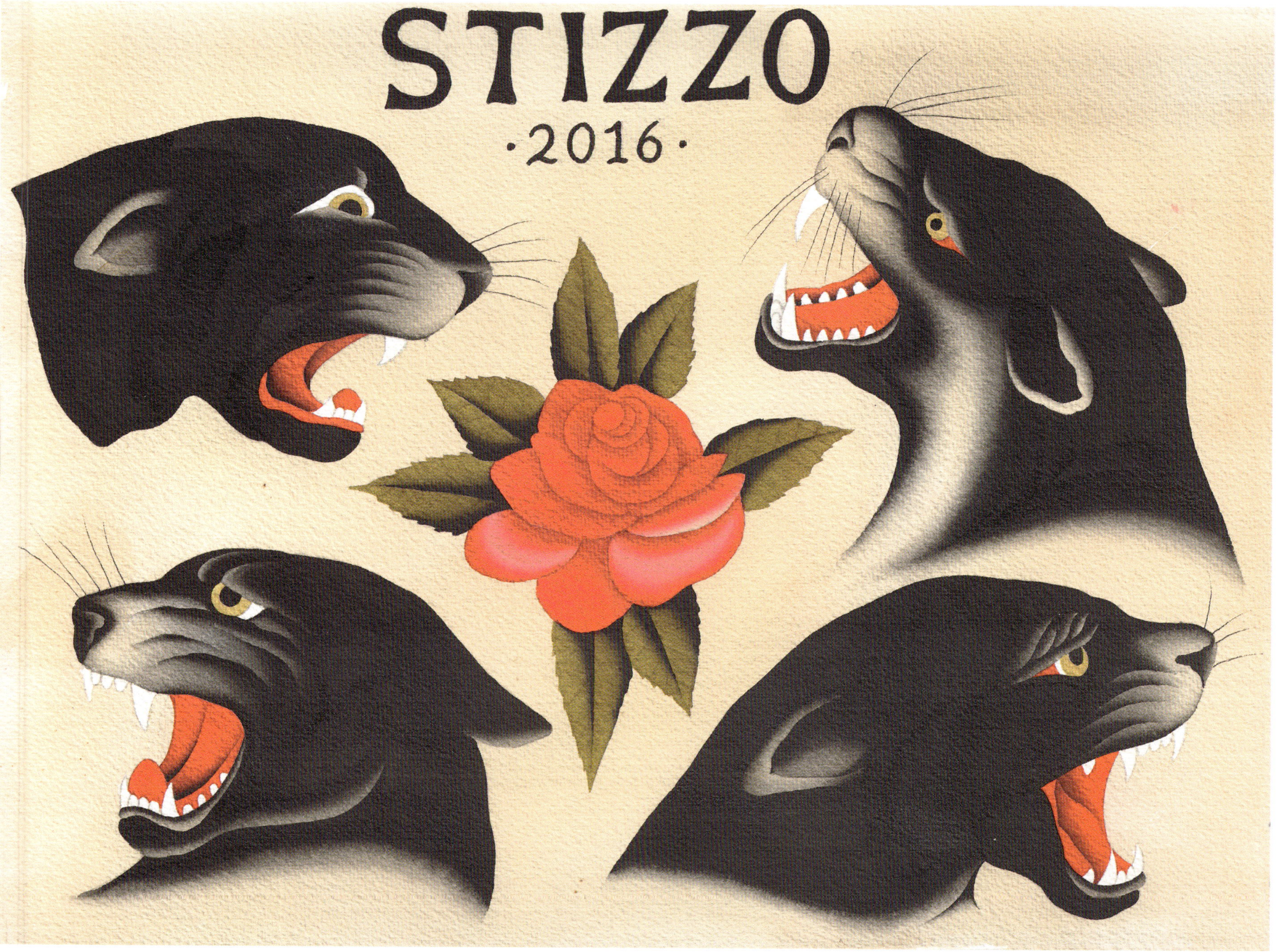

STIZZO

·2016·

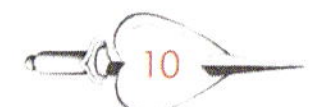

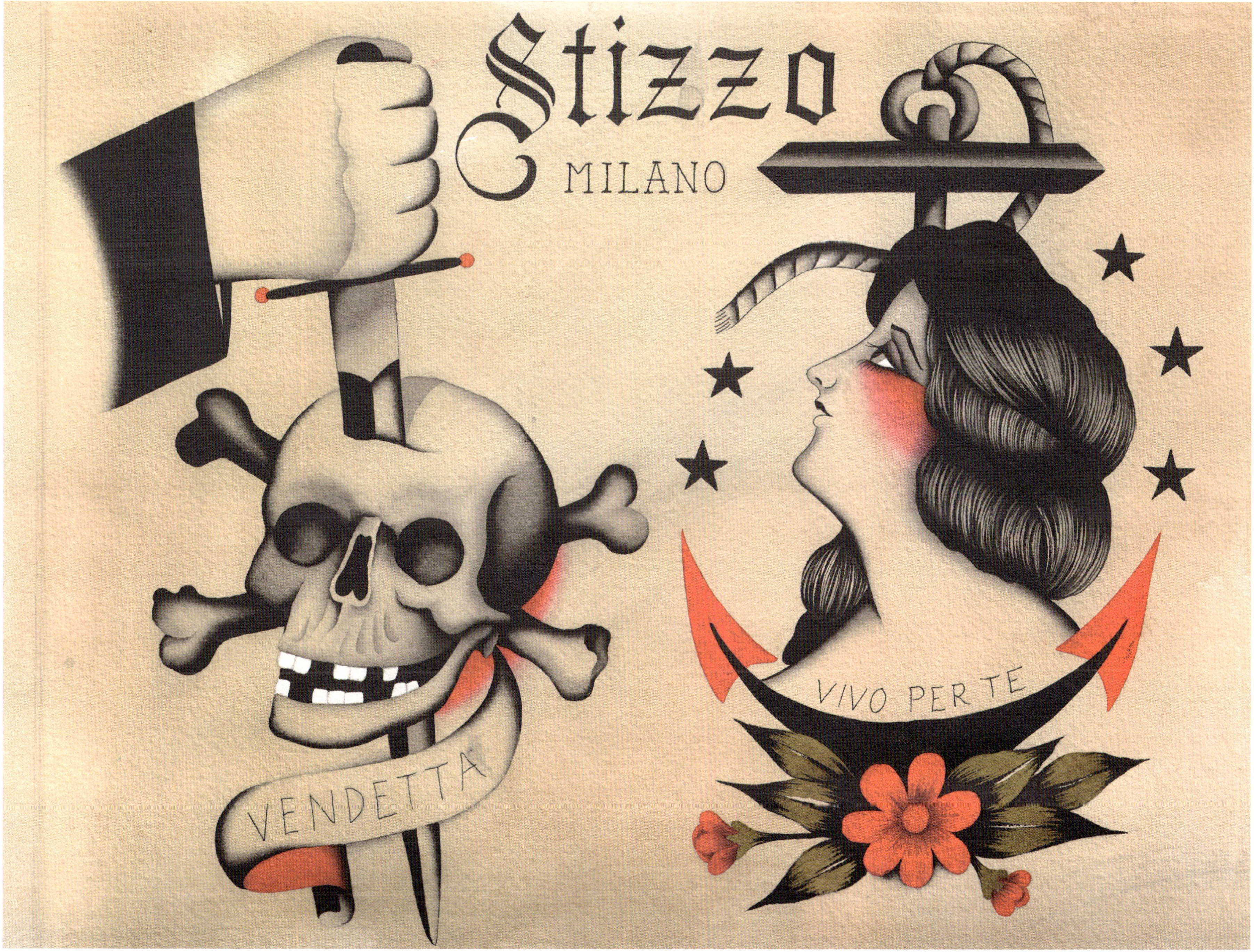

Stizzo

MILANO

VIVO PER TE

VENDETTA

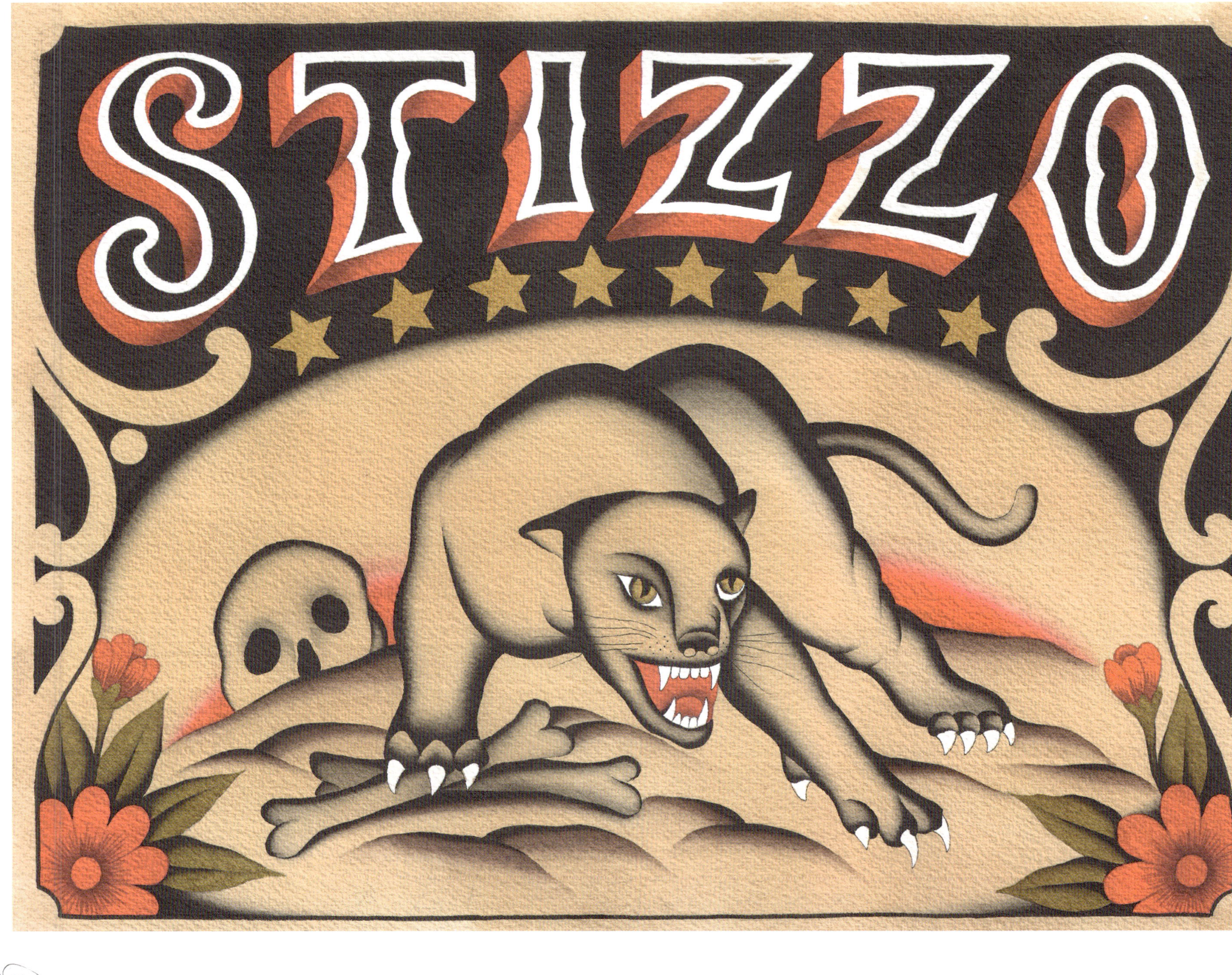

STIZZO

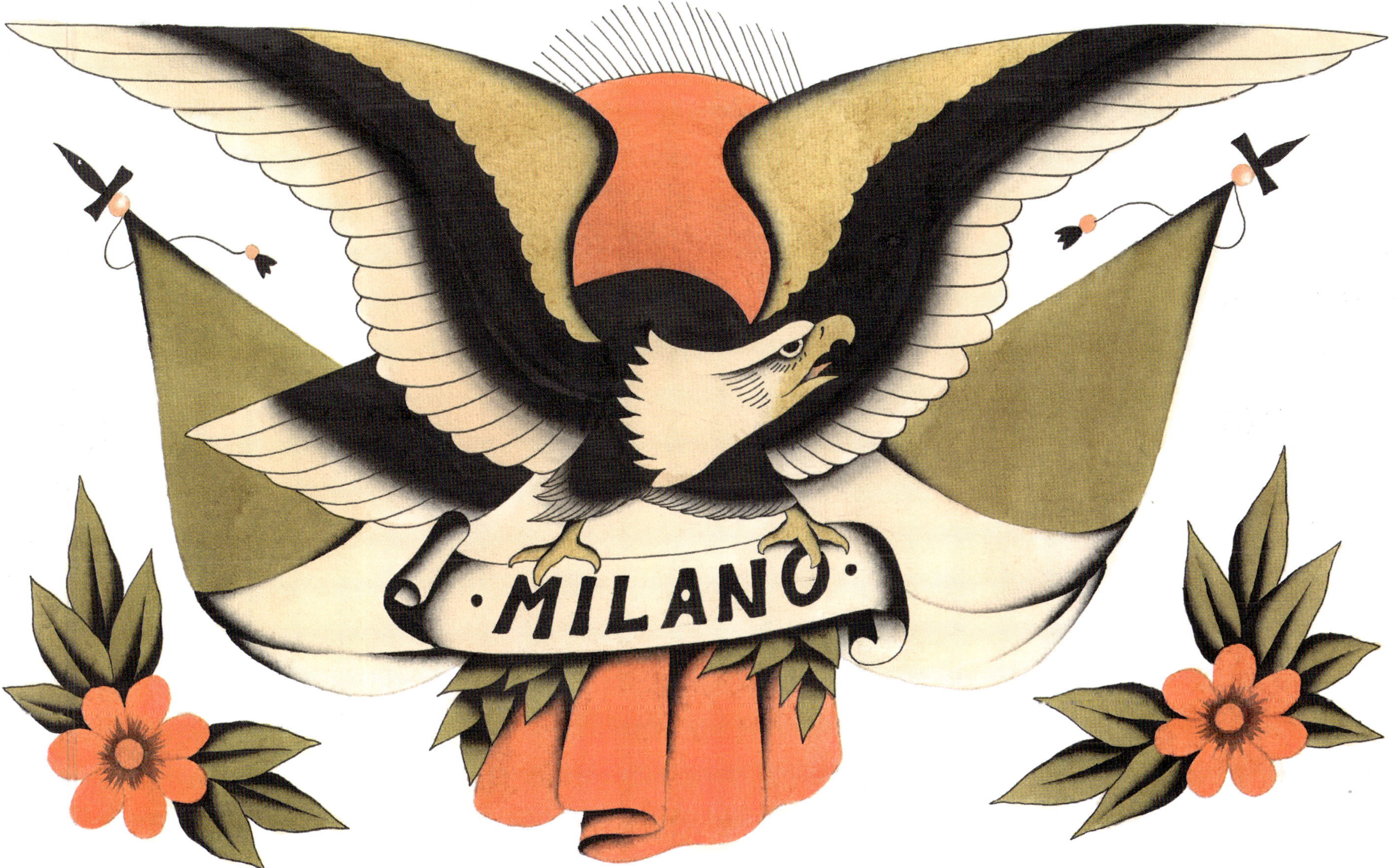
STIZZO
MILANO

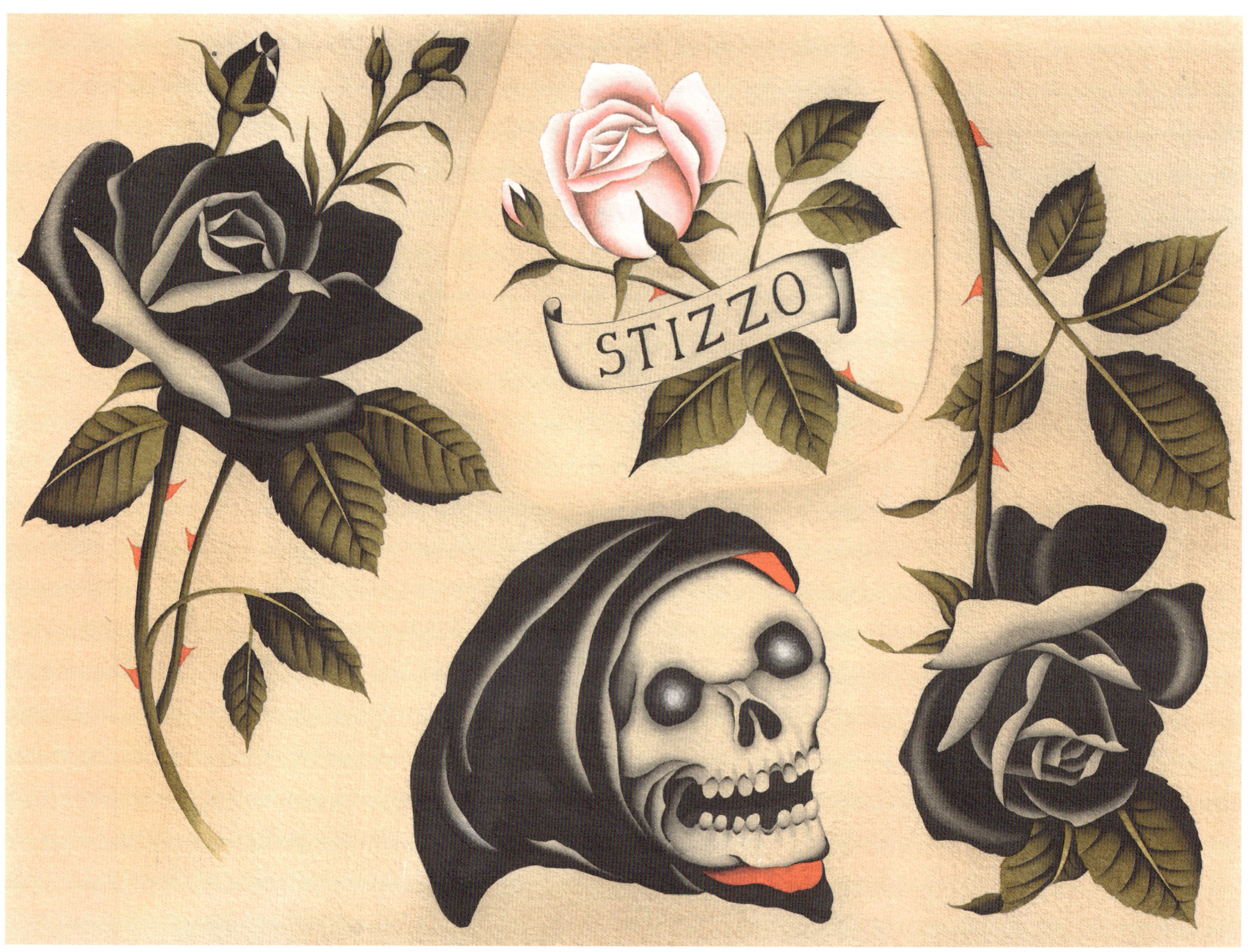
STIZZO

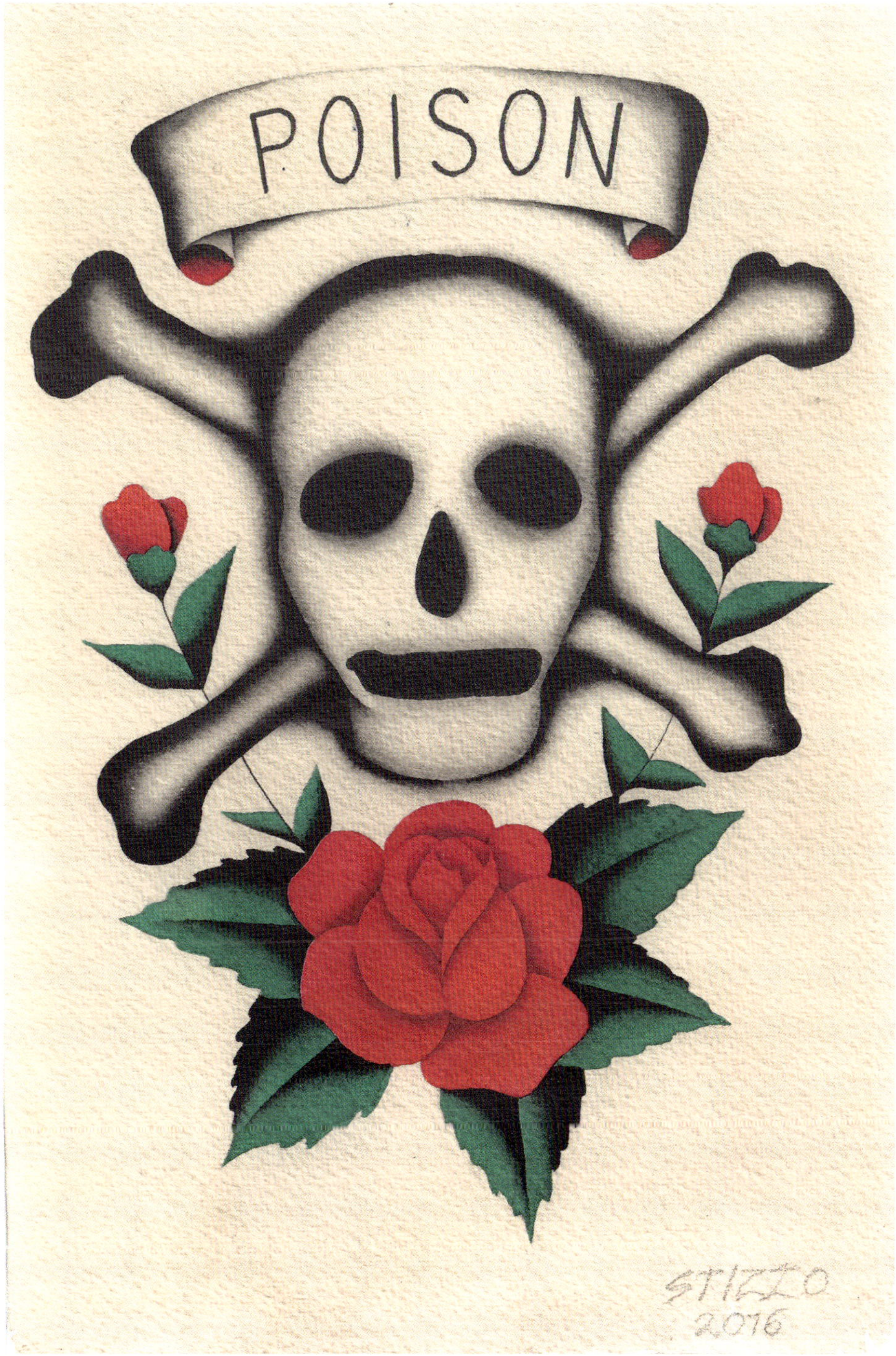

POISON
STIZZO
2016

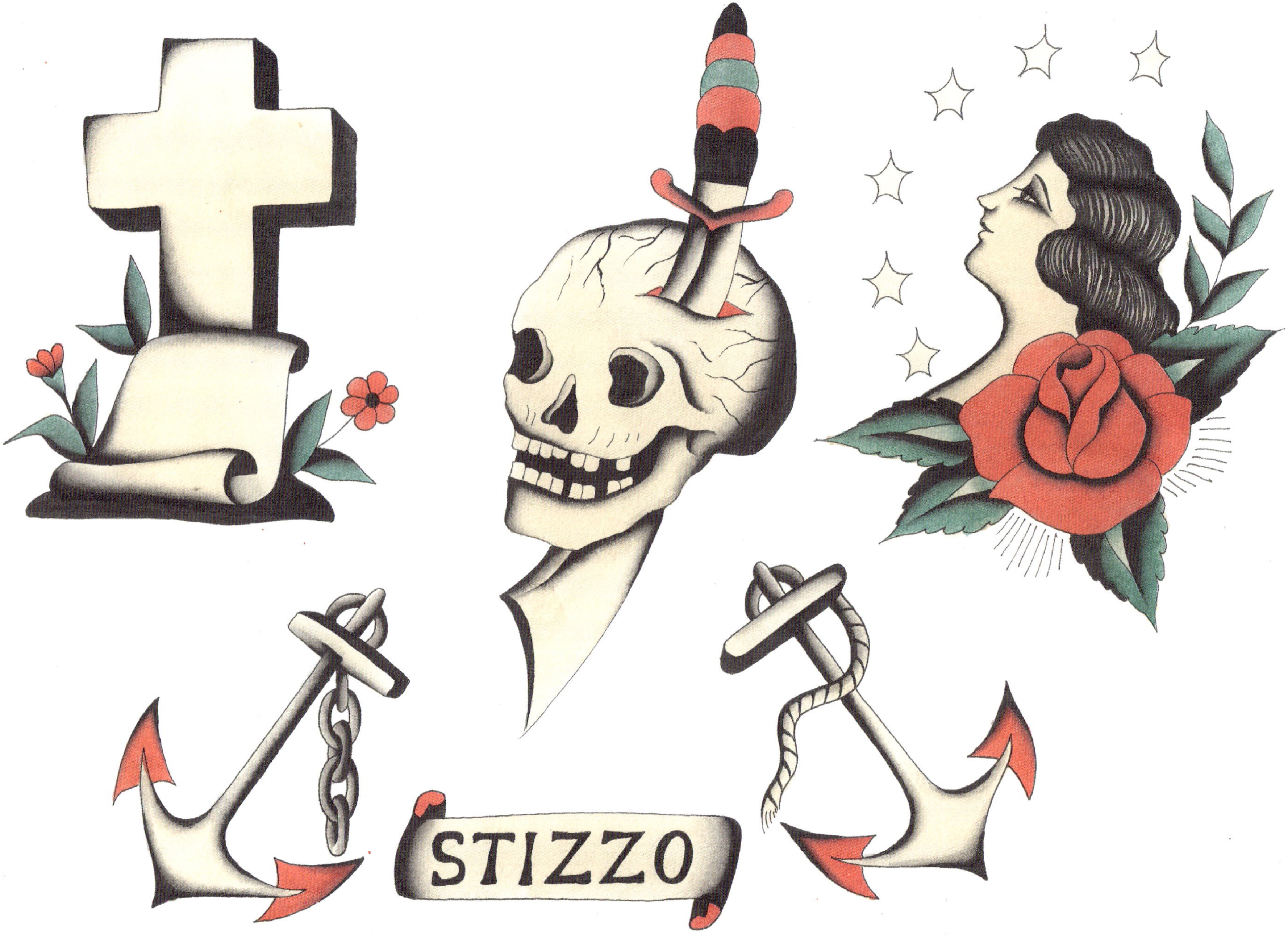

STIZZO

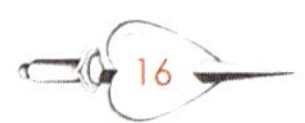

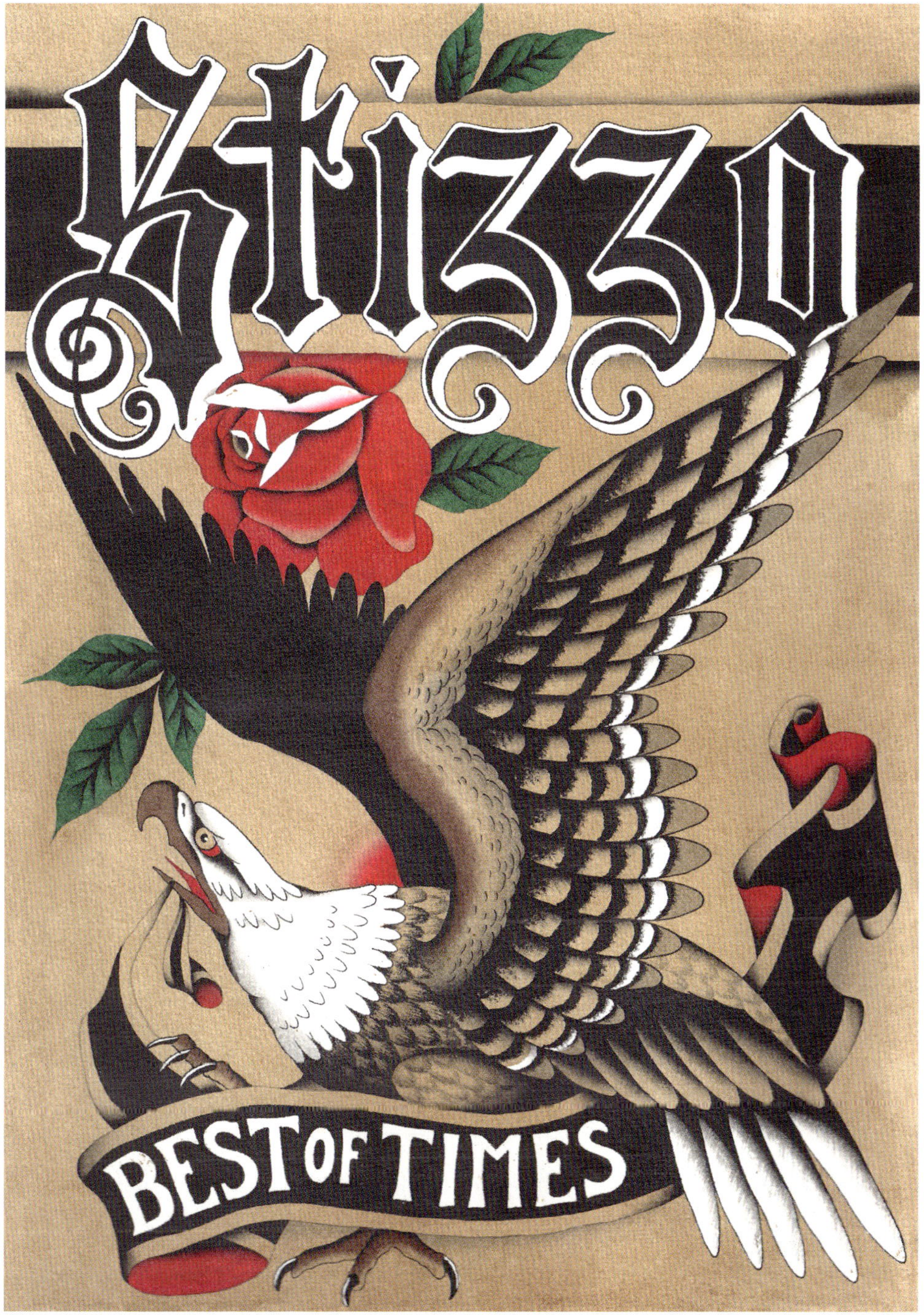

Stizzo

BEST OF TIMES

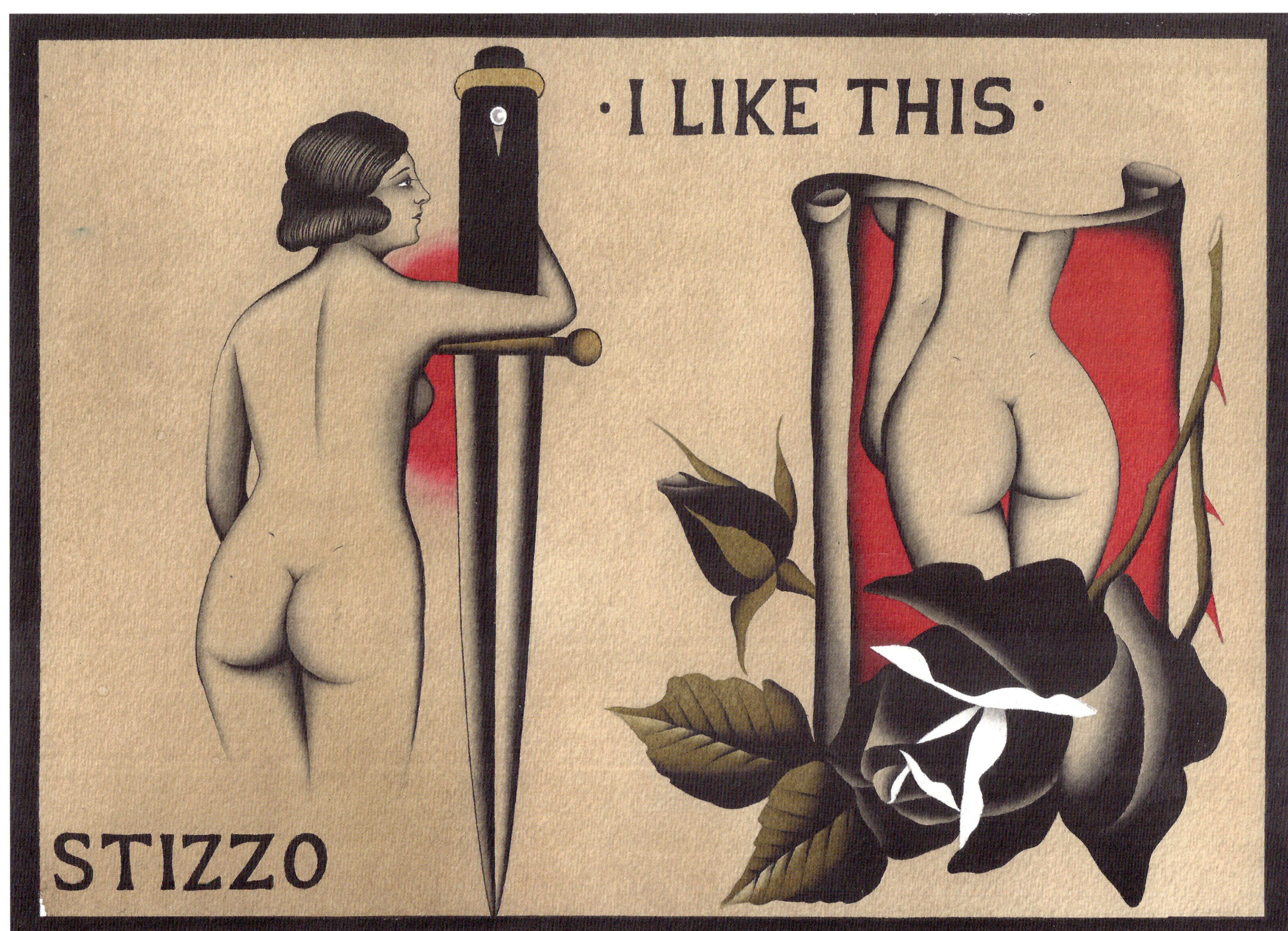
·I LIKE THIS·
STIZZO

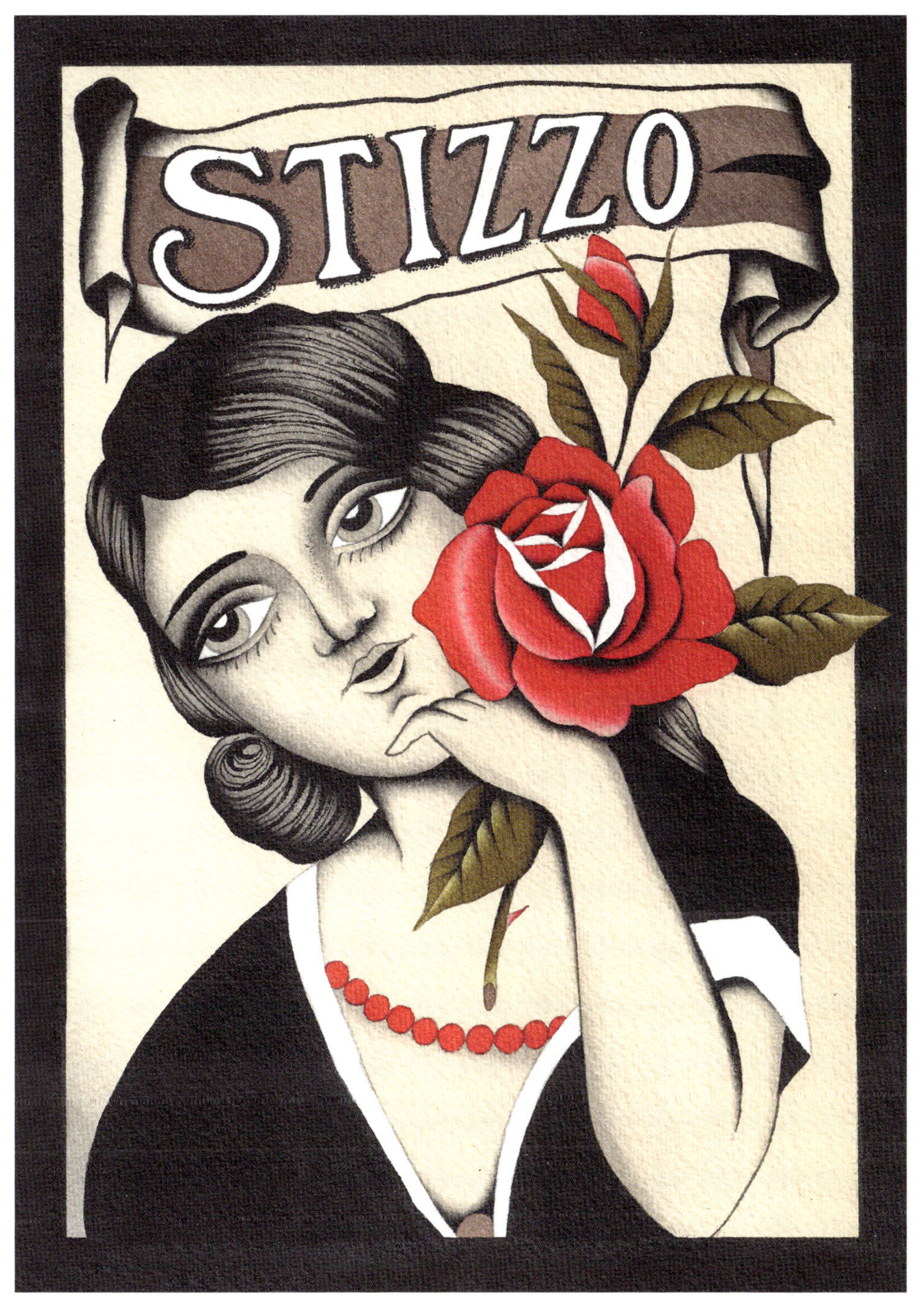
STIZZO

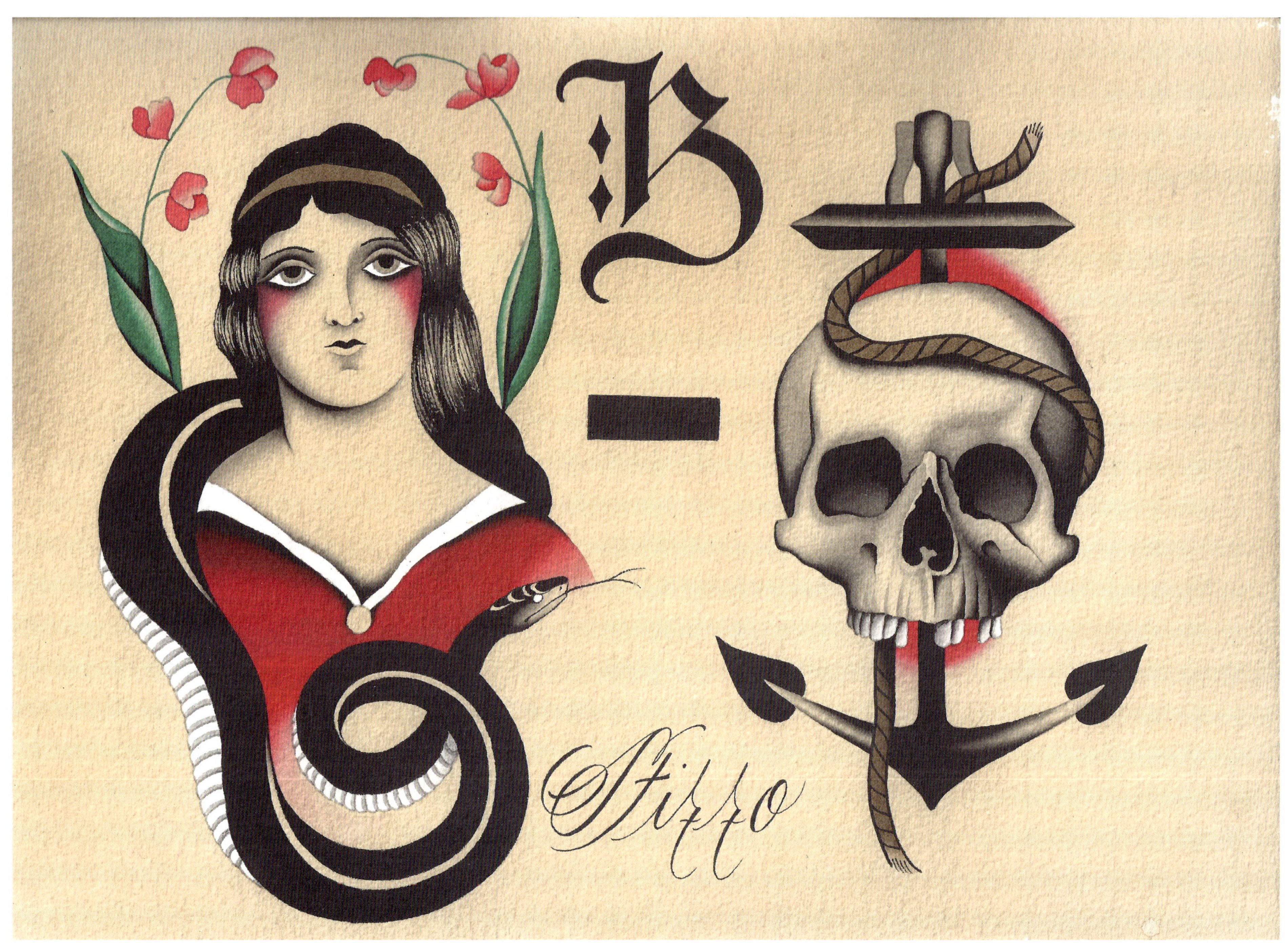

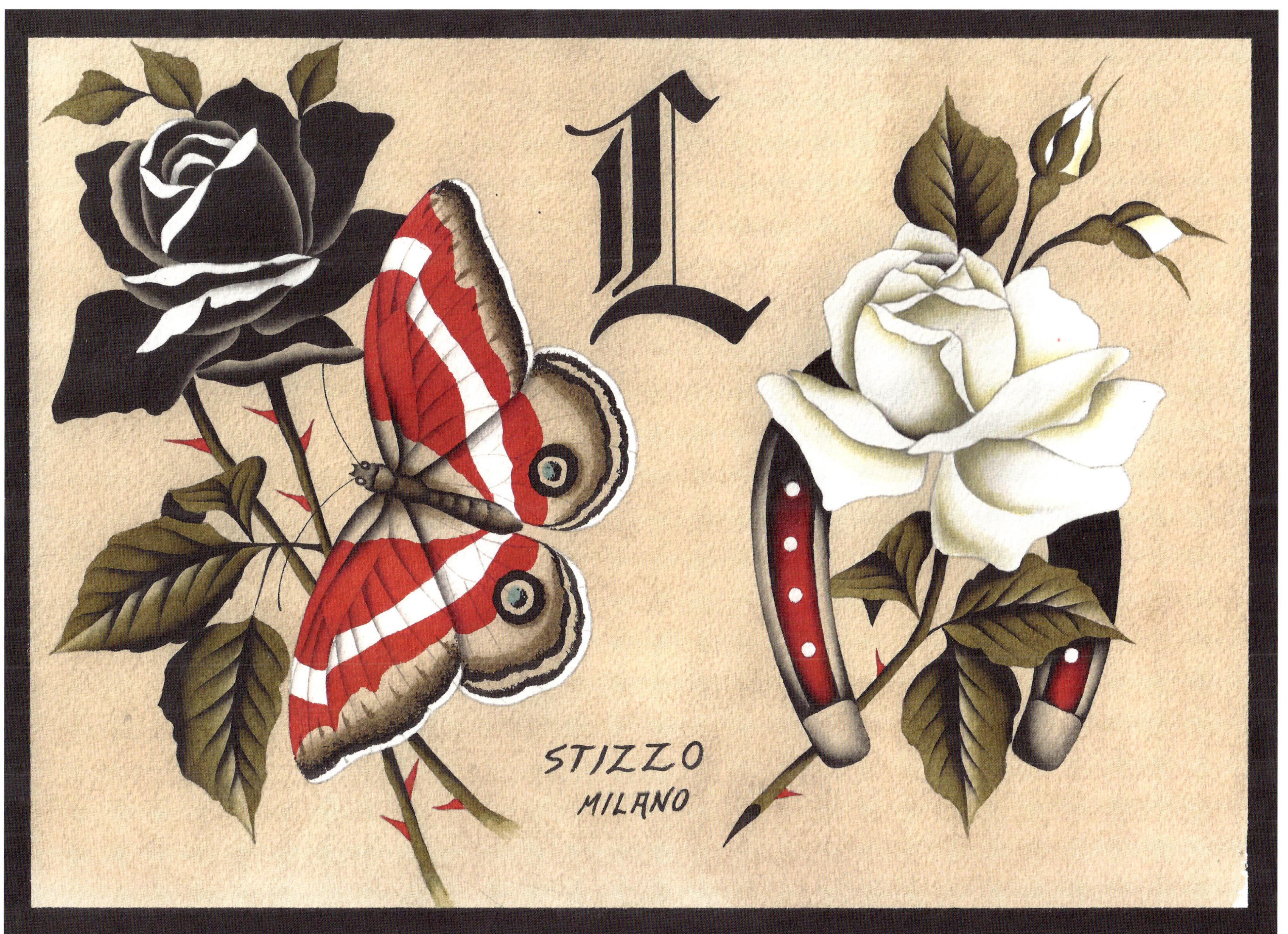
L
STIZZO
MILANO

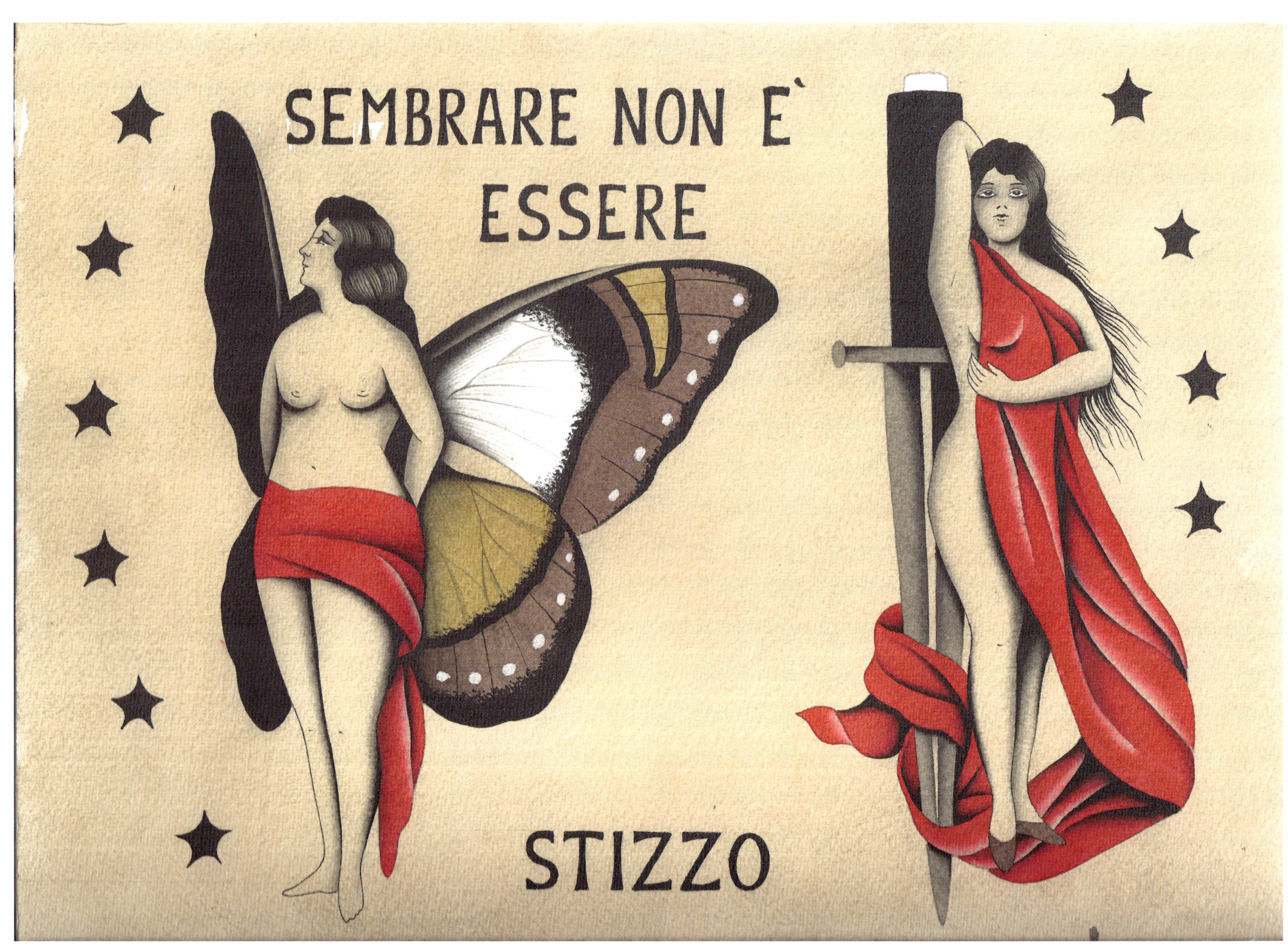
SEMBRARE NON E`
ESSERE
STIZZO

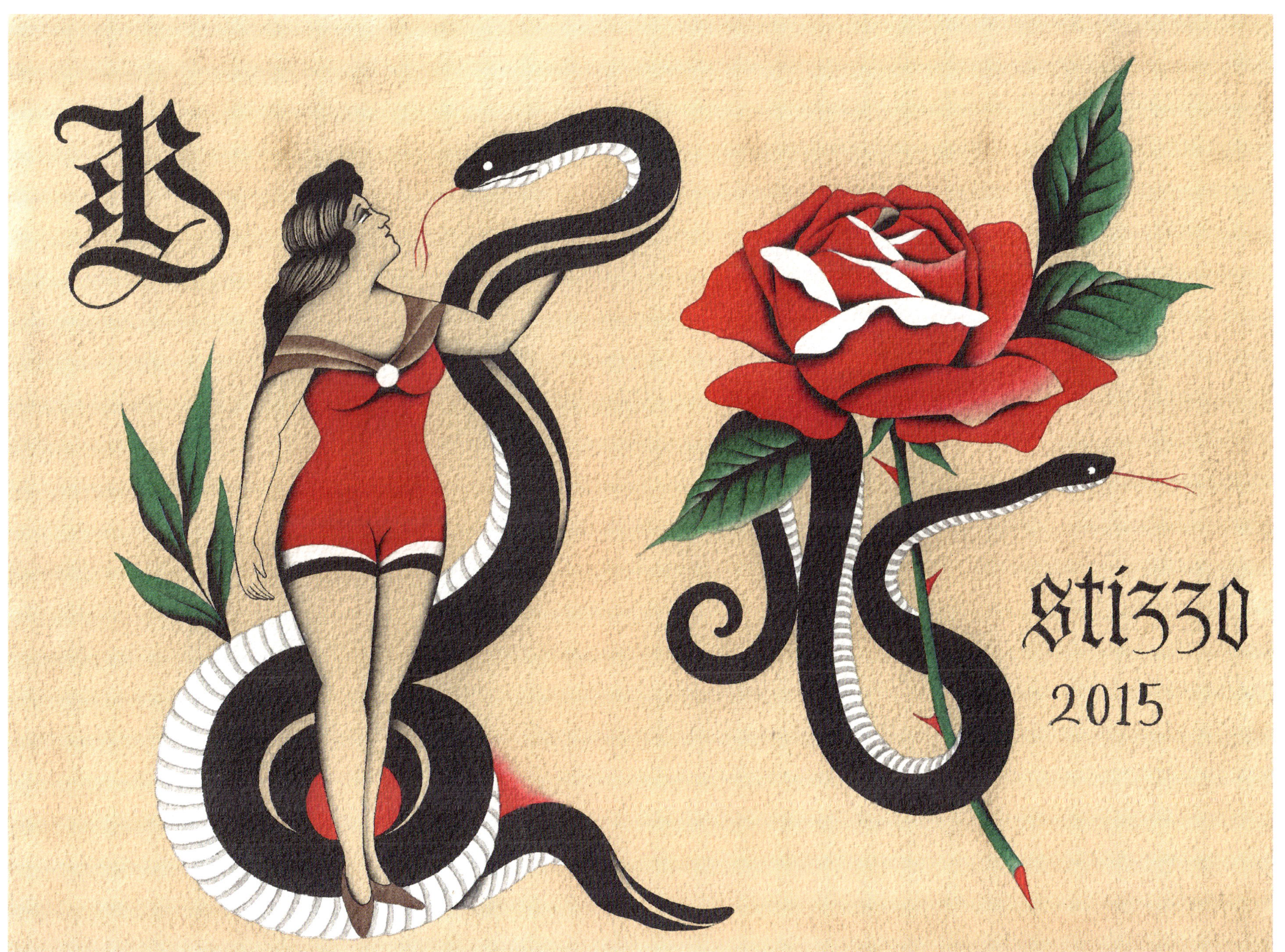
Stizzo
2015

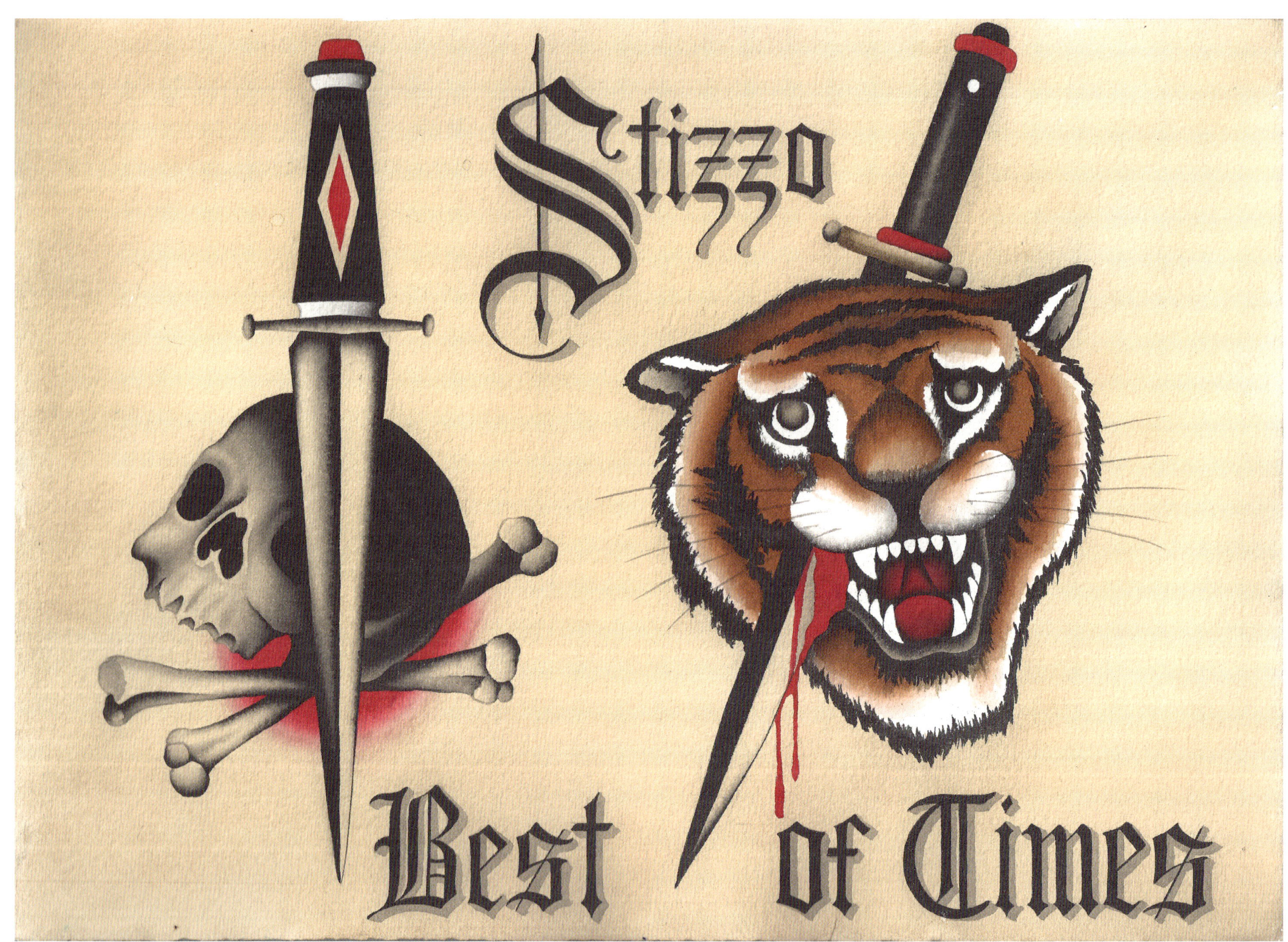
Stizzo
Best of Times

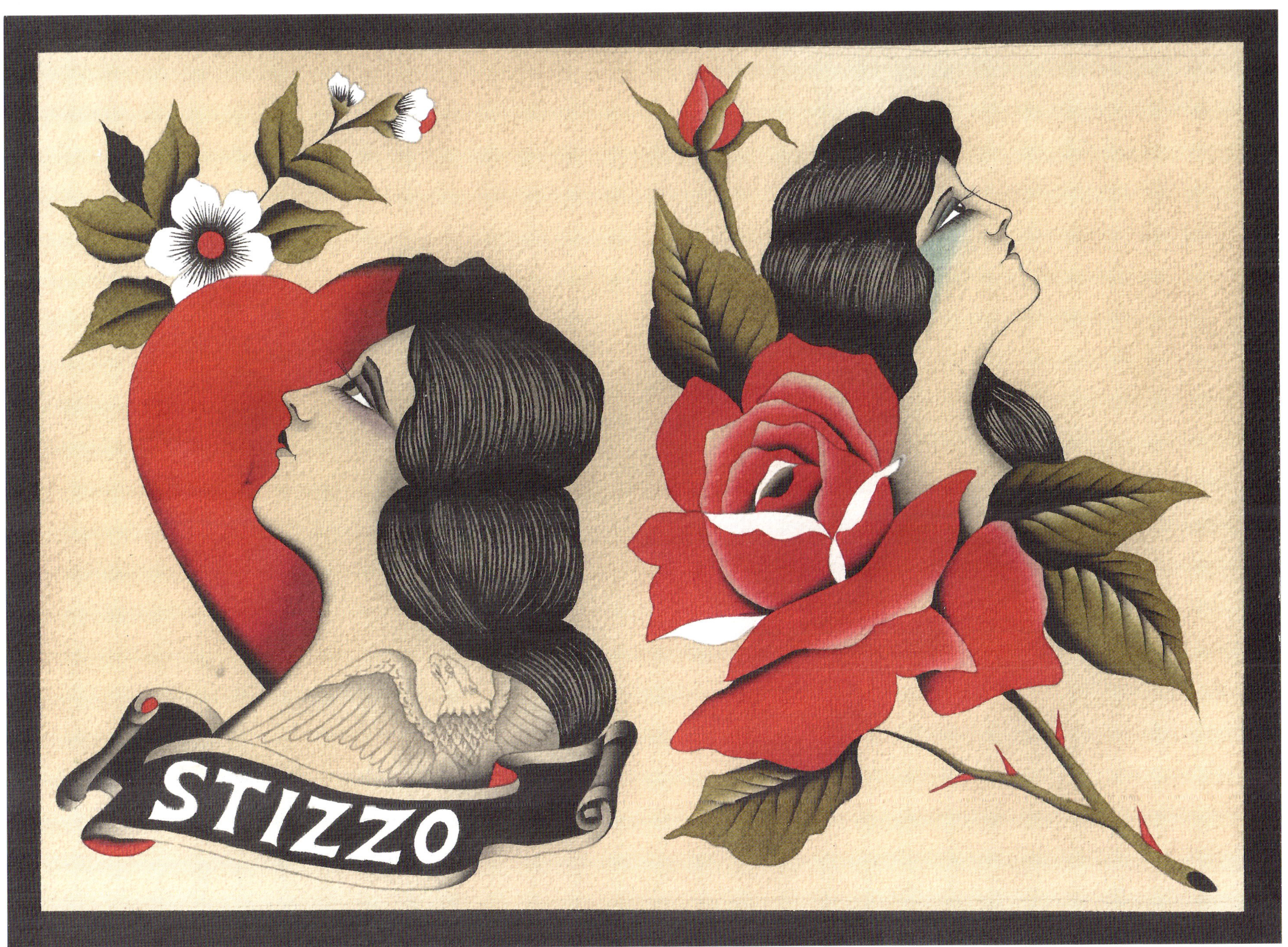
STIZZO

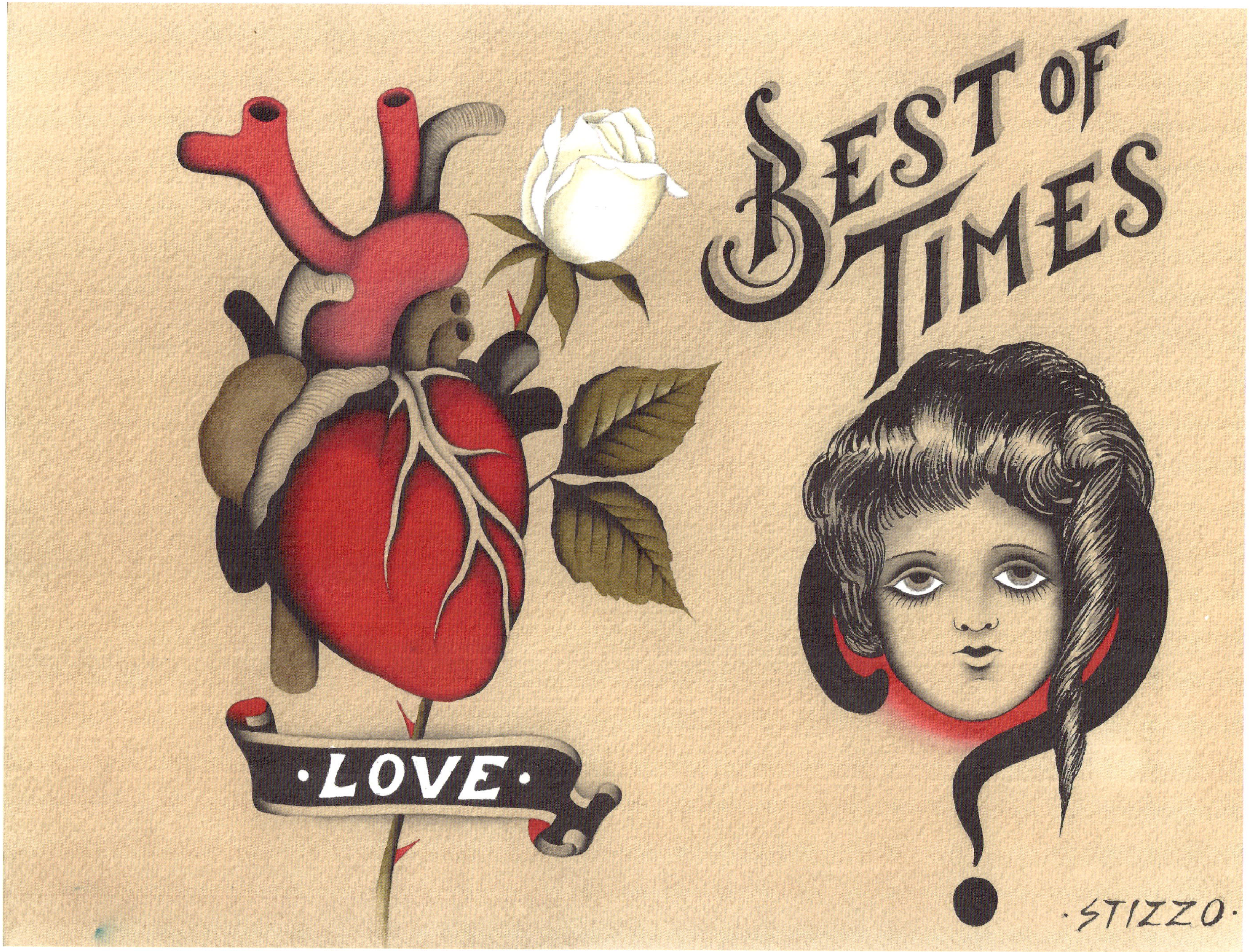

BEST OF TIMES

LOVE

STIZZO

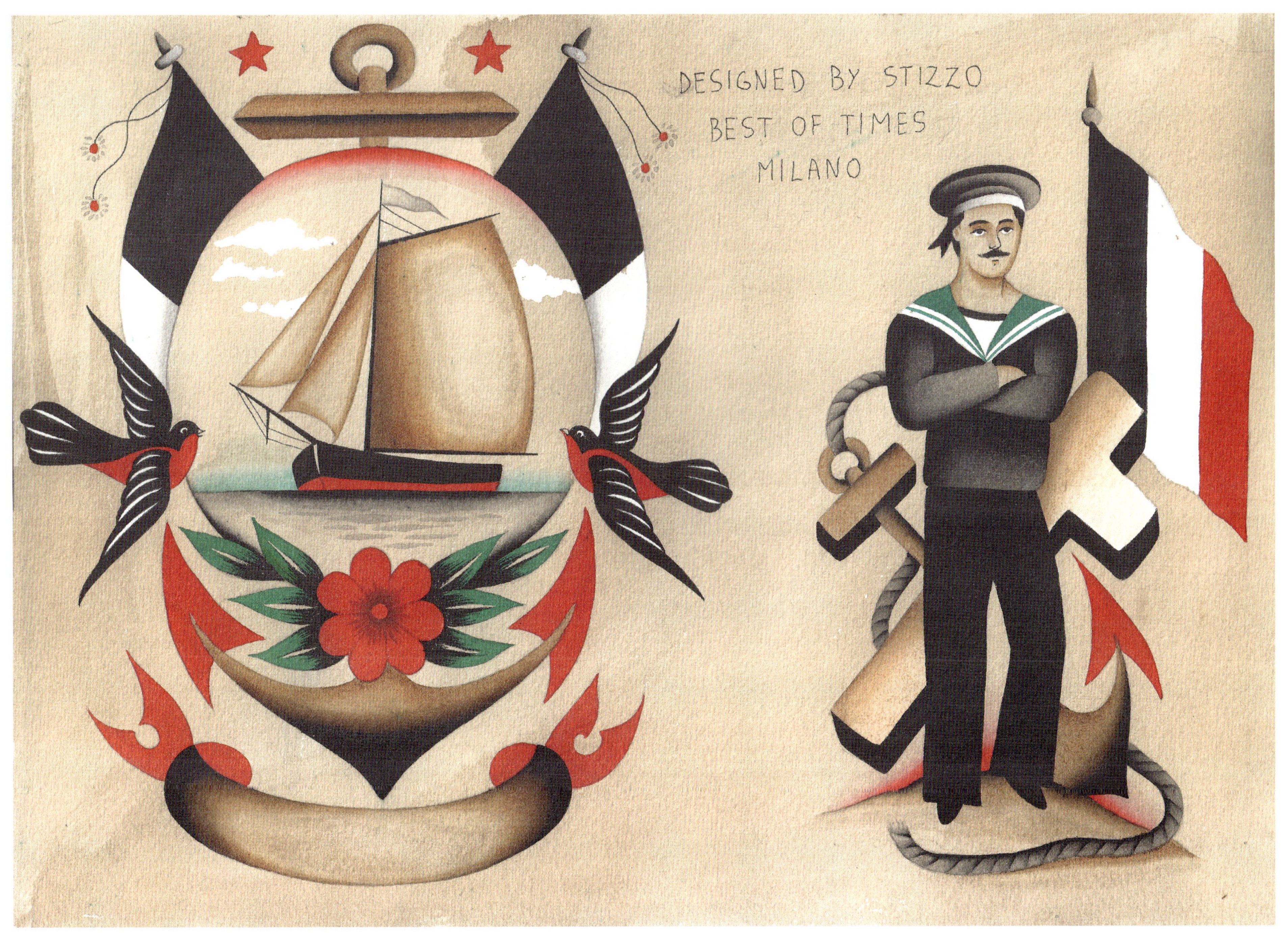
DESIGNED BY STIZZO
BEST OF TIMES
MILANO

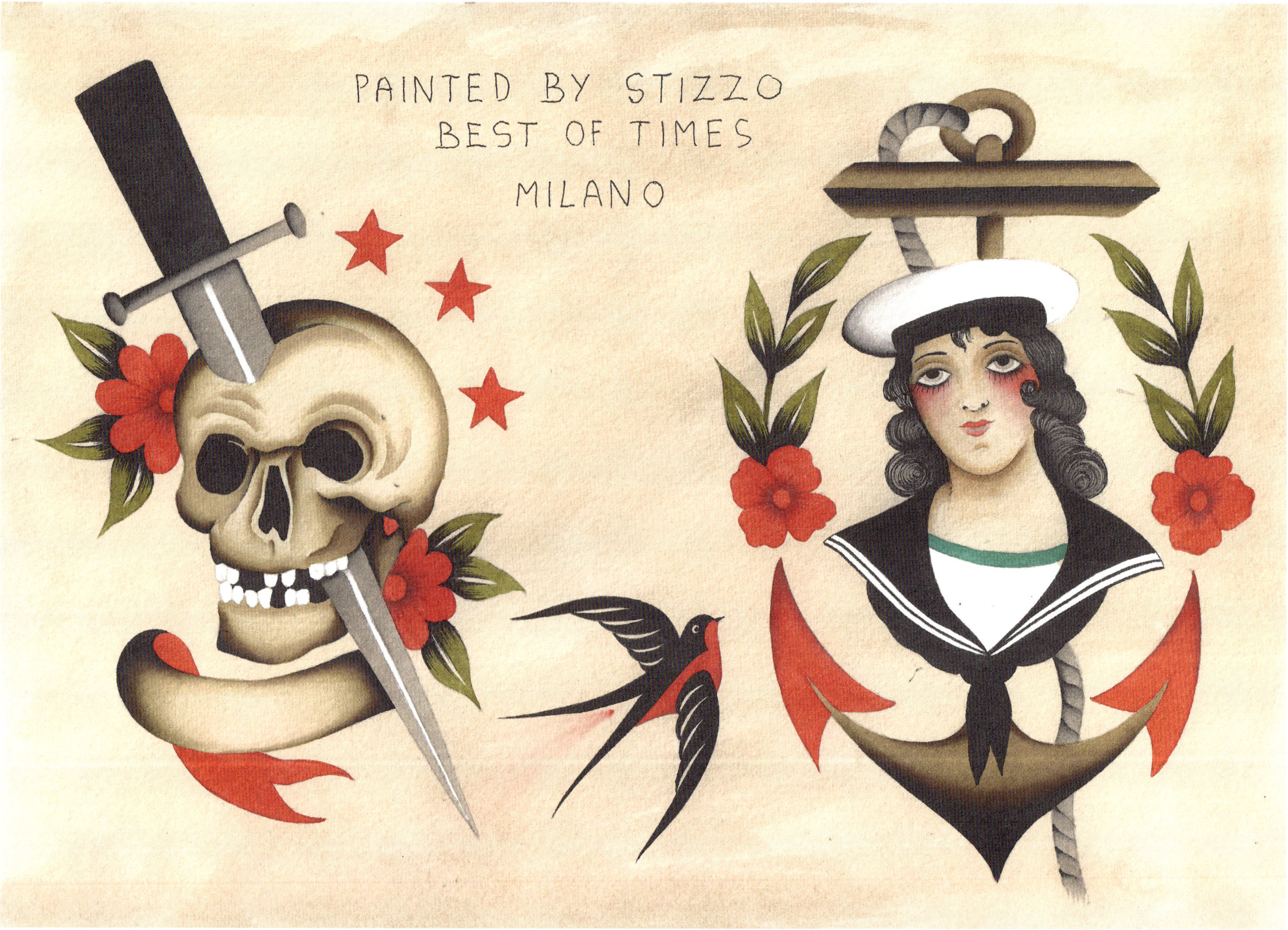

PAINTED BY STIZZO
BEST OF TIMES
MILANO

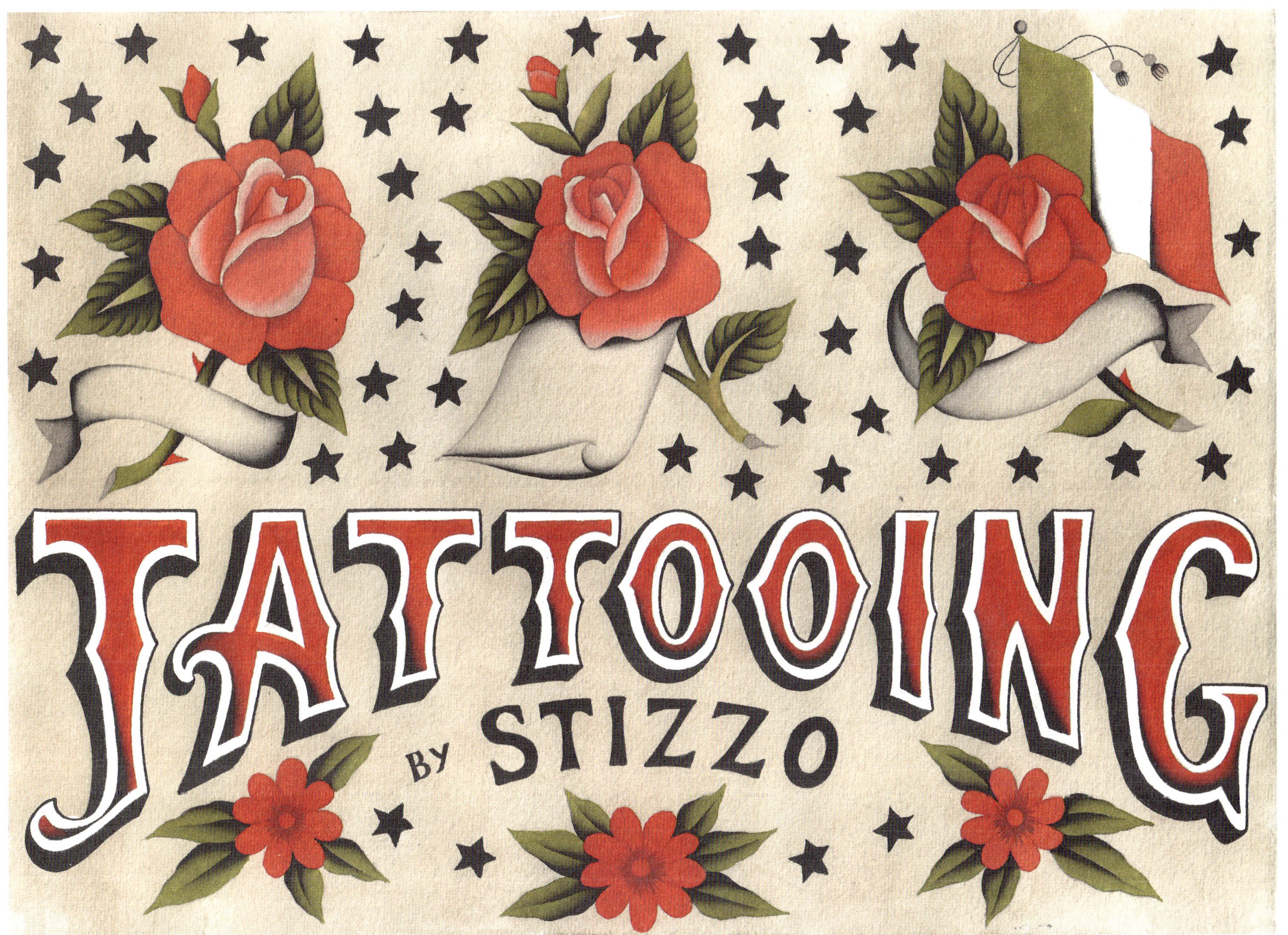
TATTOOING
BY STIZZO

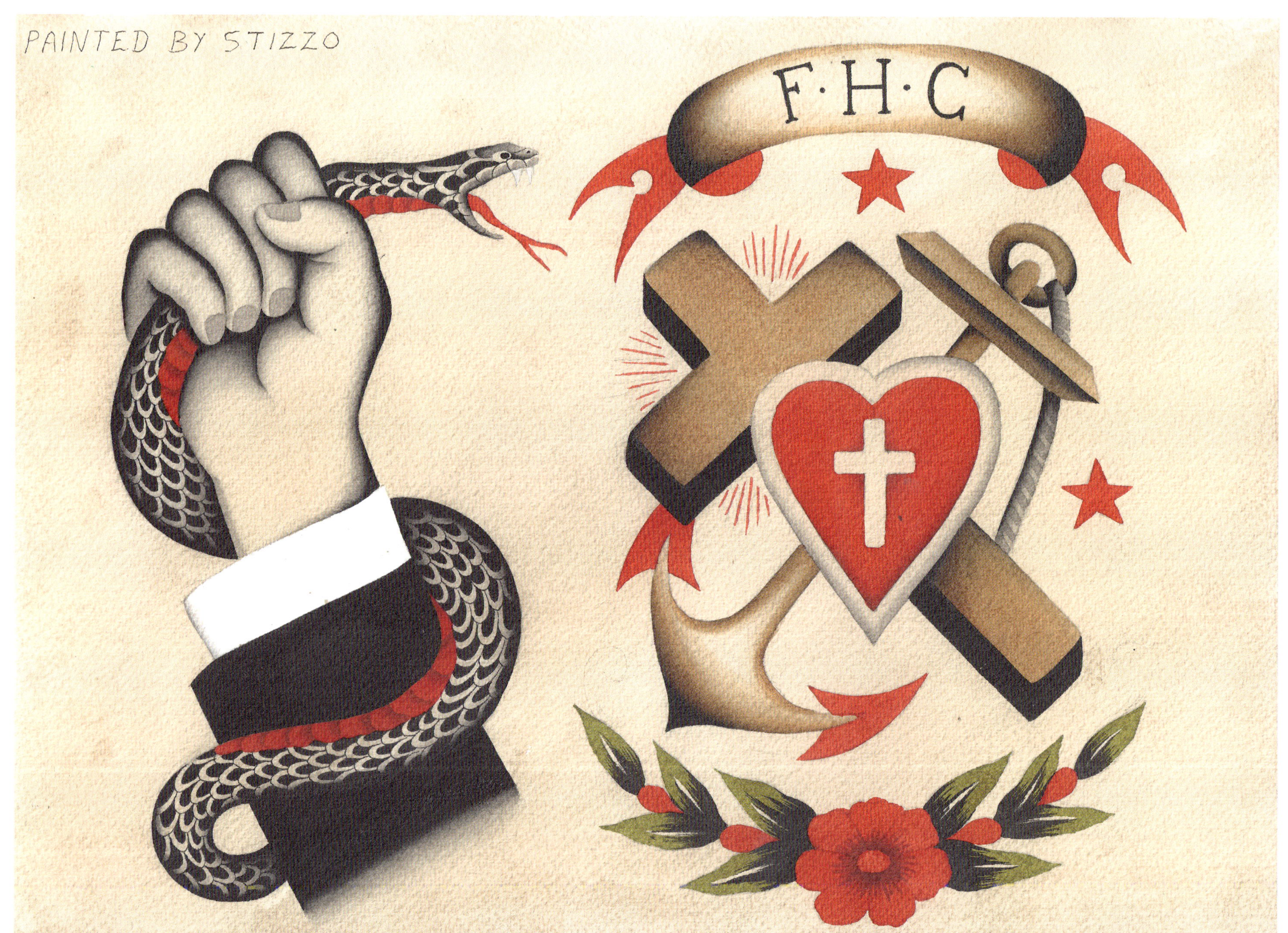
PAINTED BY STIZZO
F·H·C

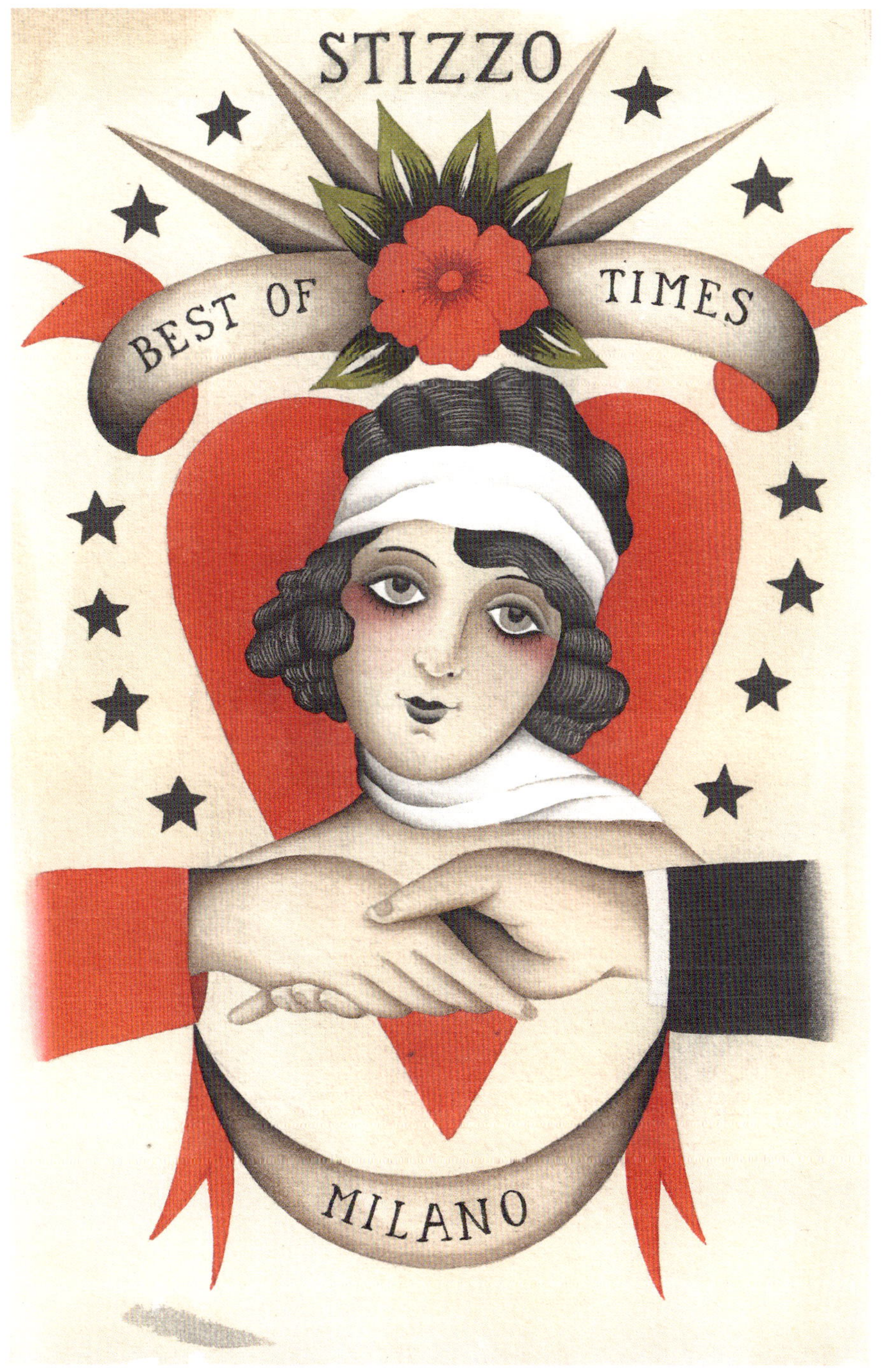
STIZZO
BEST OF
TIMES
MILANO

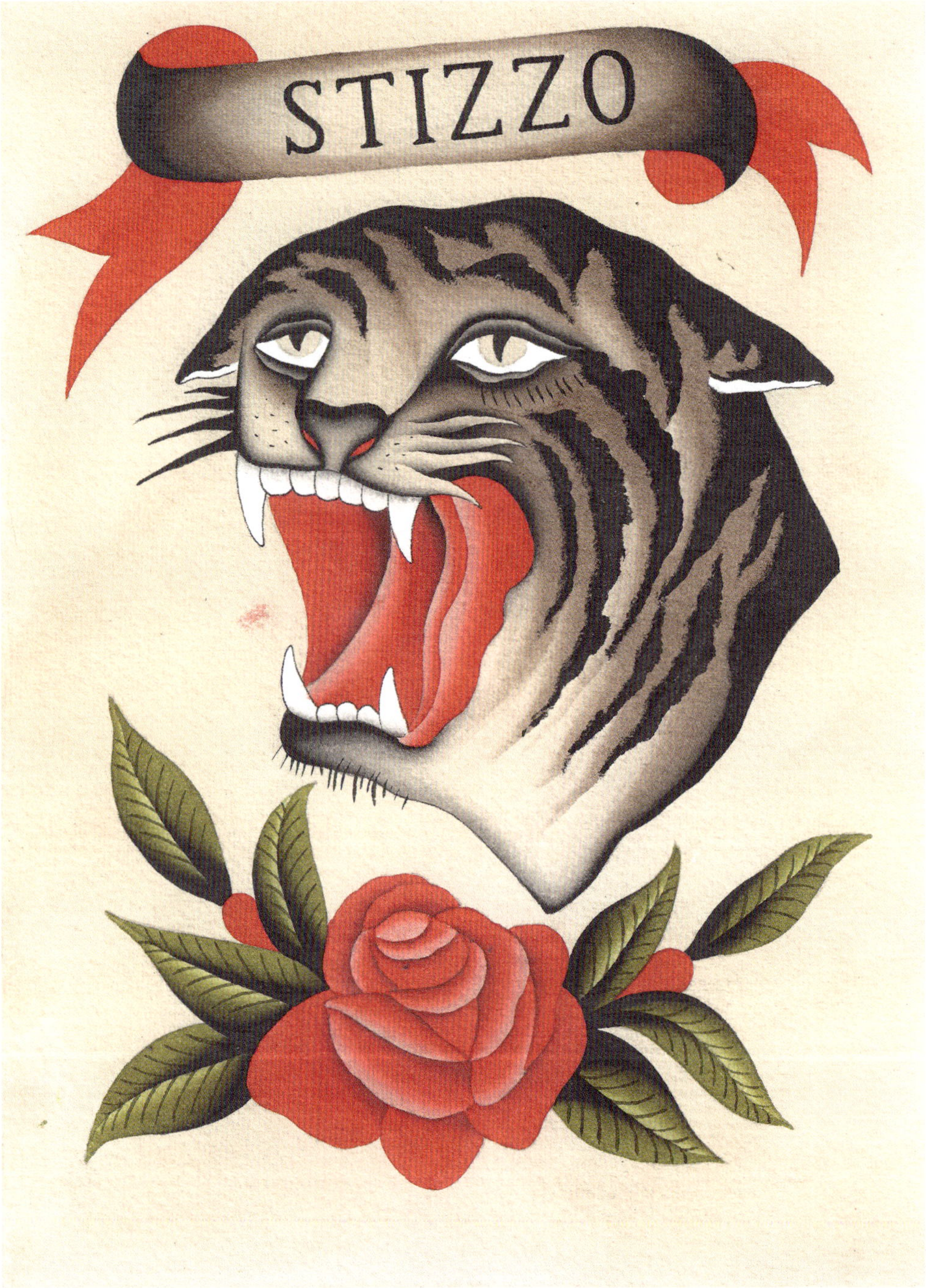

STIZZO

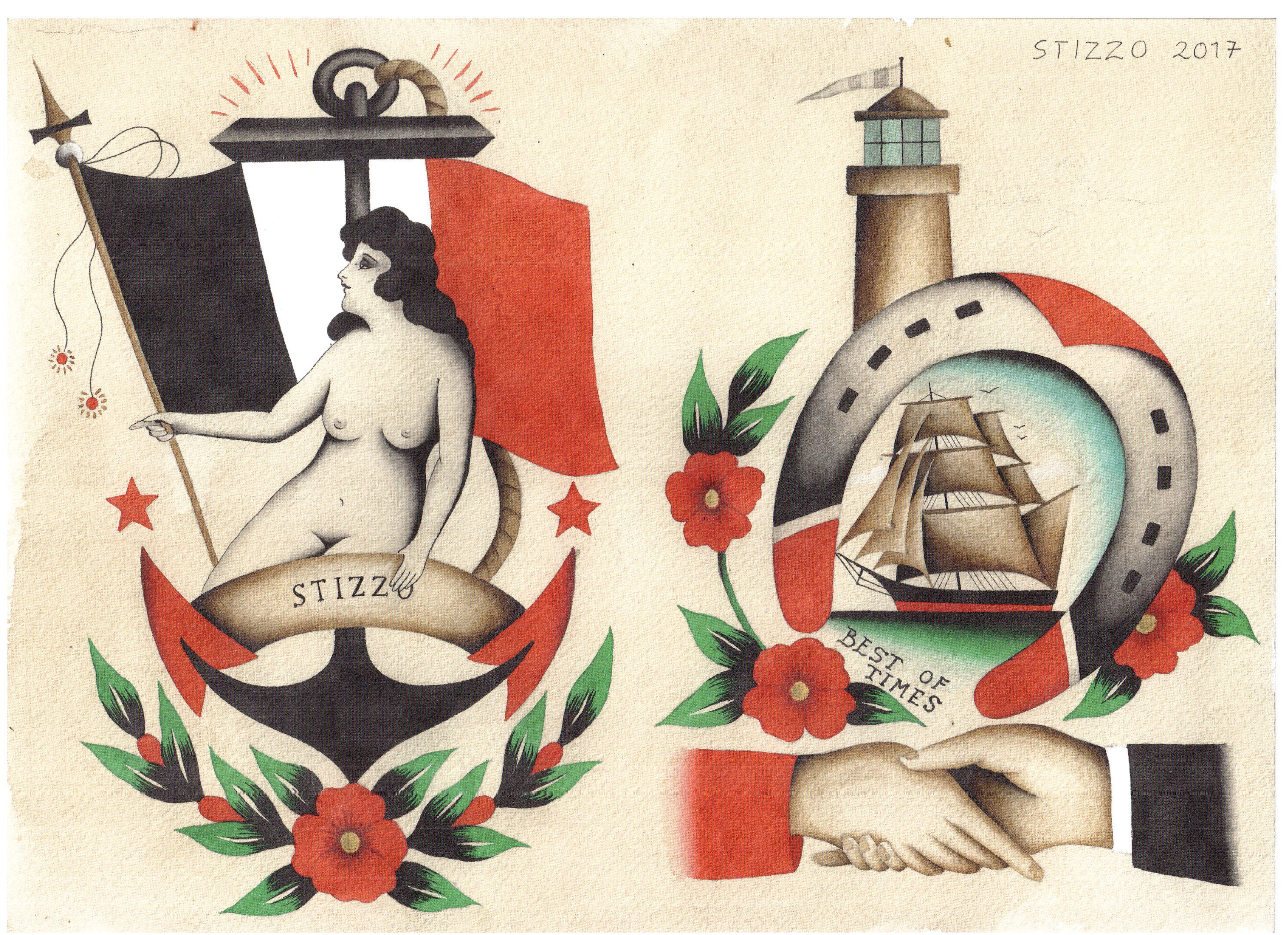
STIZZO 2017
STIZZO
BEST OF TIMES

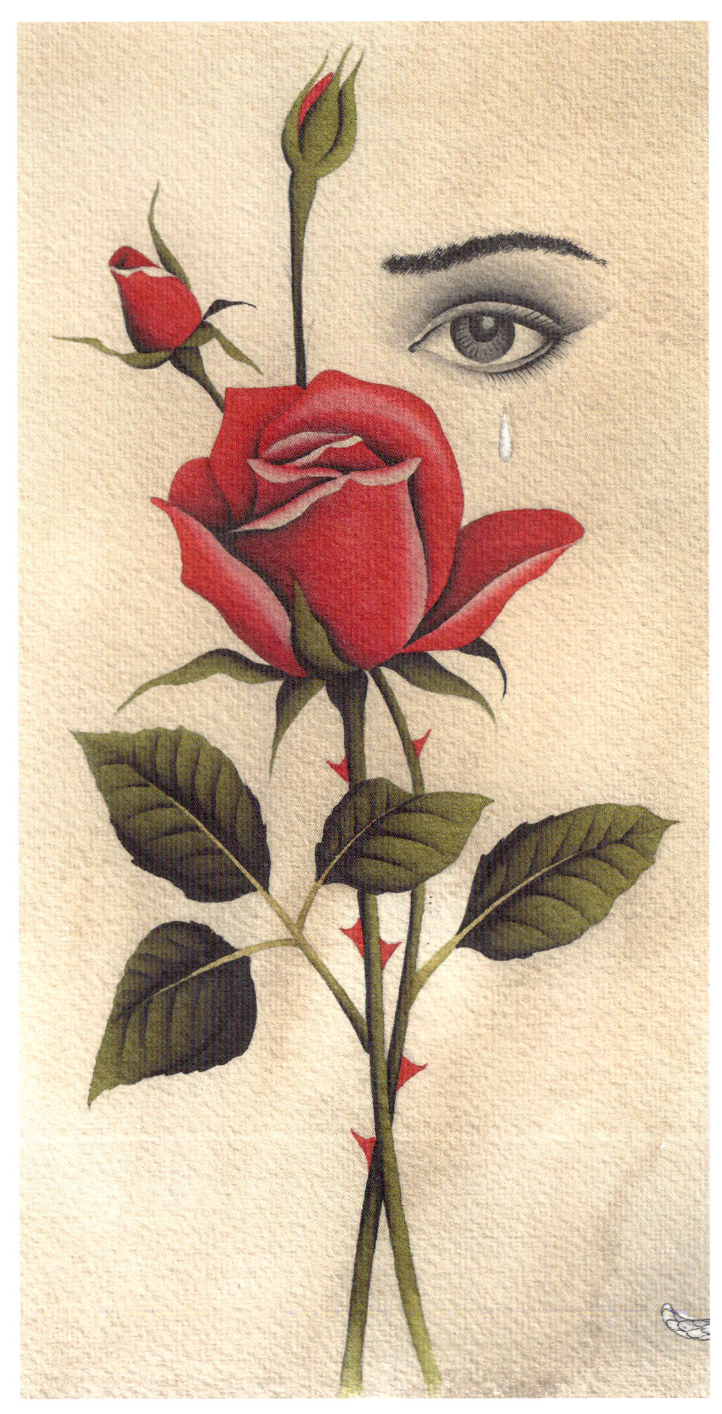

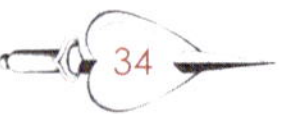

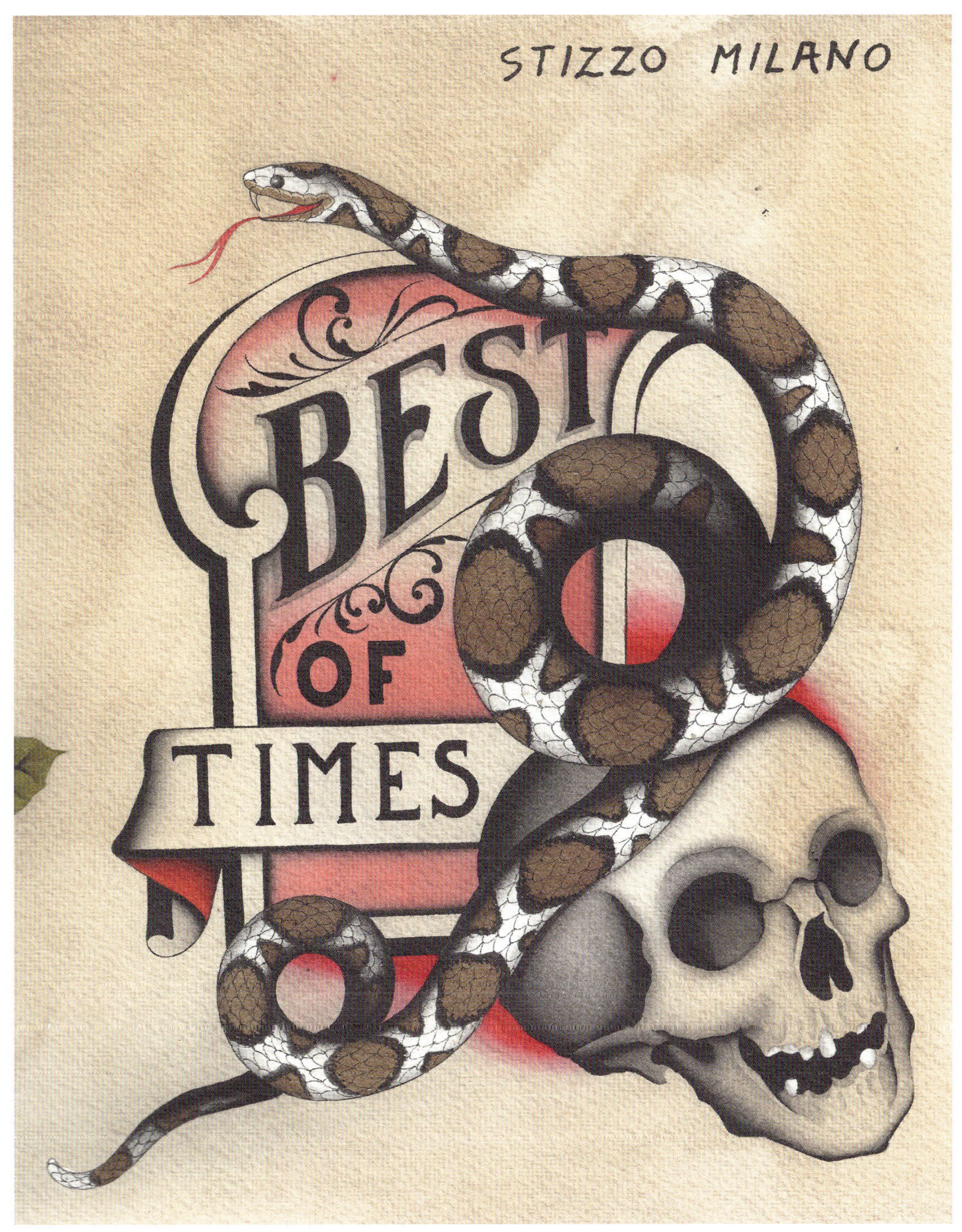
STIZZO MILANO
BEST
OF
TIMES

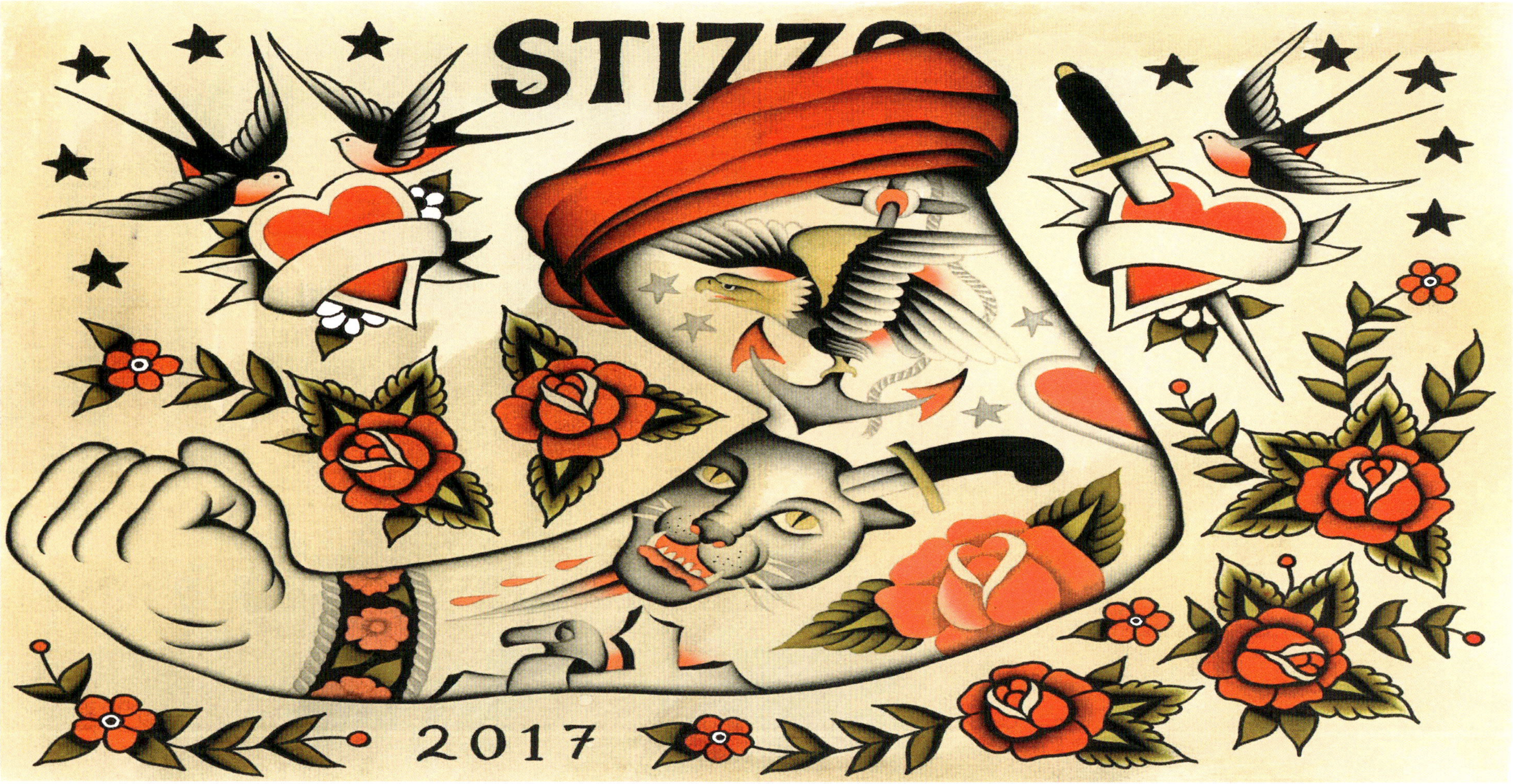

STIZZ

2017

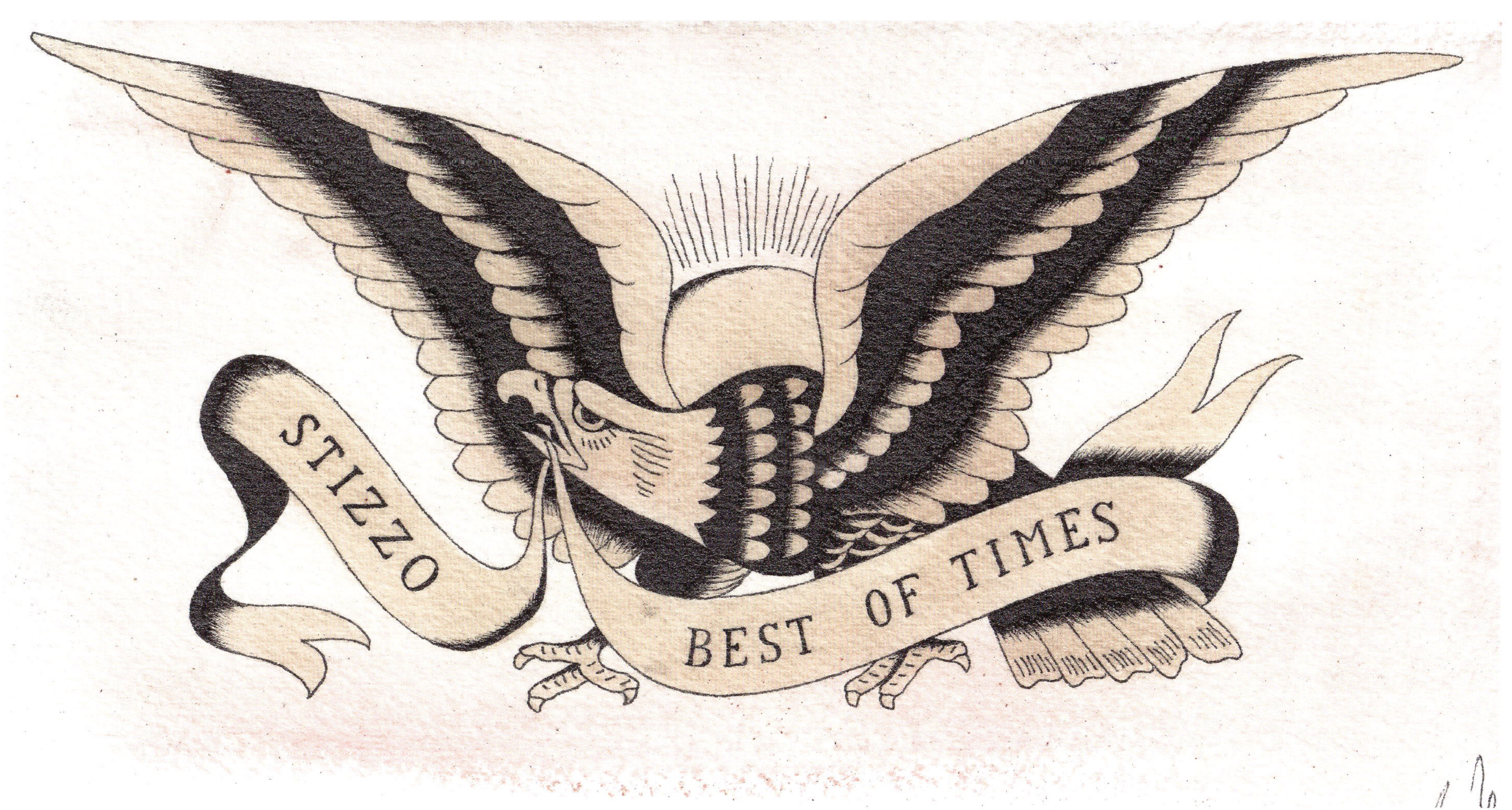
STIZZO
BEST OF TIMES

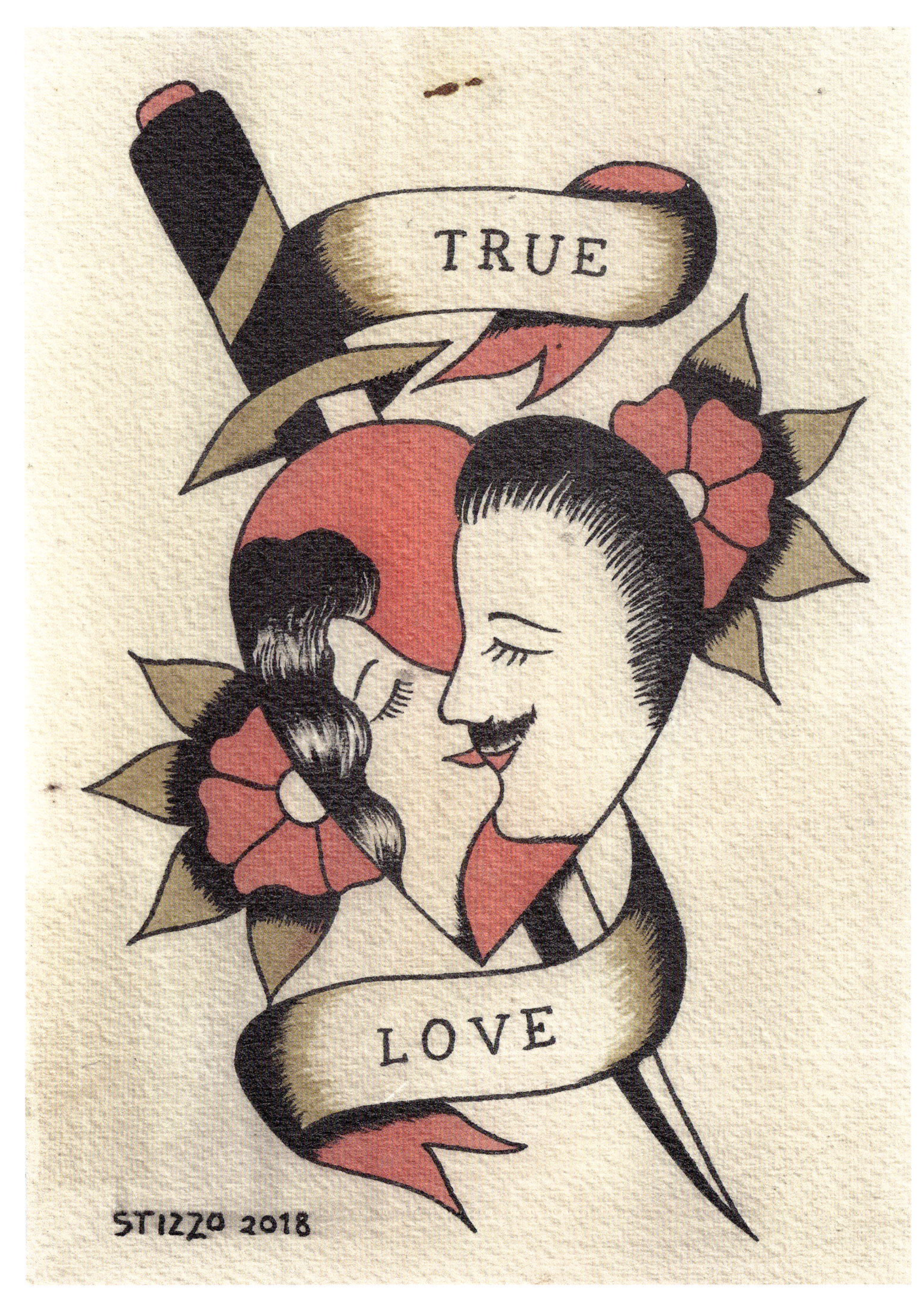
TRUE
LOVE
STIZZO 2018

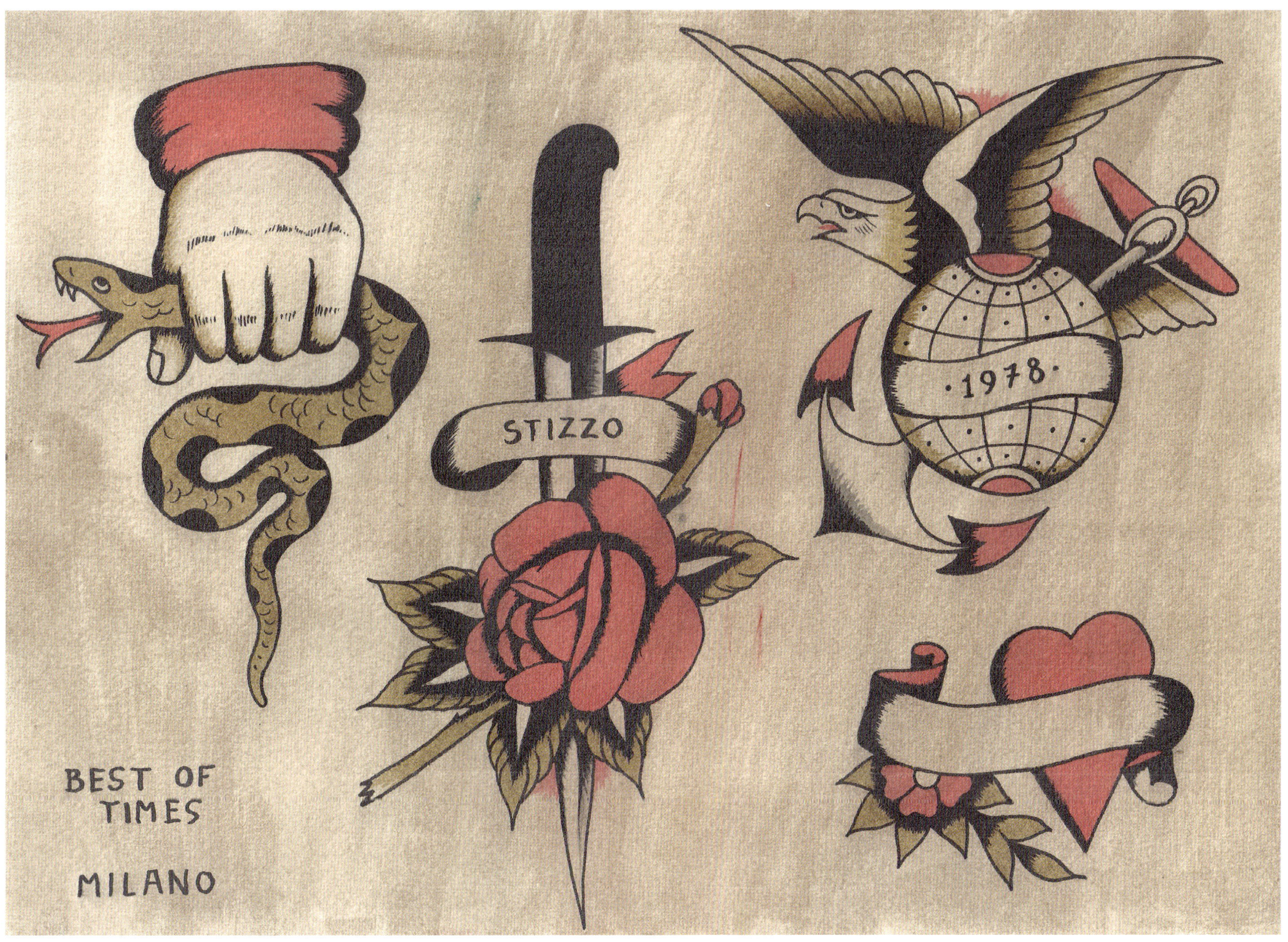
STIZZO
·1978·
BEST OF
TIMES
MILANO

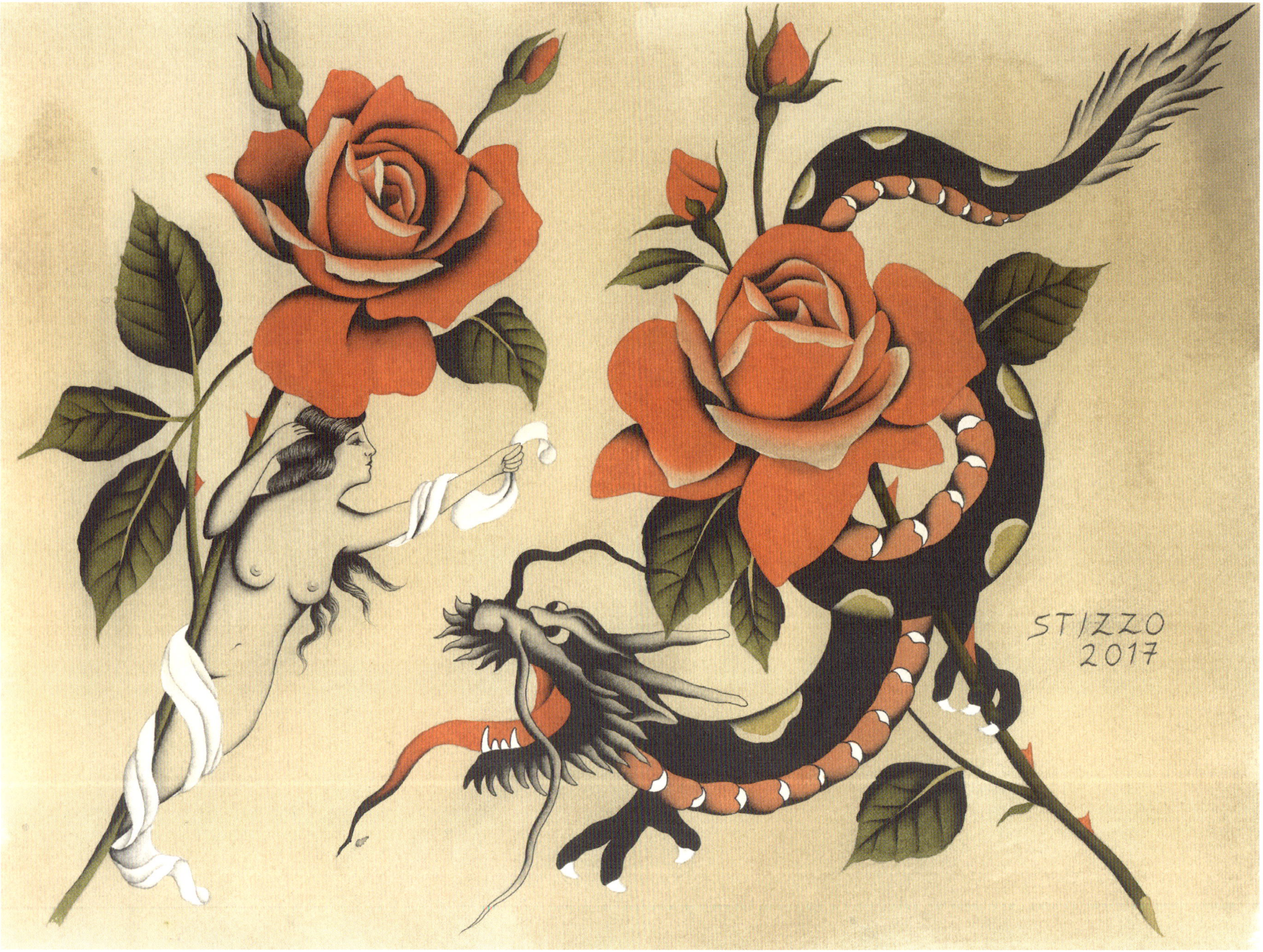

STIZZO
2017

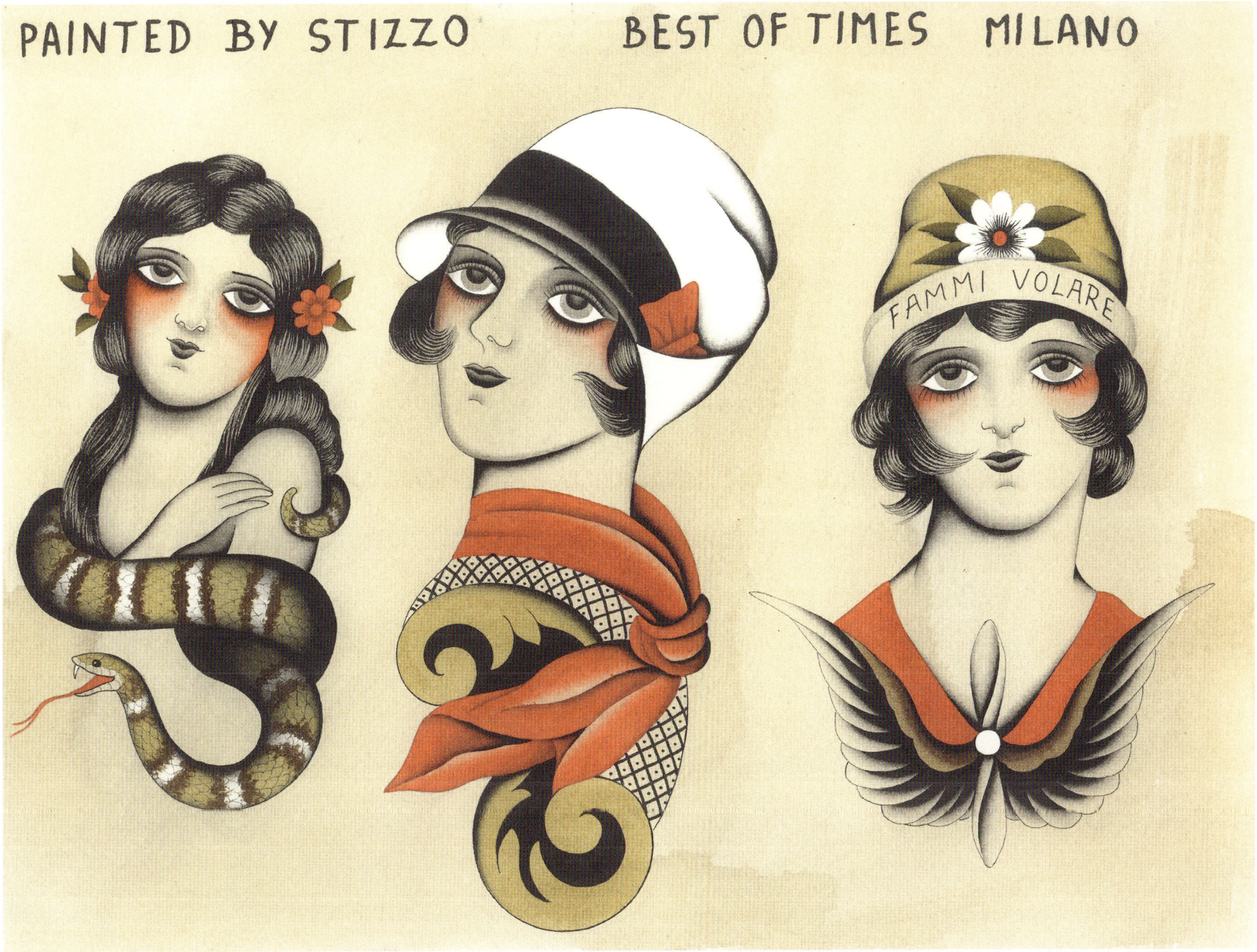

PAINTED BY STIZZO BEST OF TIMES MILANO

FAMMI VOLARE

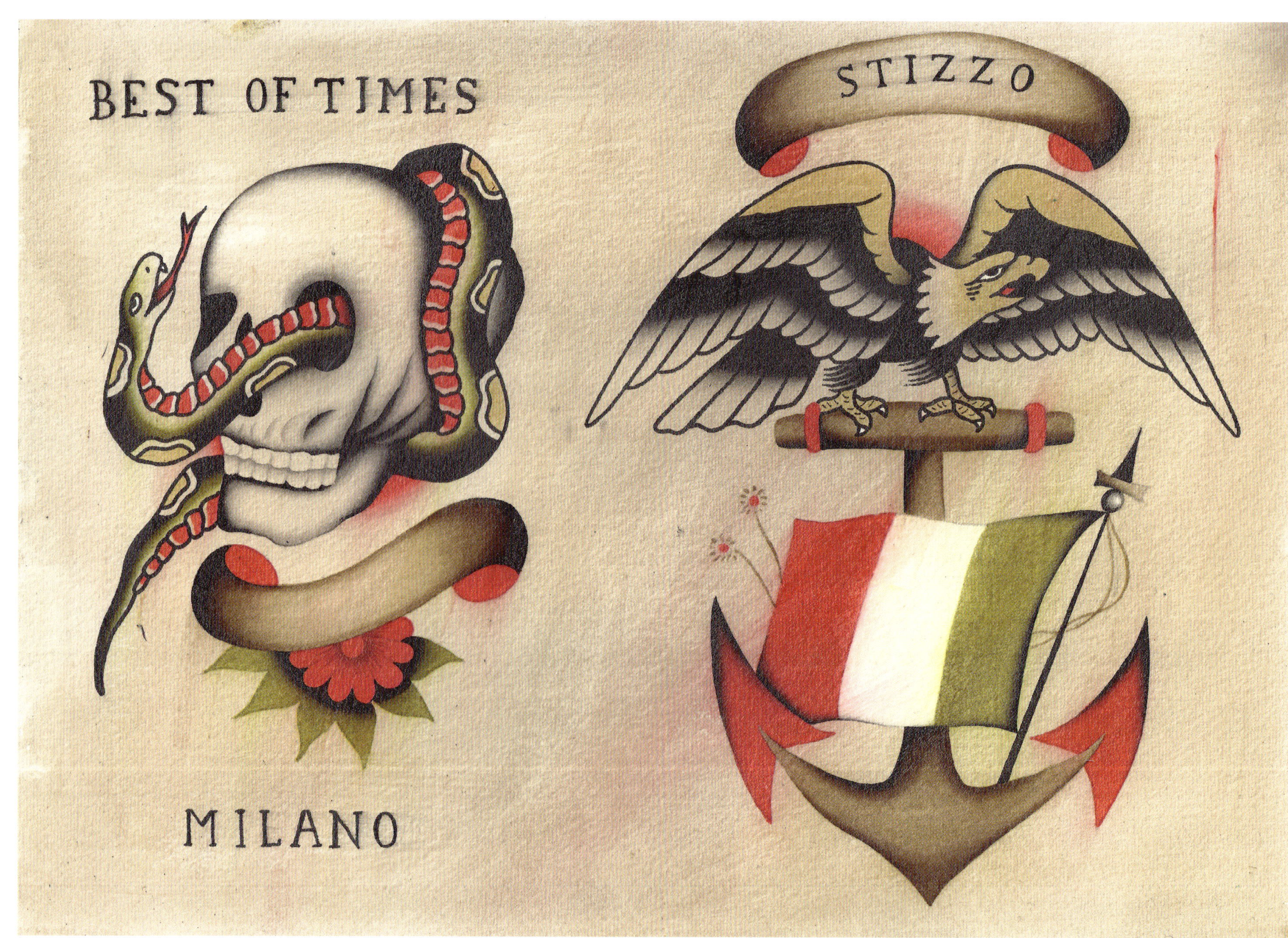
BEST OF TIMES
STIZZO
MILANO

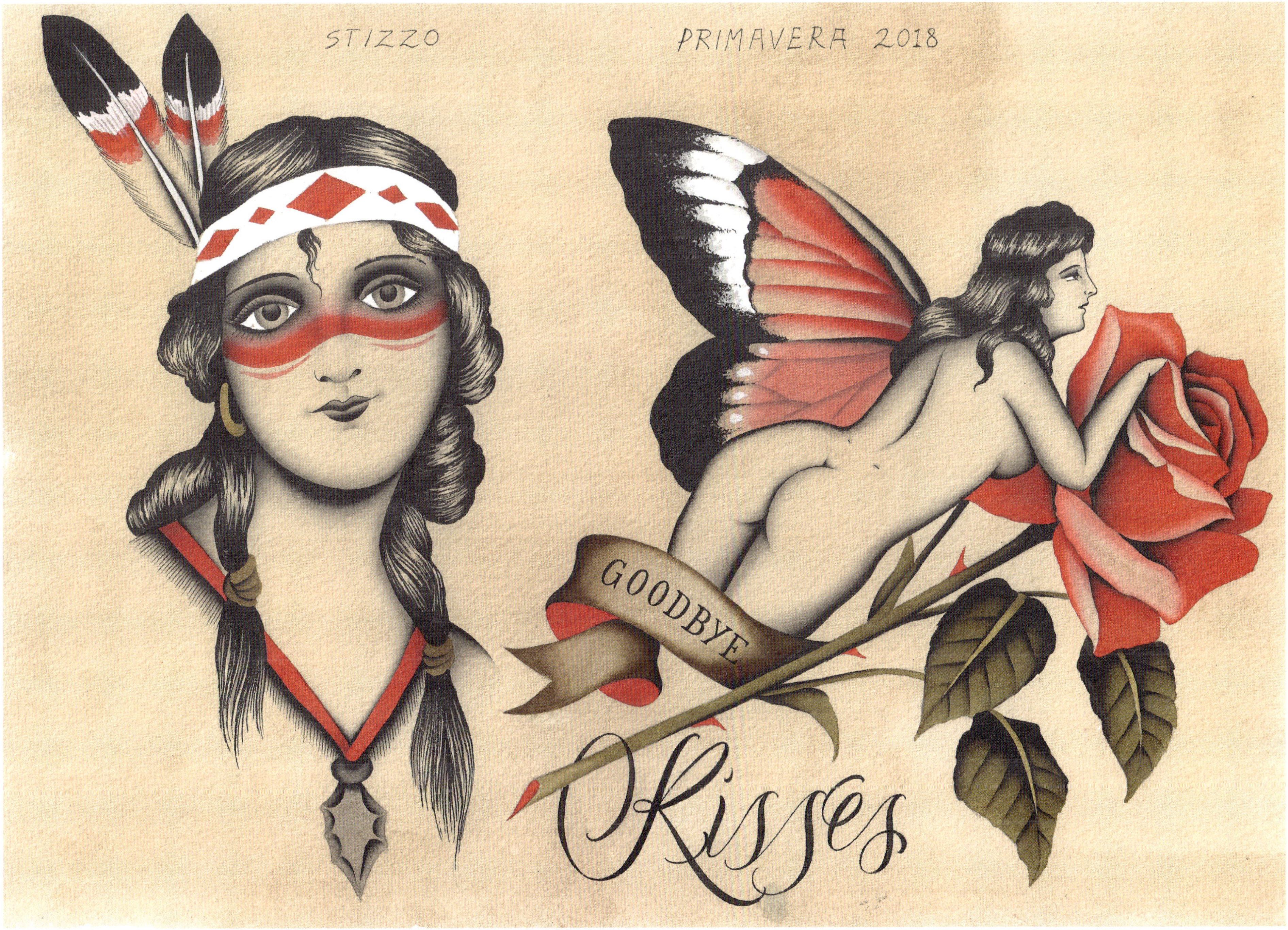

STIZZO PRIMAVERA 2018

GOODBYE

Kisses

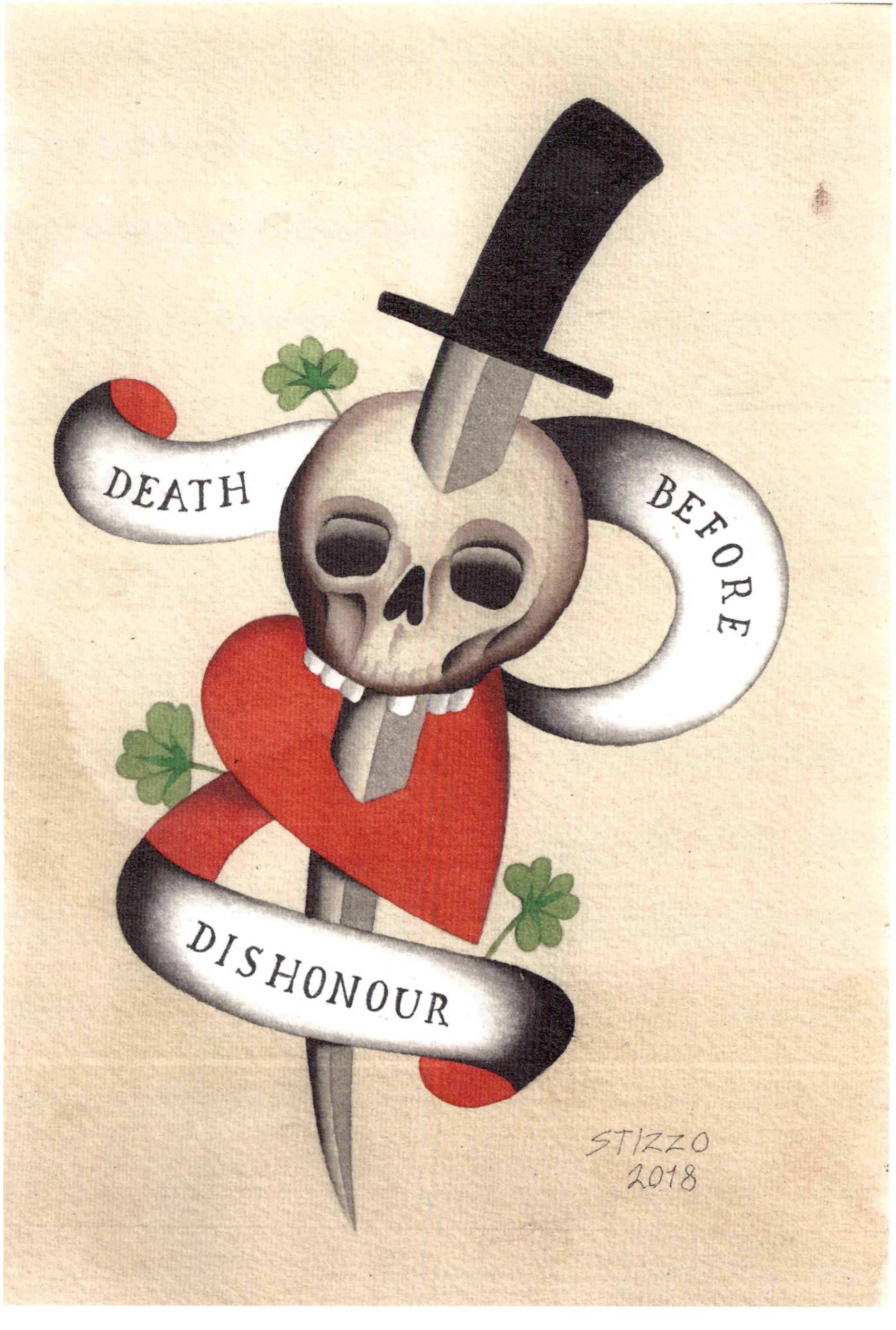

DEATH BEFORE

DISHONOUR

STIZZO
2018

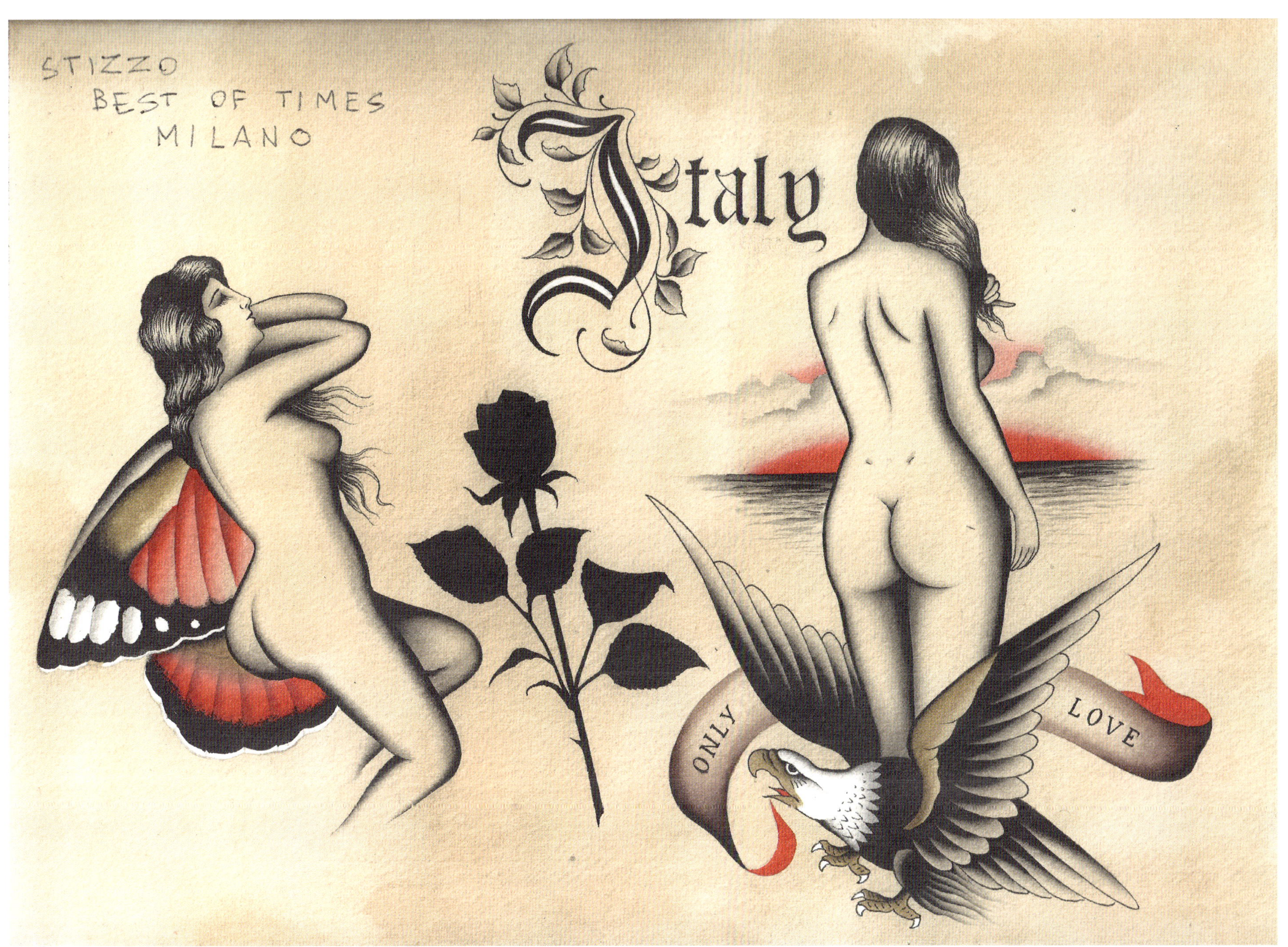
STIZZO
BEST OF TIMES
MILANO
Italy
ONLY
LOVE

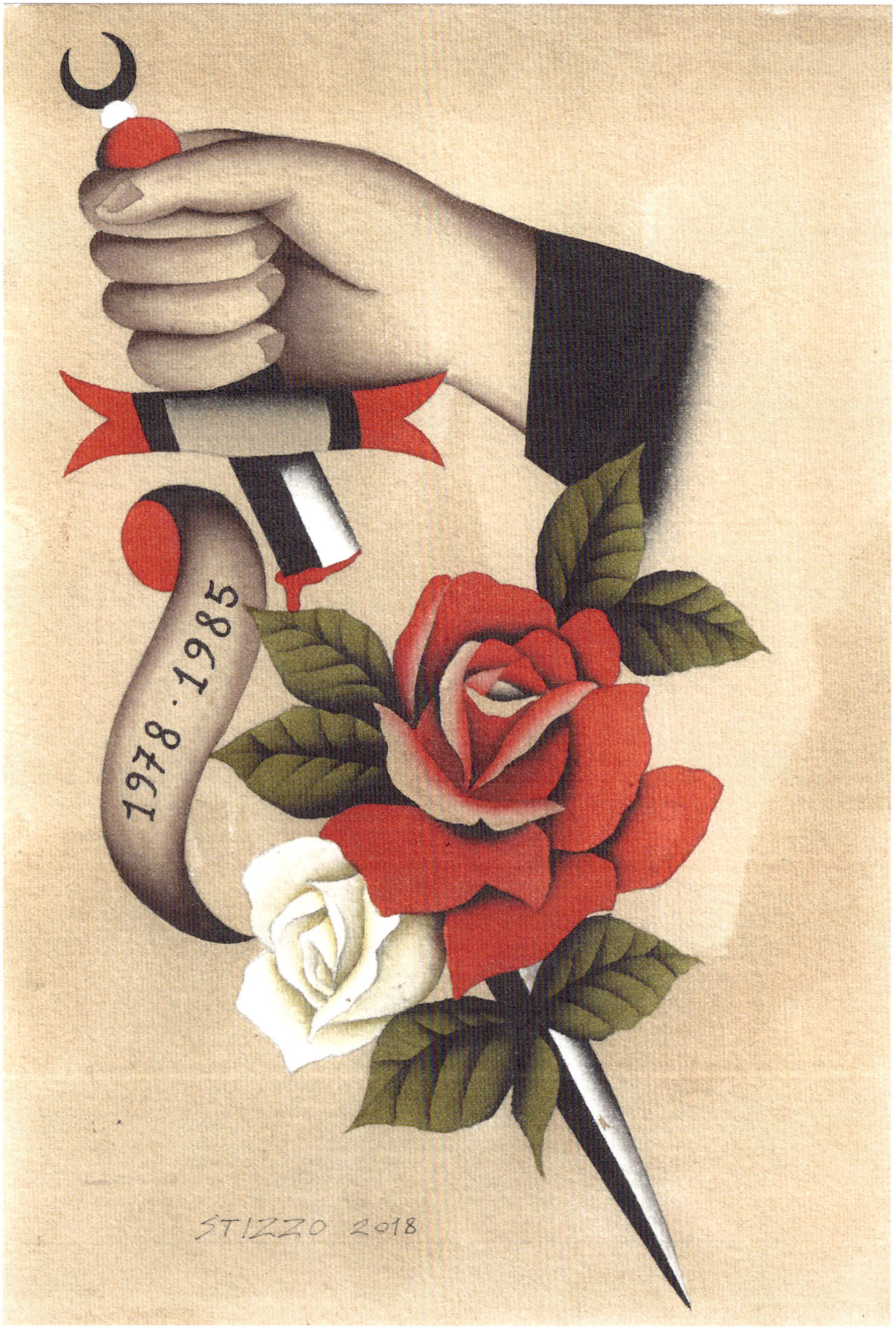

1978 · 1985

STIZZO 2018

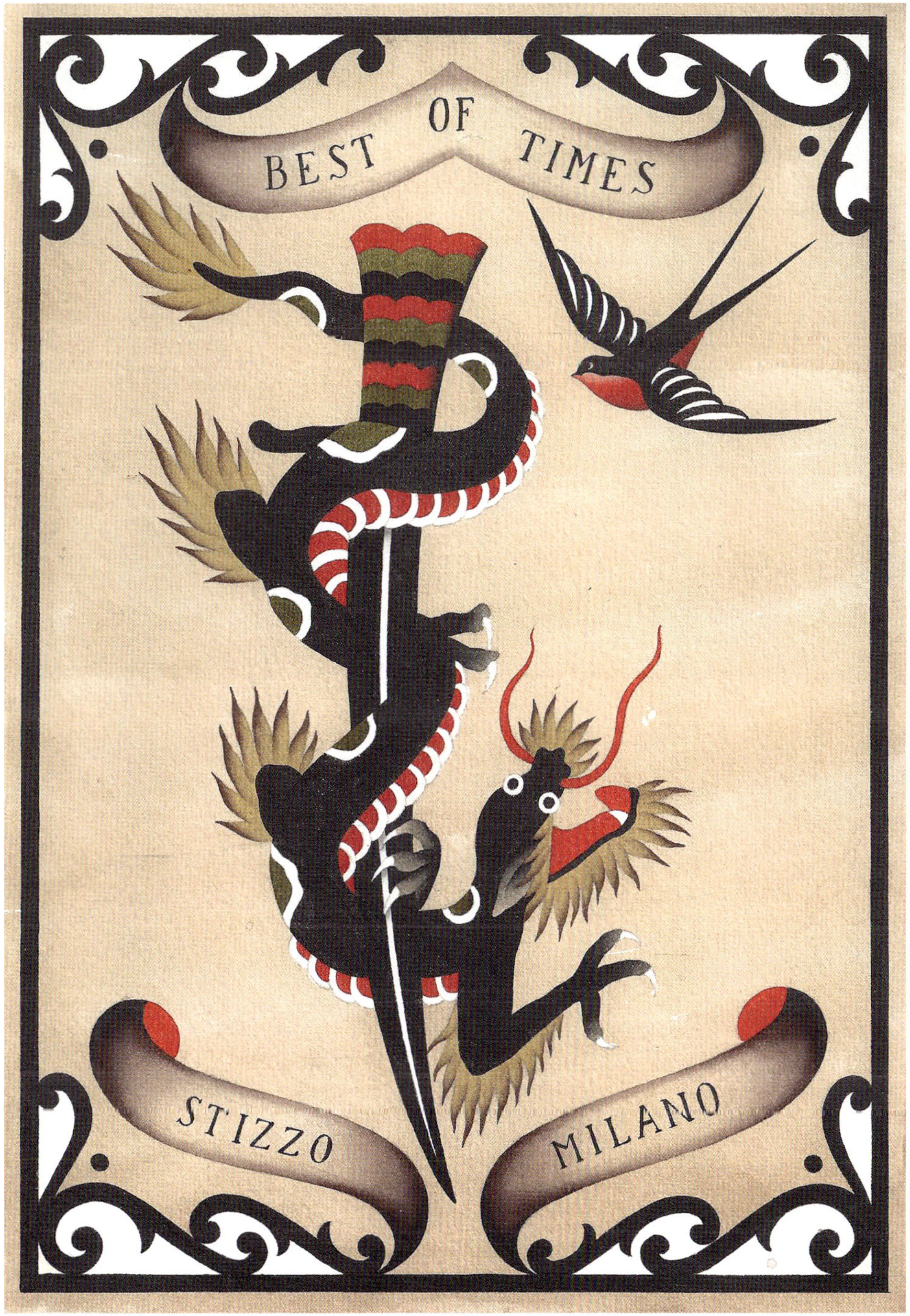

BEST OF TIMES

STIZZO MILANO

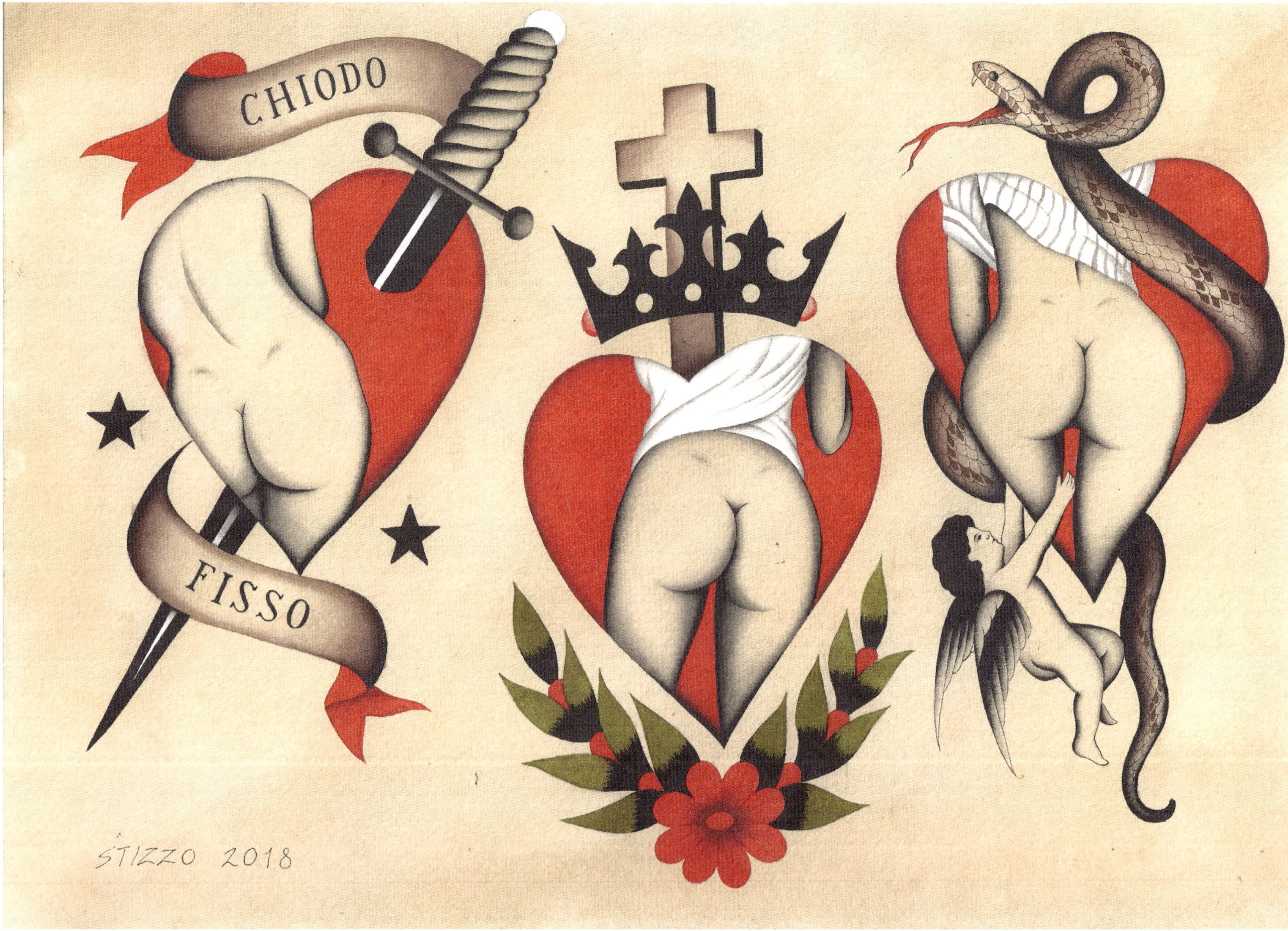

CHIODO

FISSO

STIZZO 2018

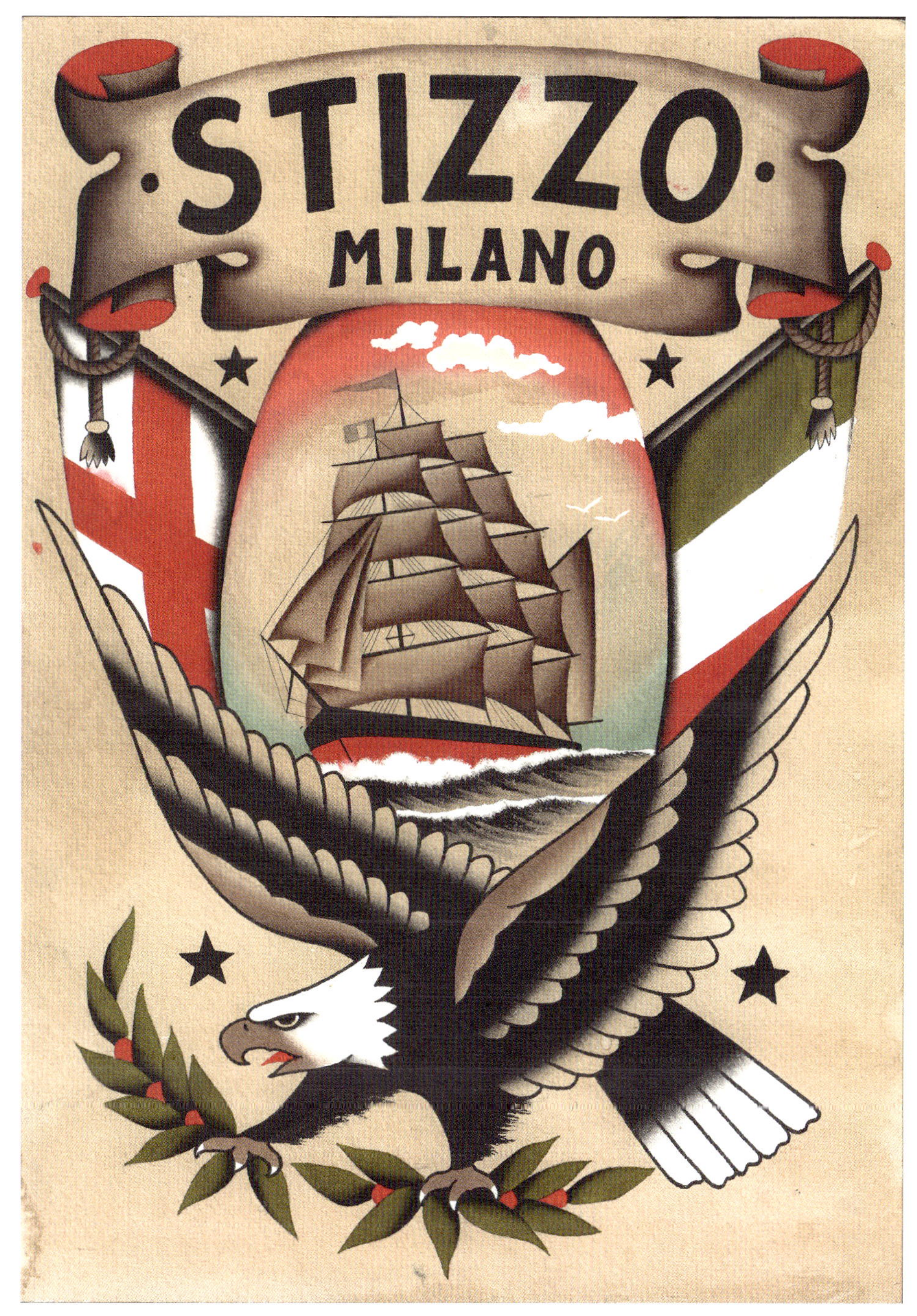
STIZZO
MILANO

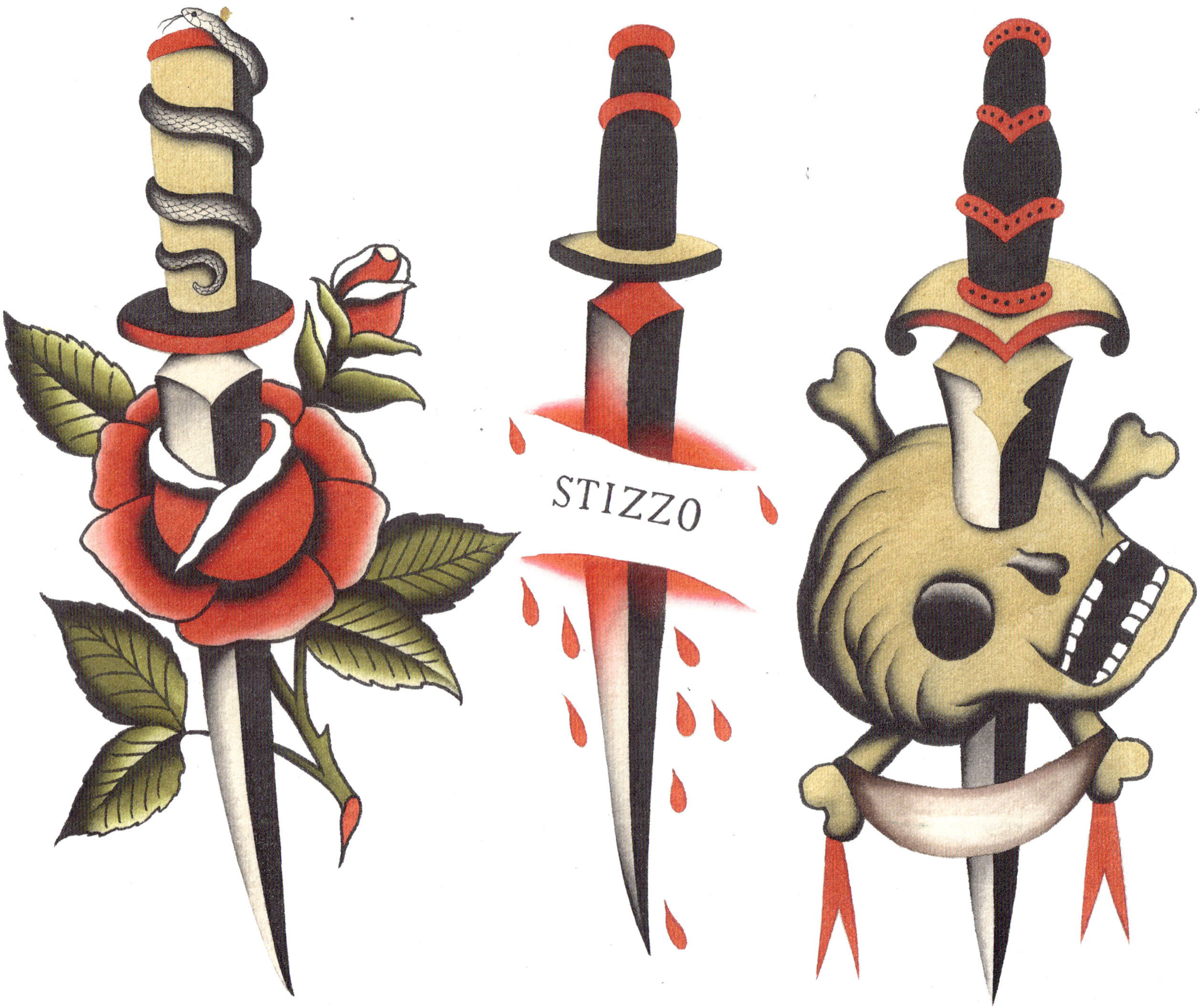

STIZZO

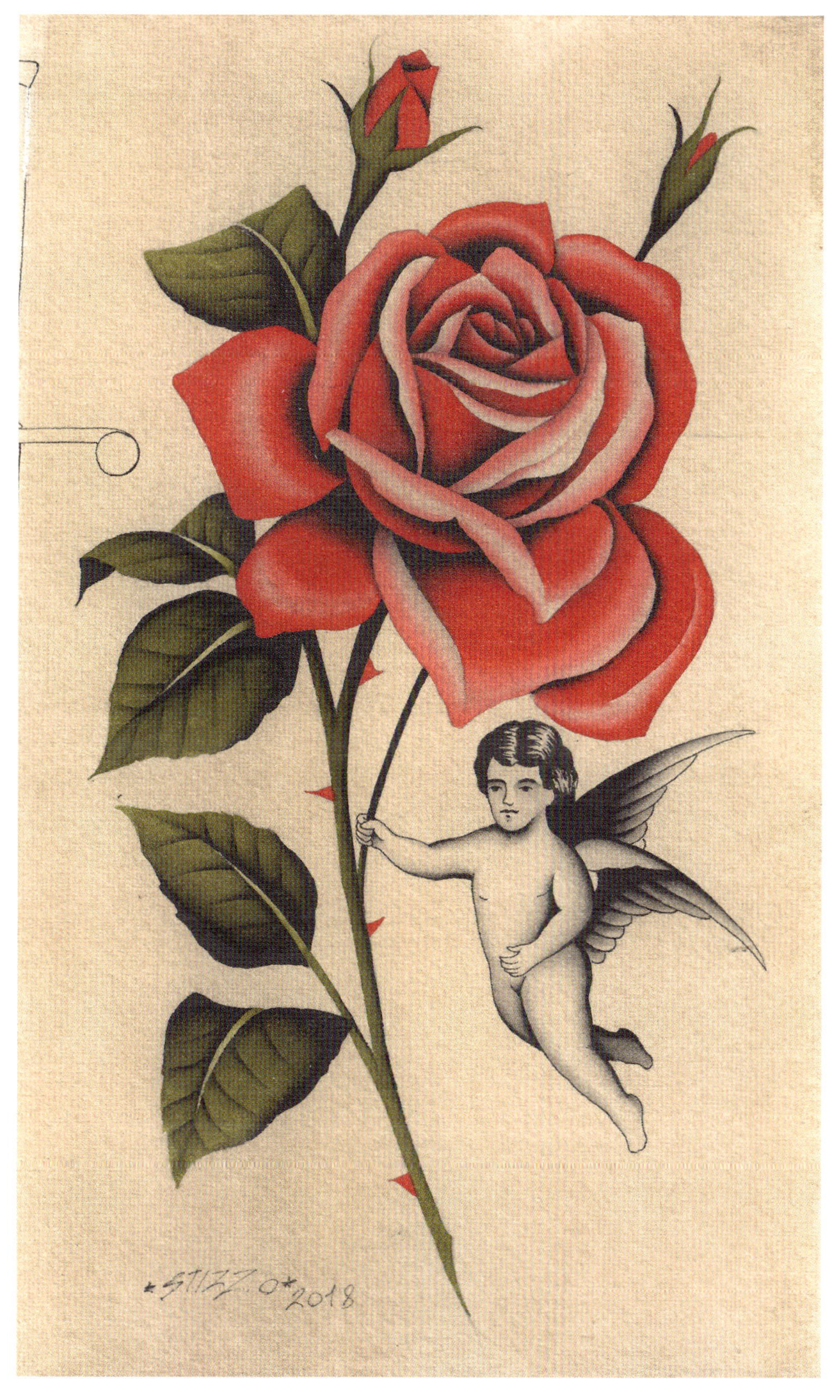
STIZZO 2018

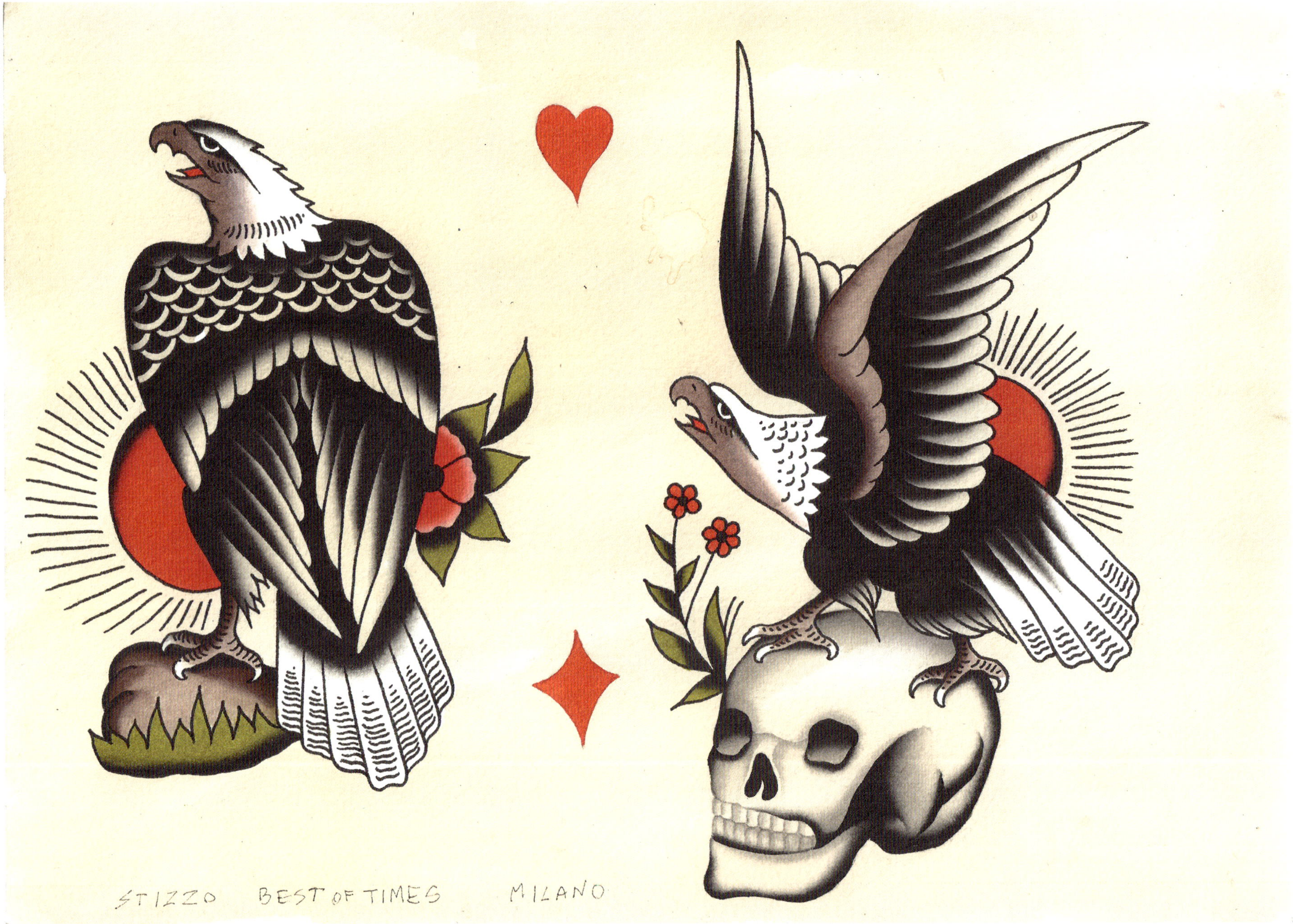

STIZZO BEST OF TIMES MILANO

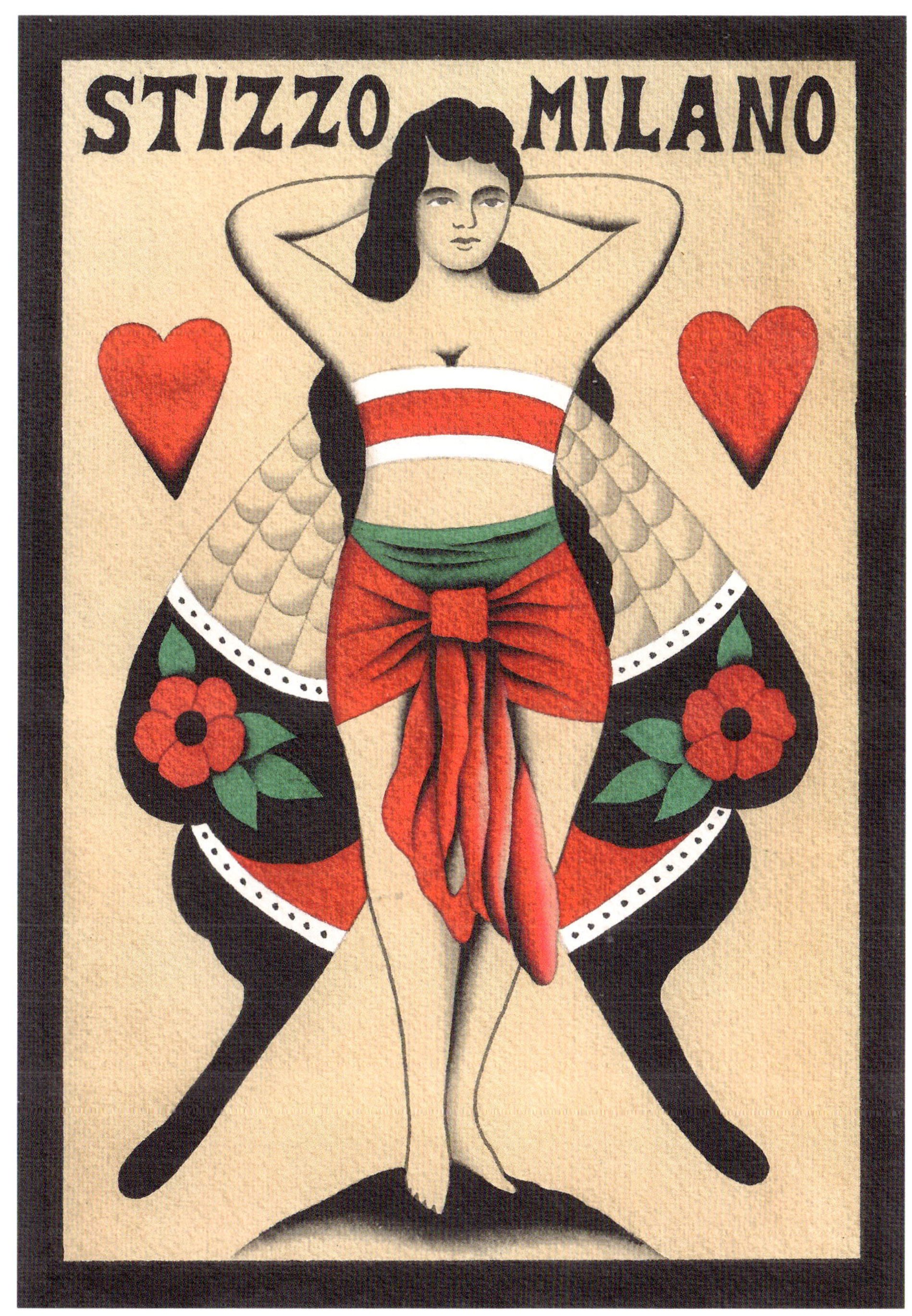
STIZZO MILANO

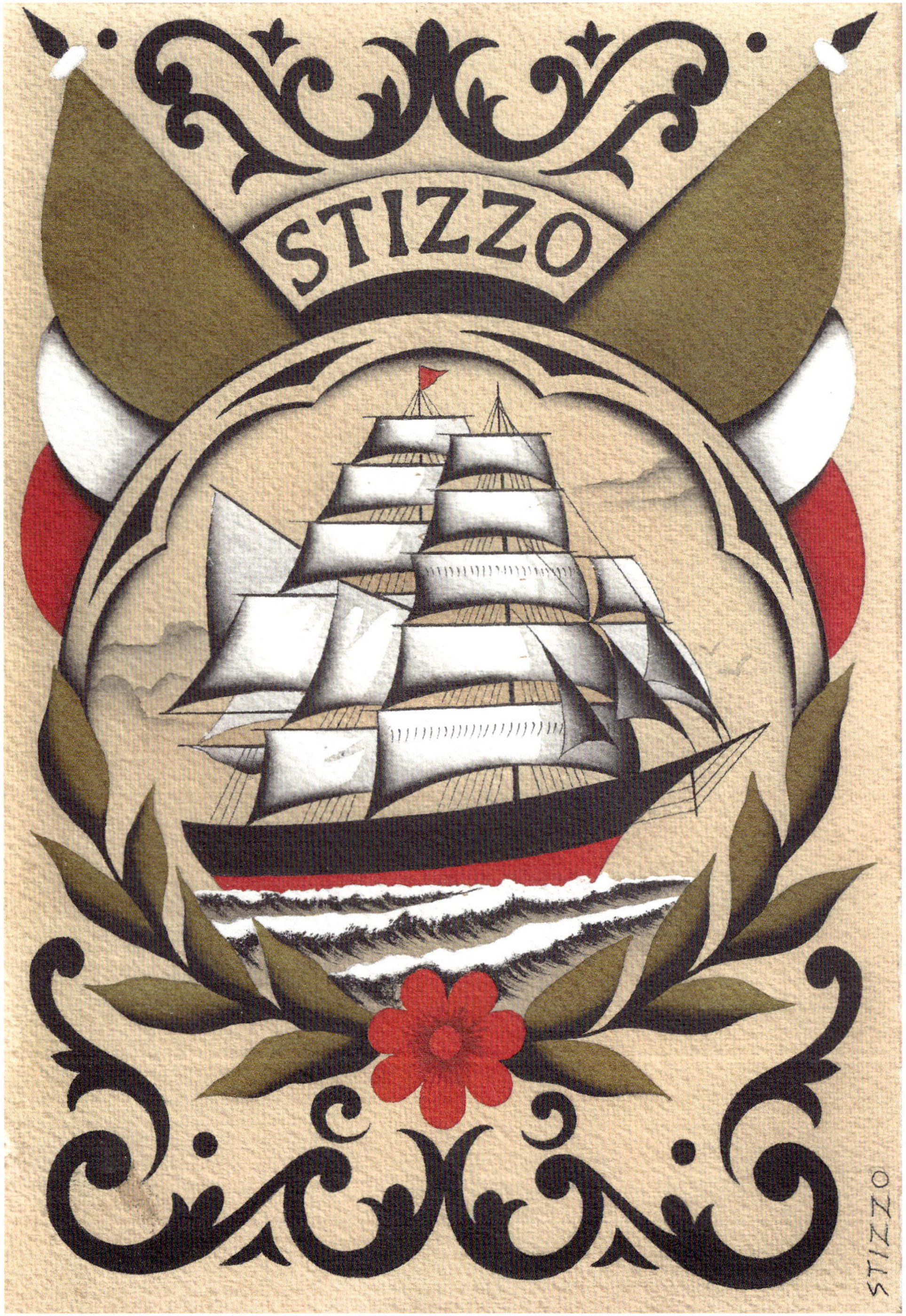

STIZZO

STIZZO

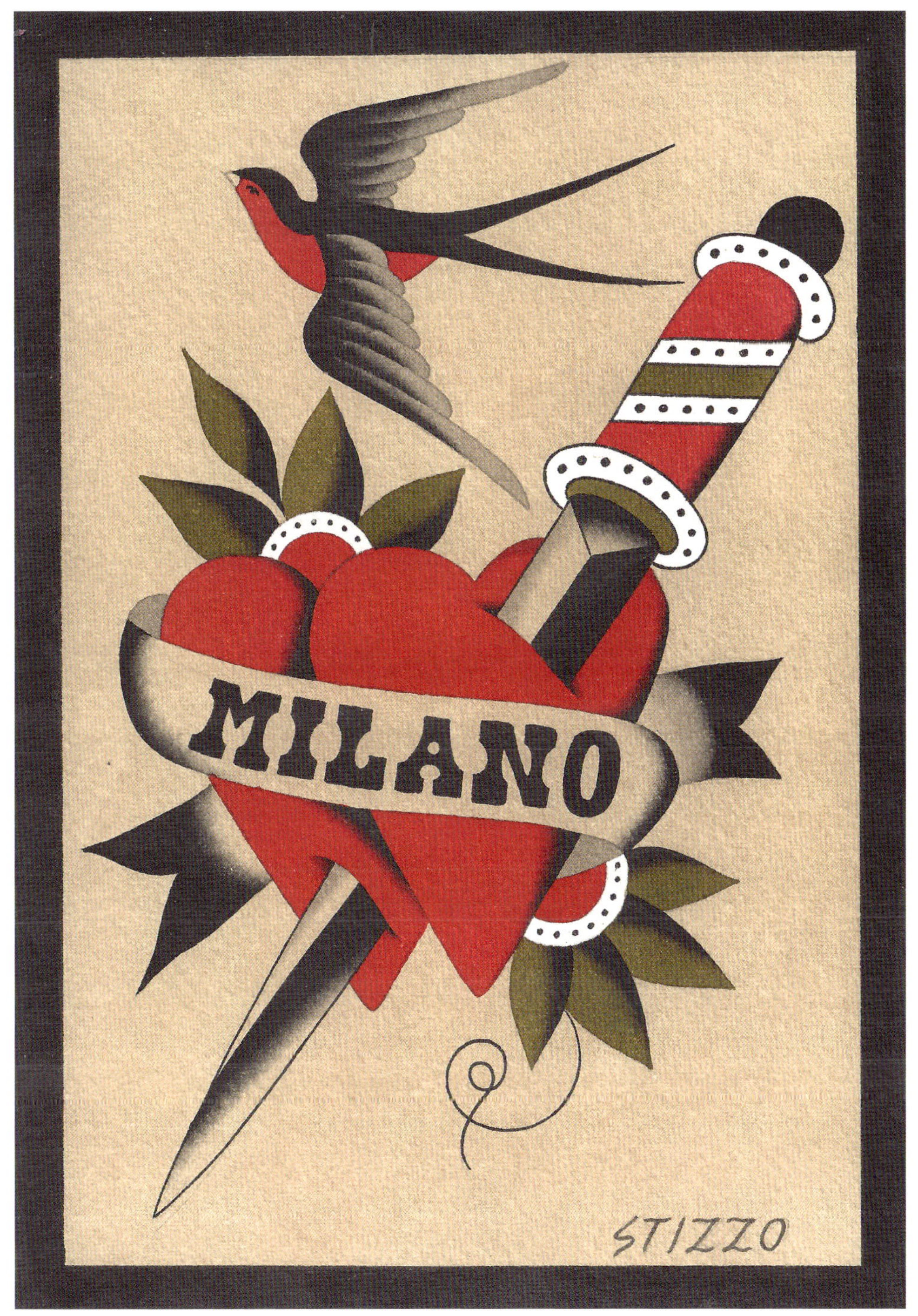
MILANO
STIZZO

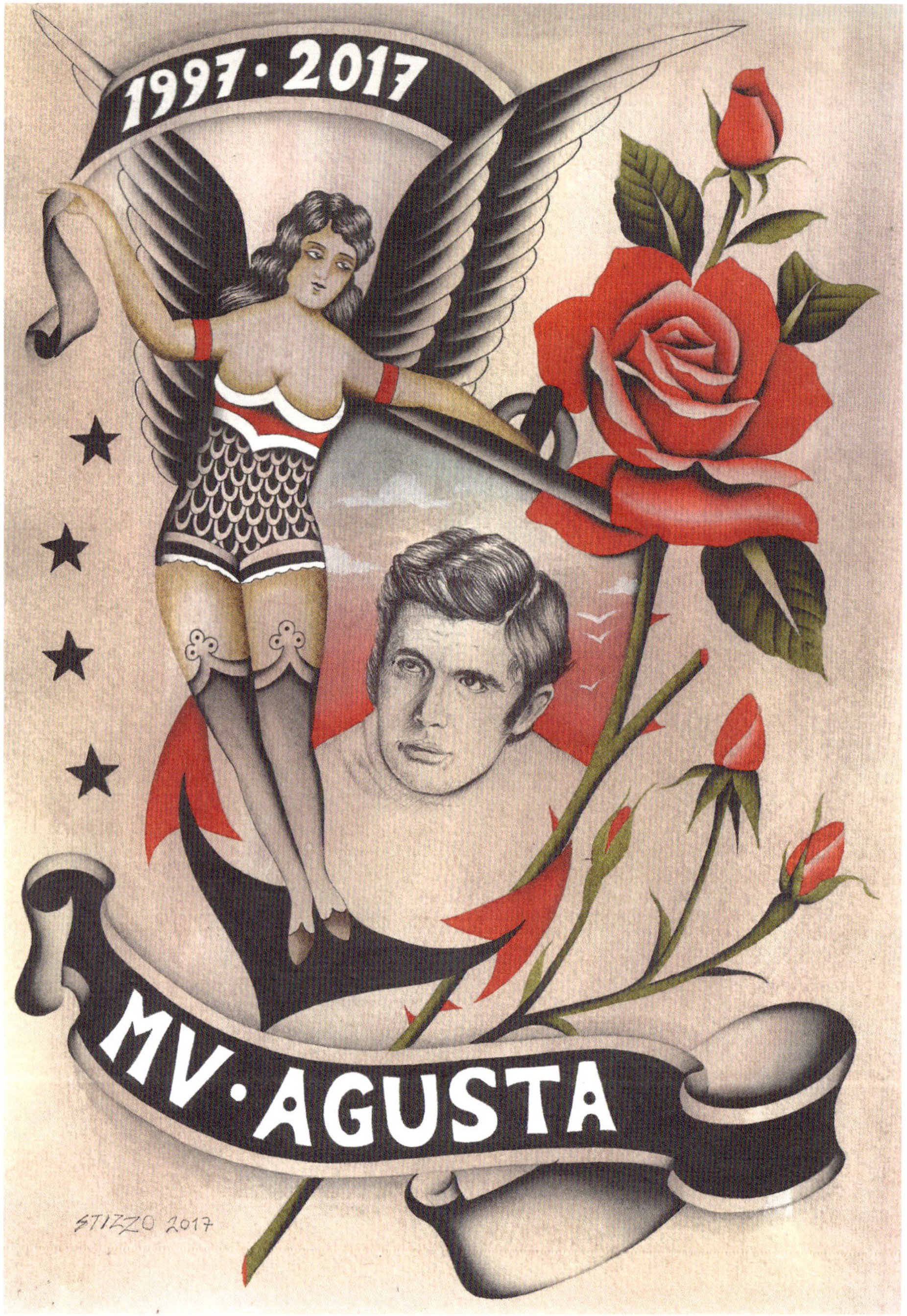

1997 · 2017

MV · AGUSTA

STIZZO 2017

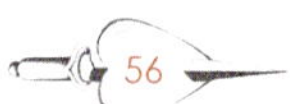

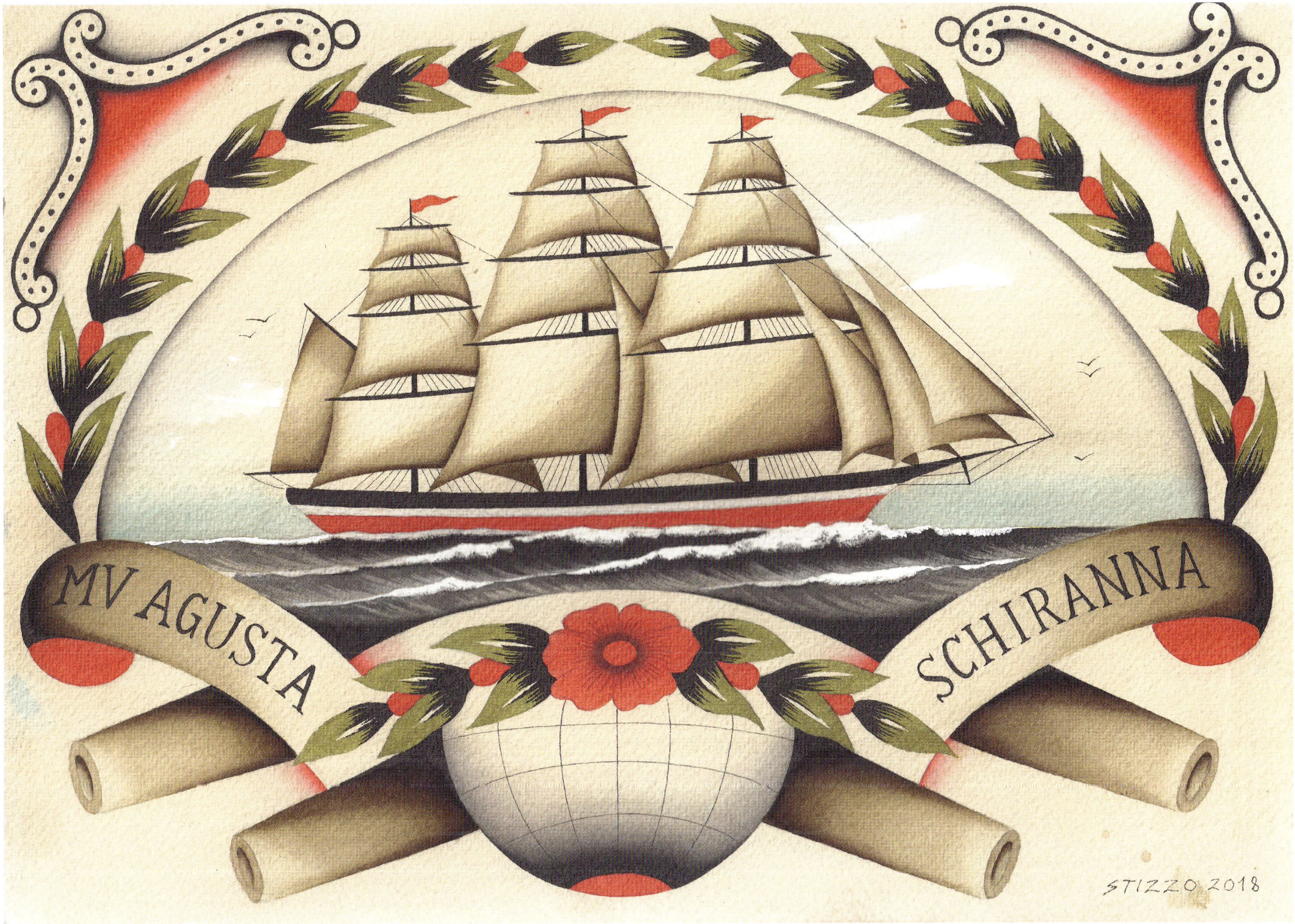

MV AGUSTA
SCHIRANNA
STIZZO 2018

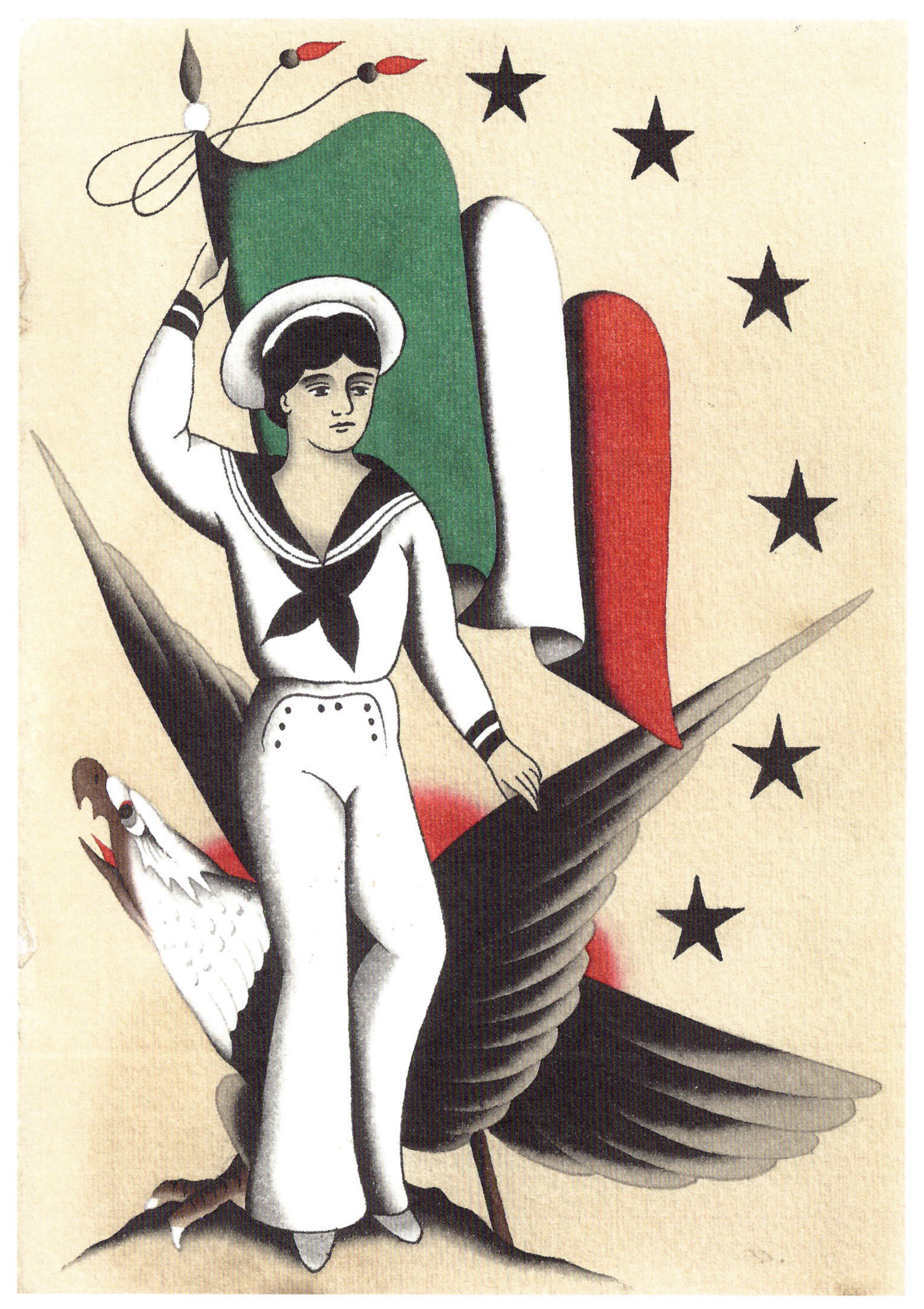

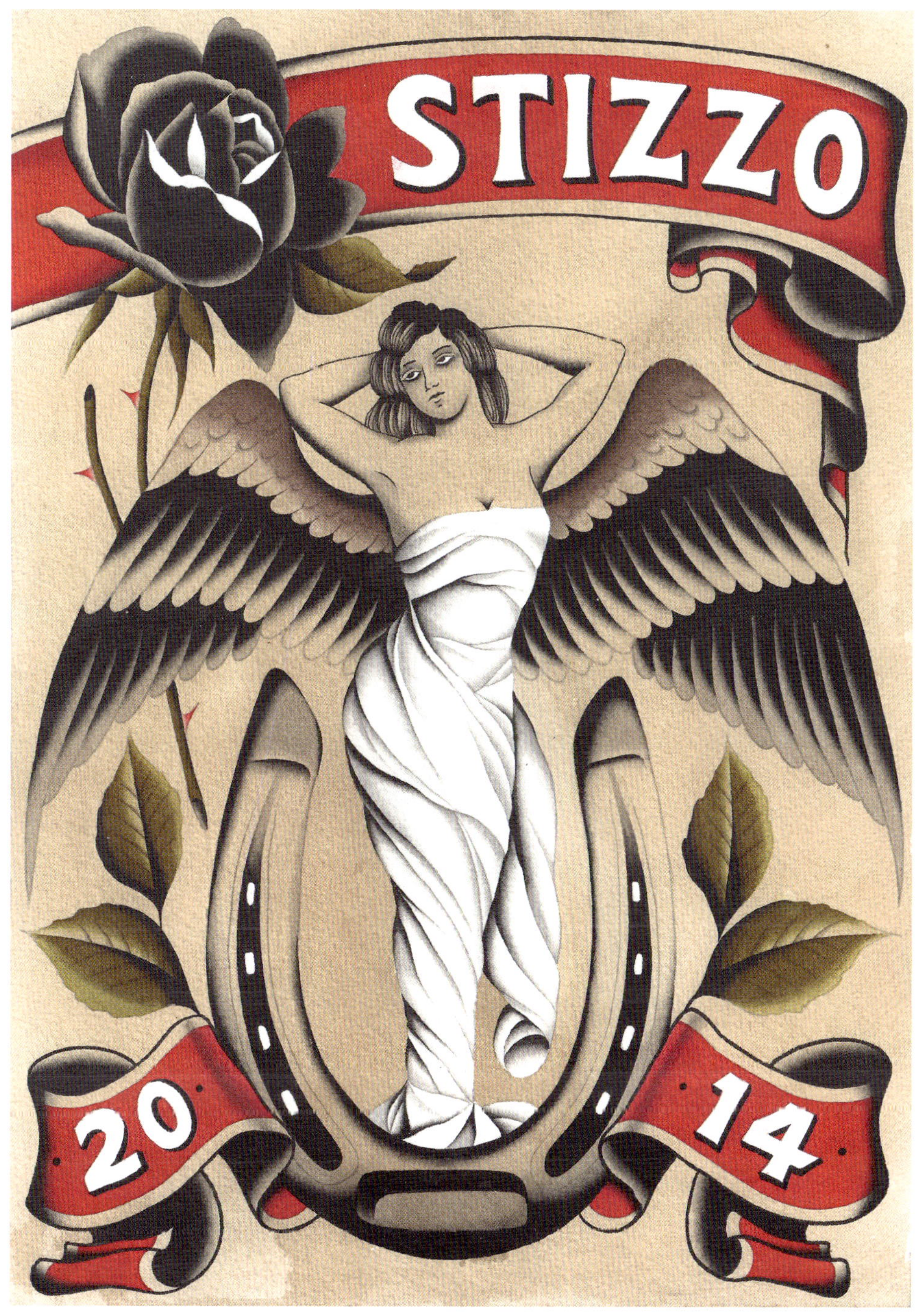
STIZZO
20
14

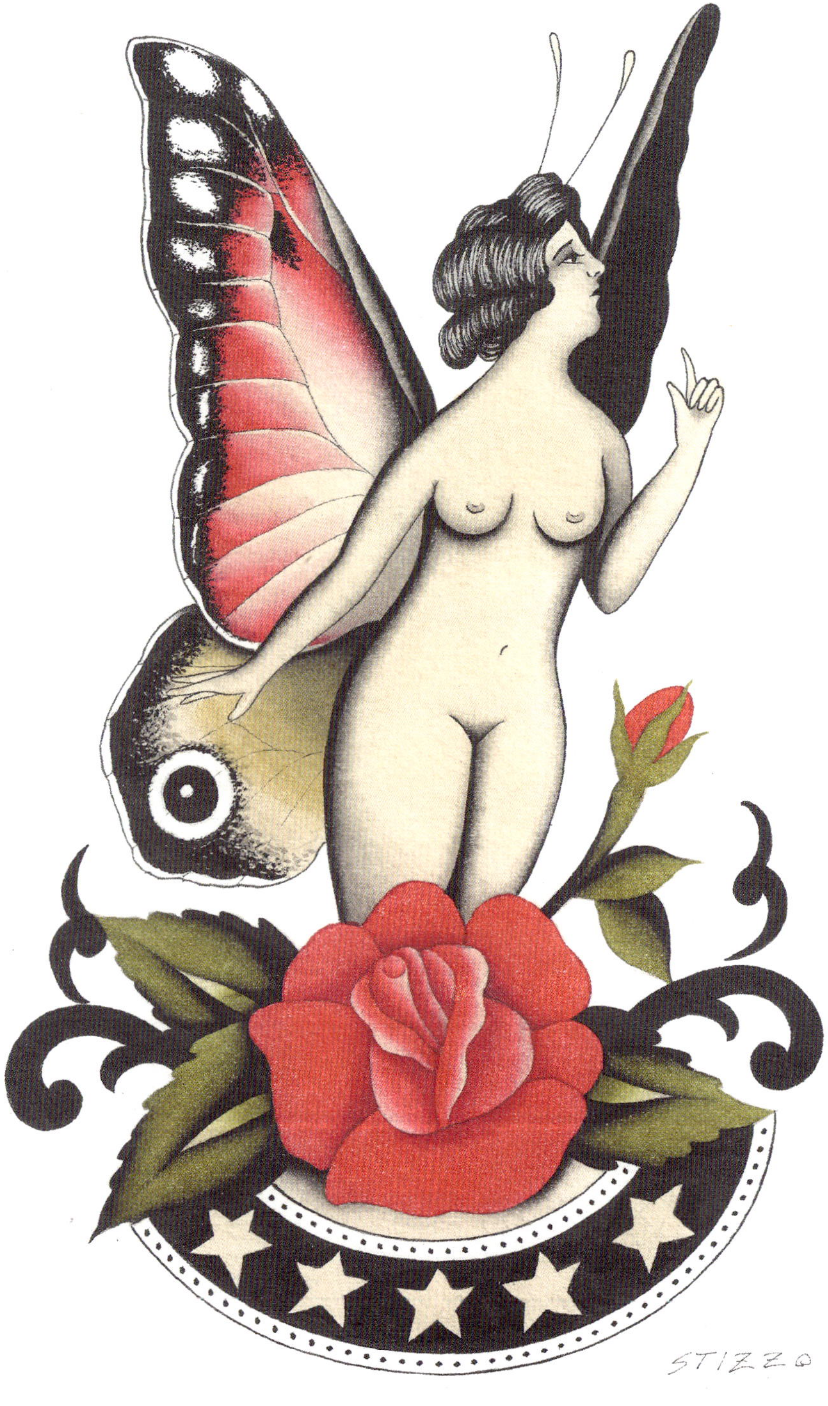

STIZZO

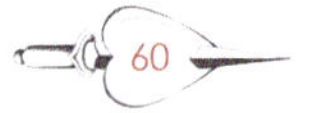

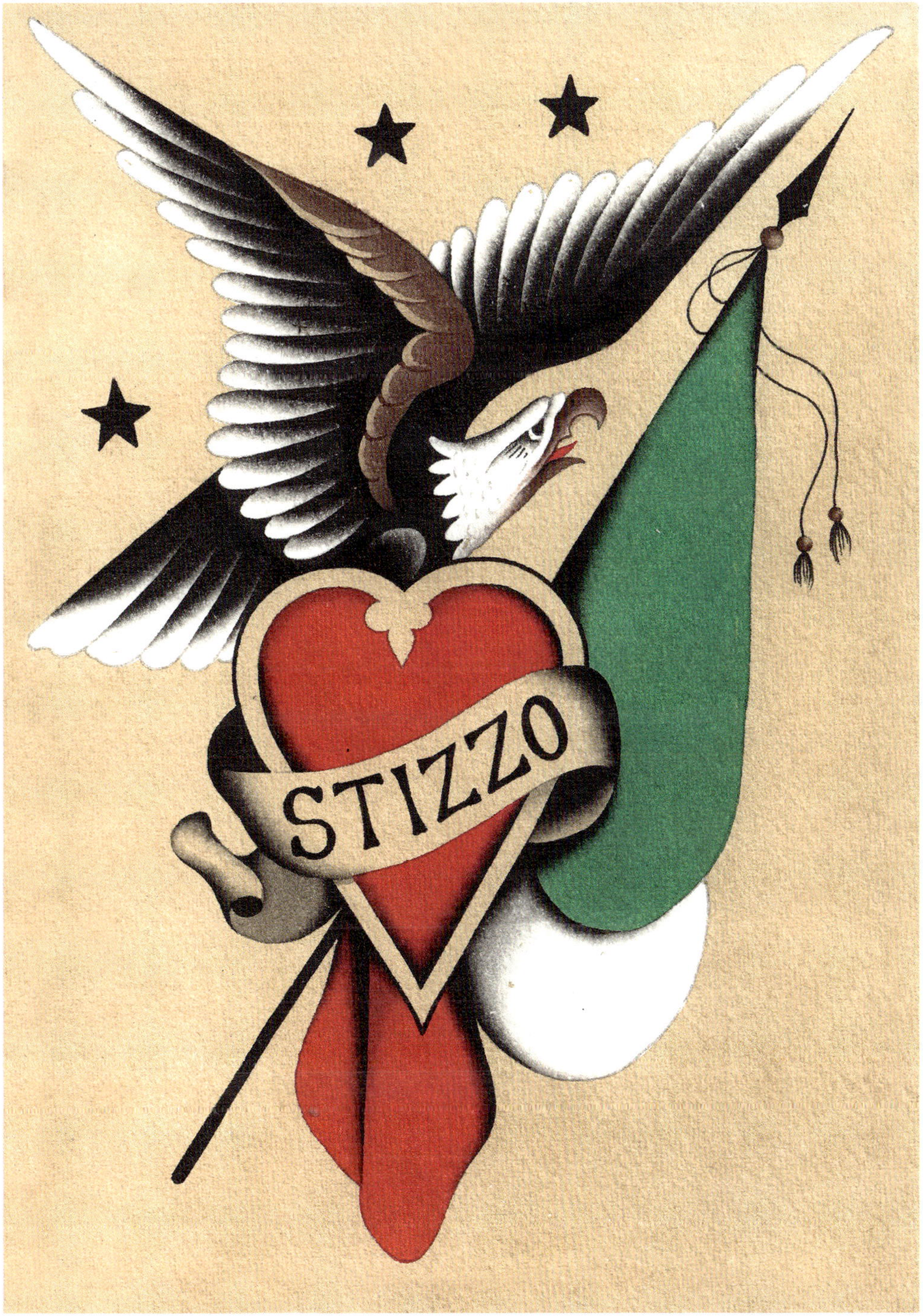

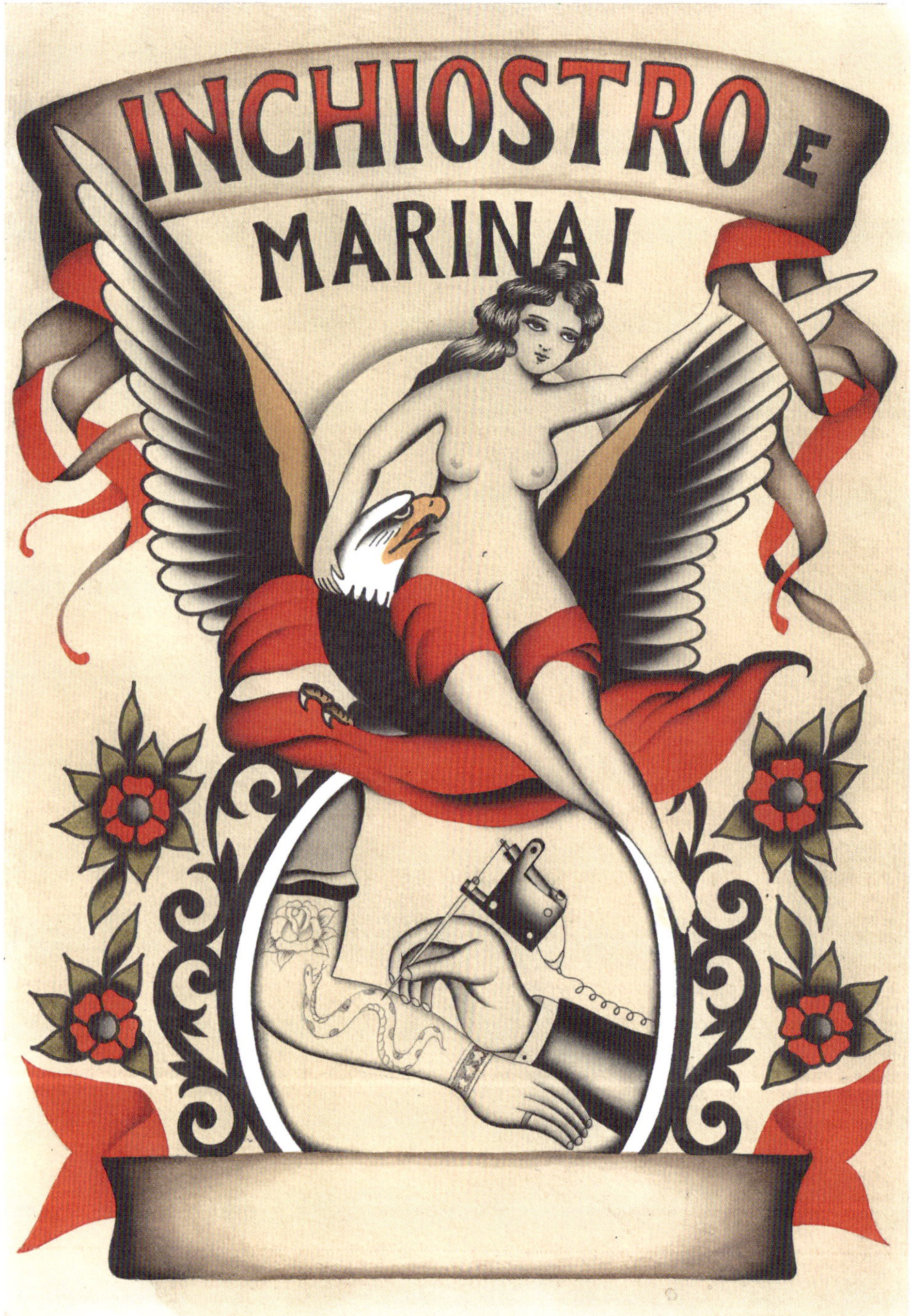

INCHIOSTRO E

MARINAI

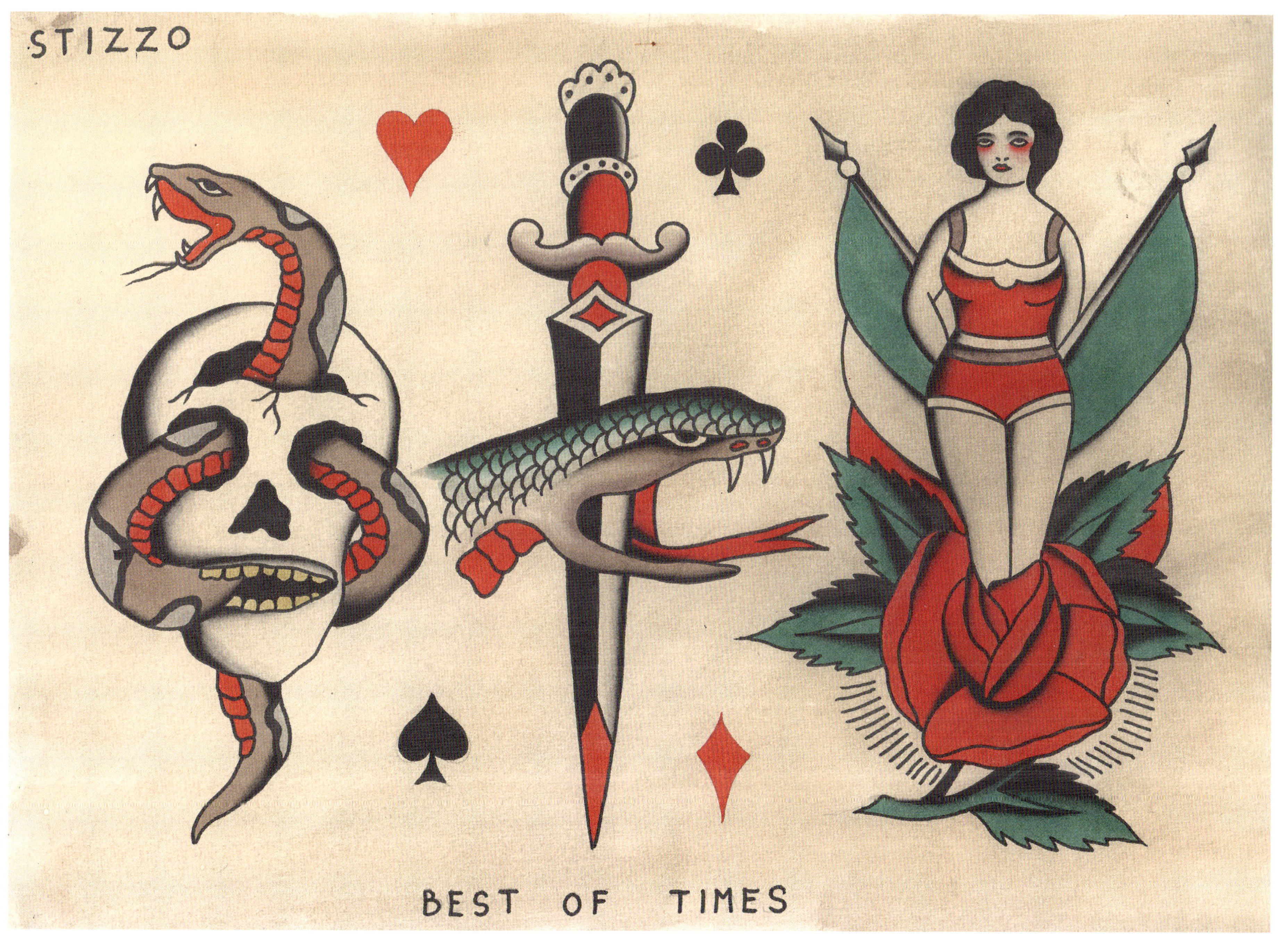
STIZZO
BEST OF TIMES

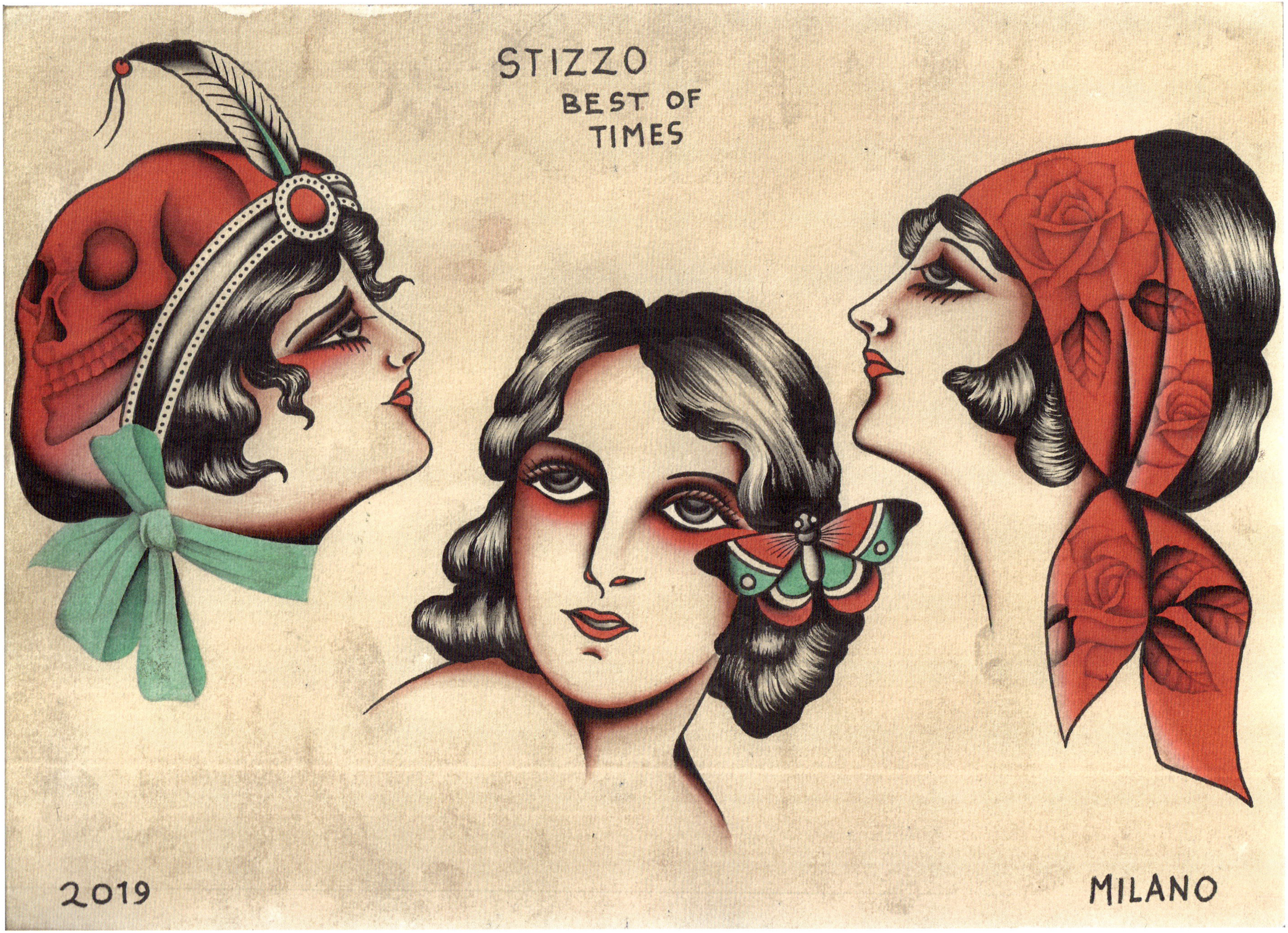

STIZZO

BEST OF TIMES

2019

MILANO

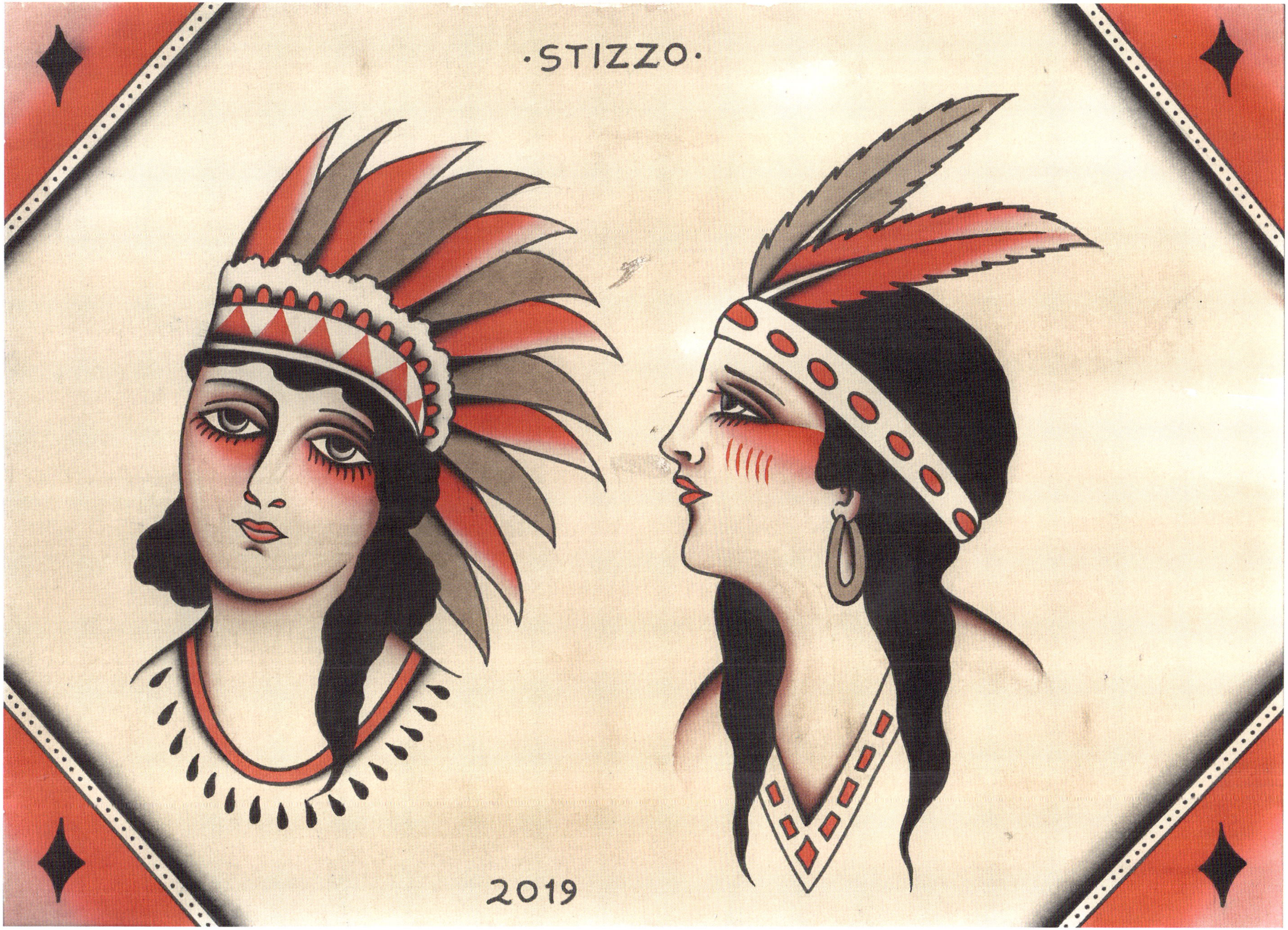

·STIZZO·

2019

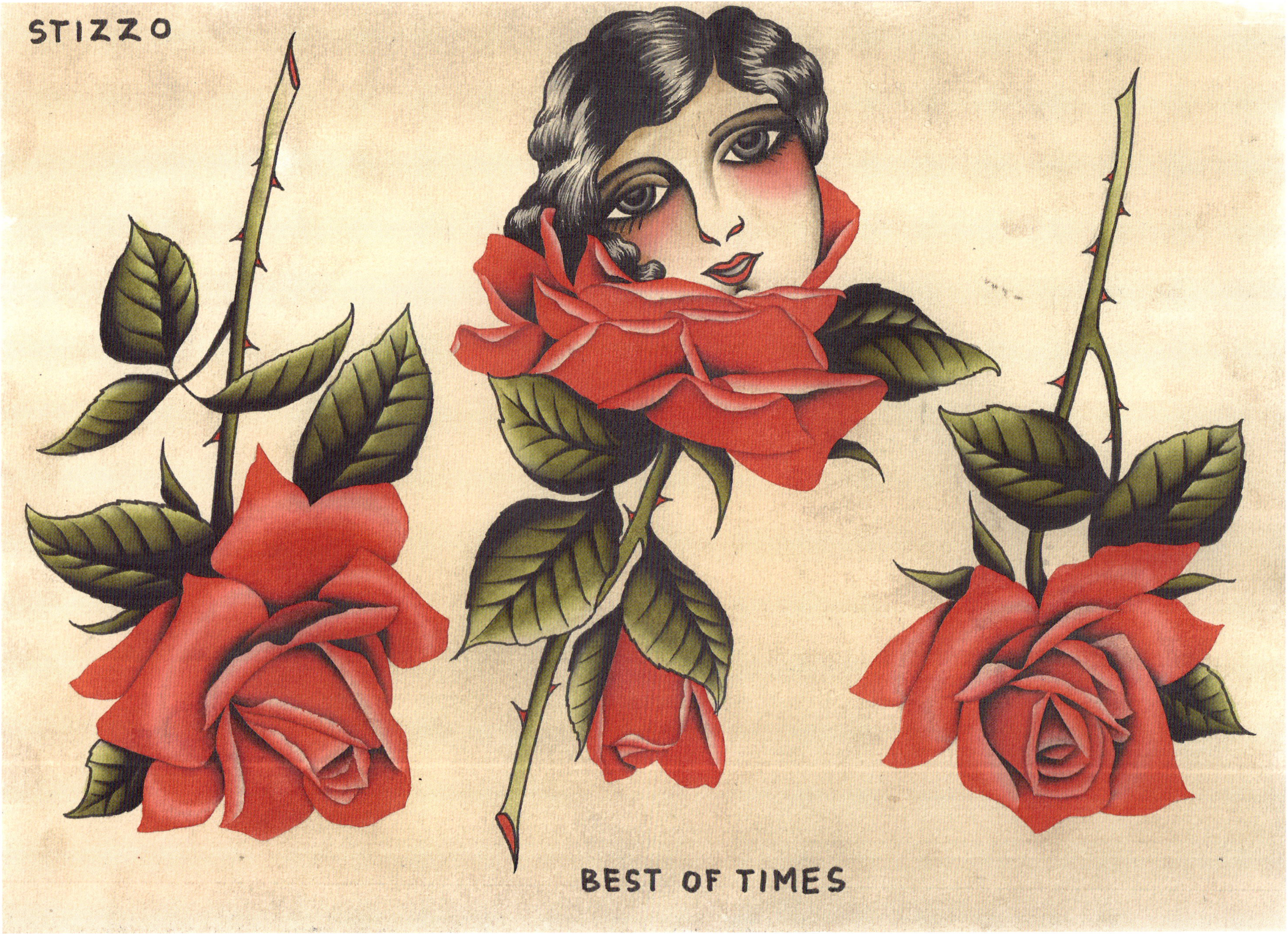

STIZZO

BEST OF TIMES

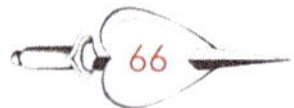

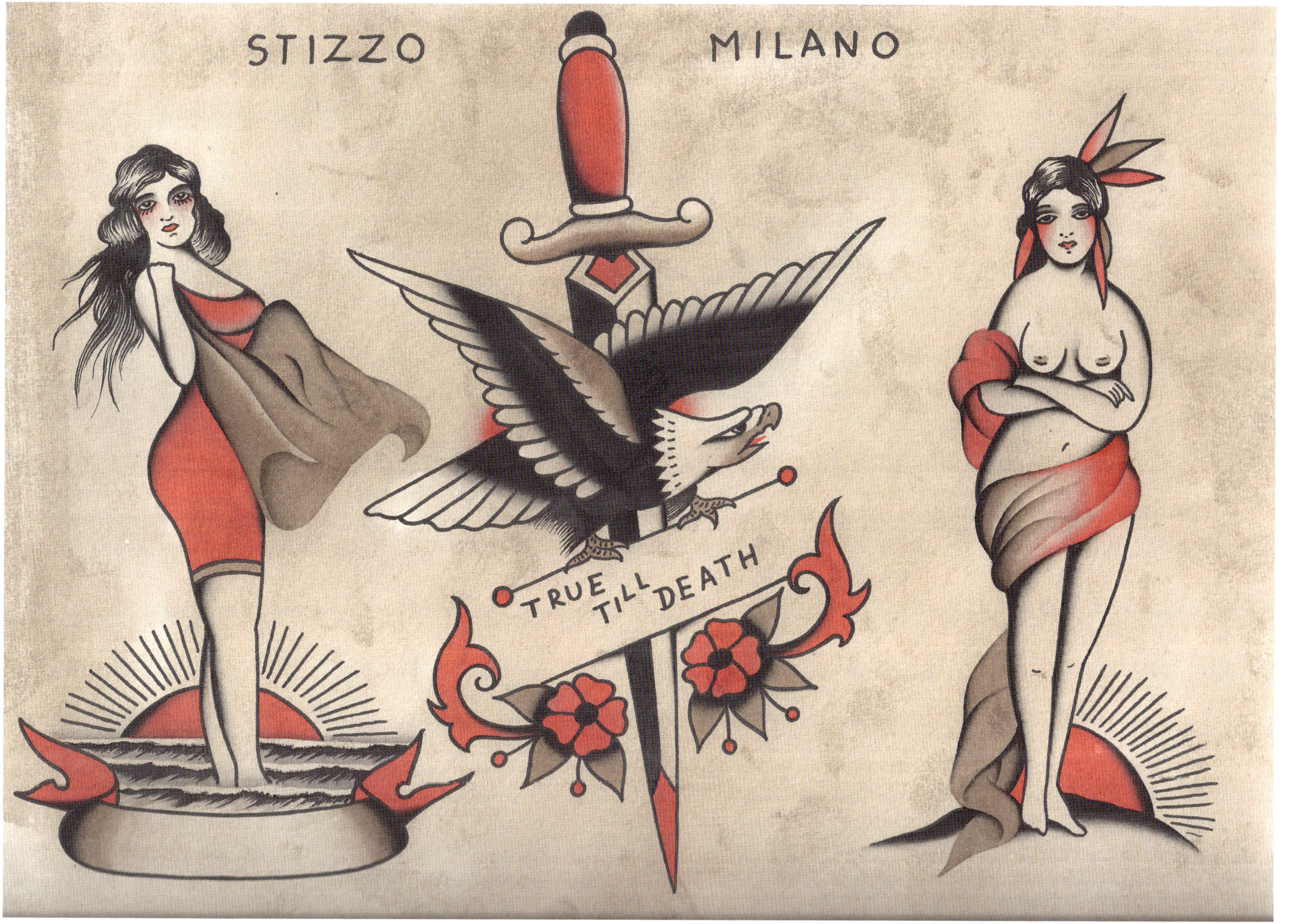

STIZZO MILANO
TRUE TILL DEATH

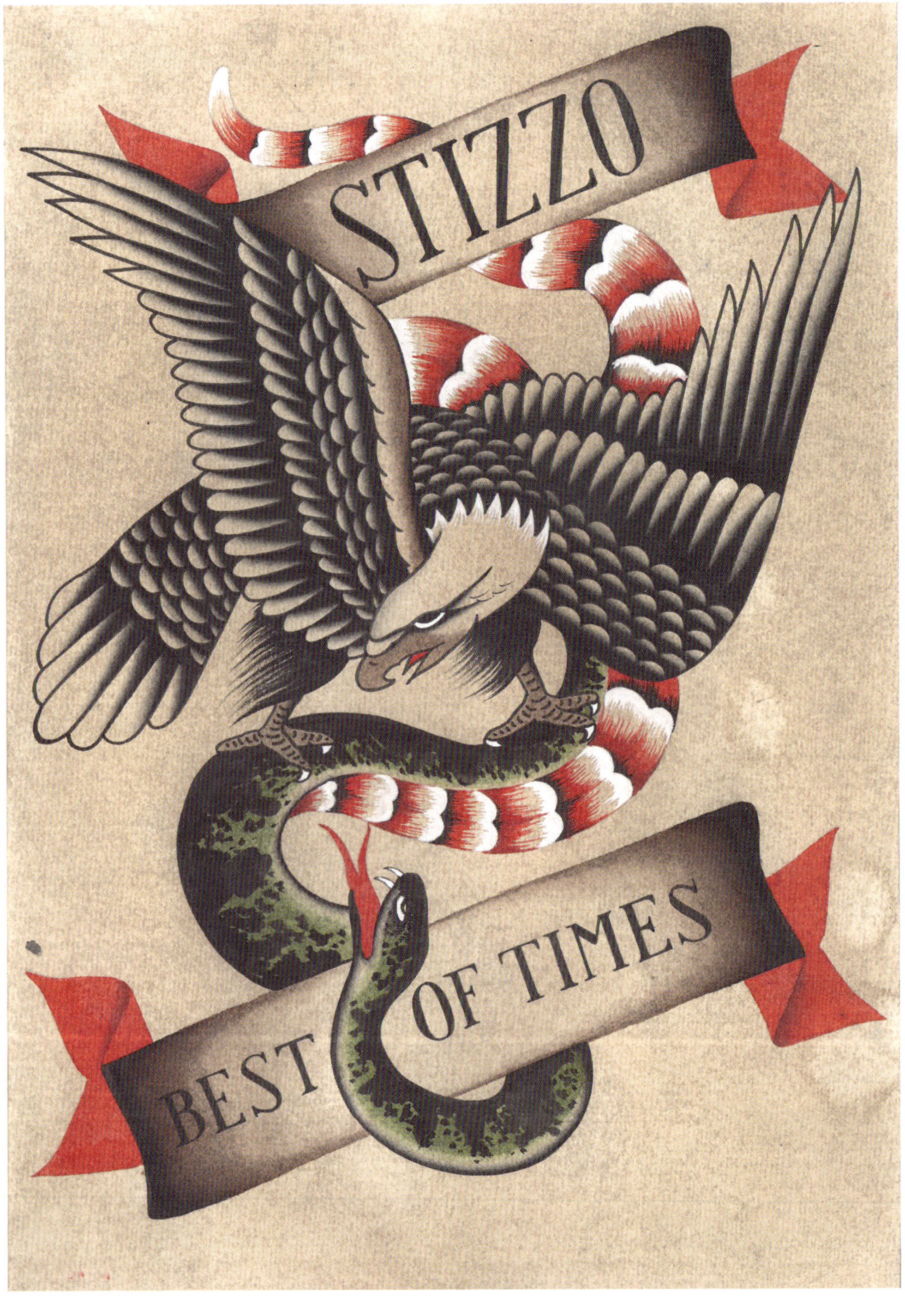

STIZZO

BEST OF TIMES

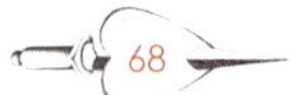

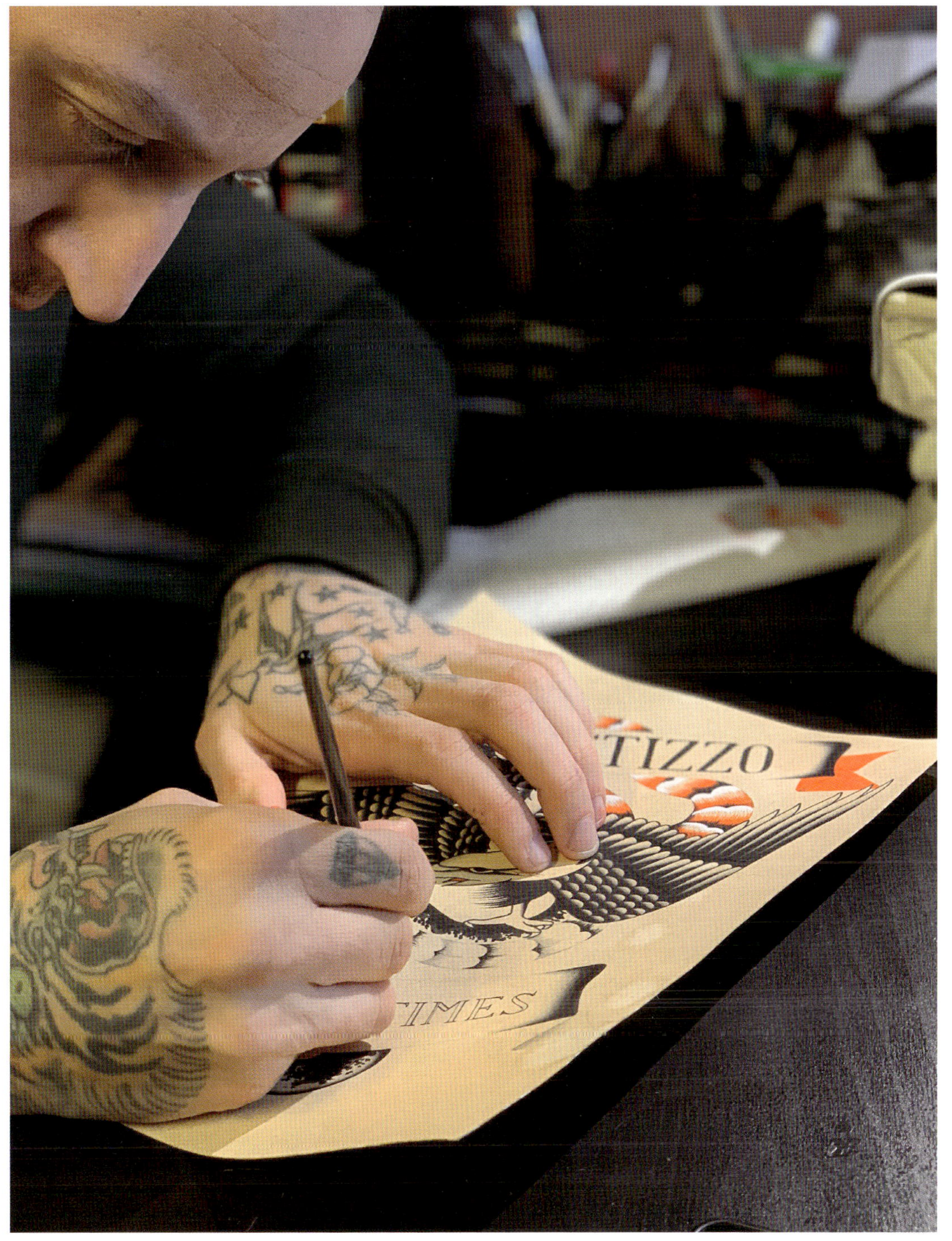
STIZZO
TIMES

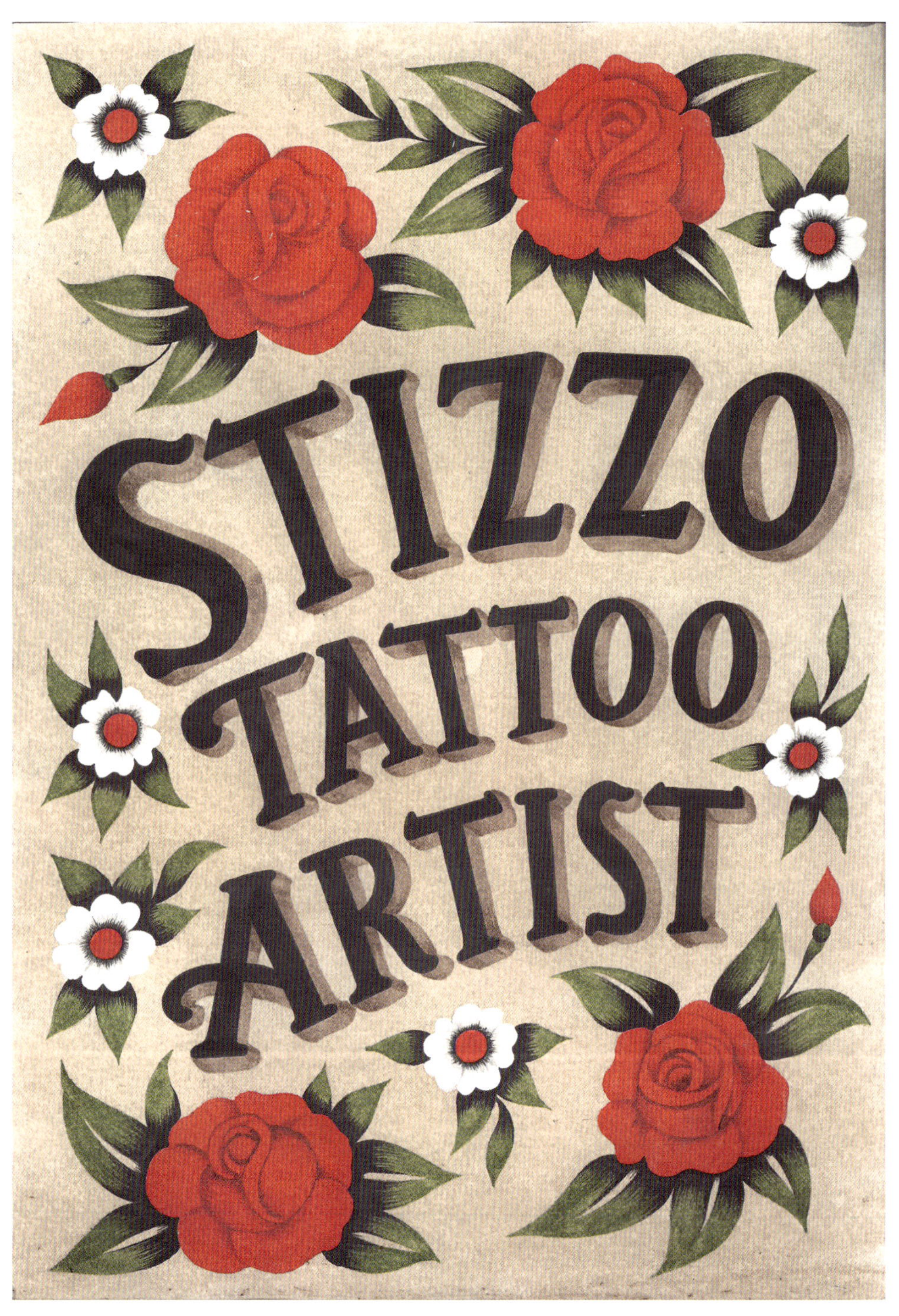
STIZZO
TATTOO
ARTIST

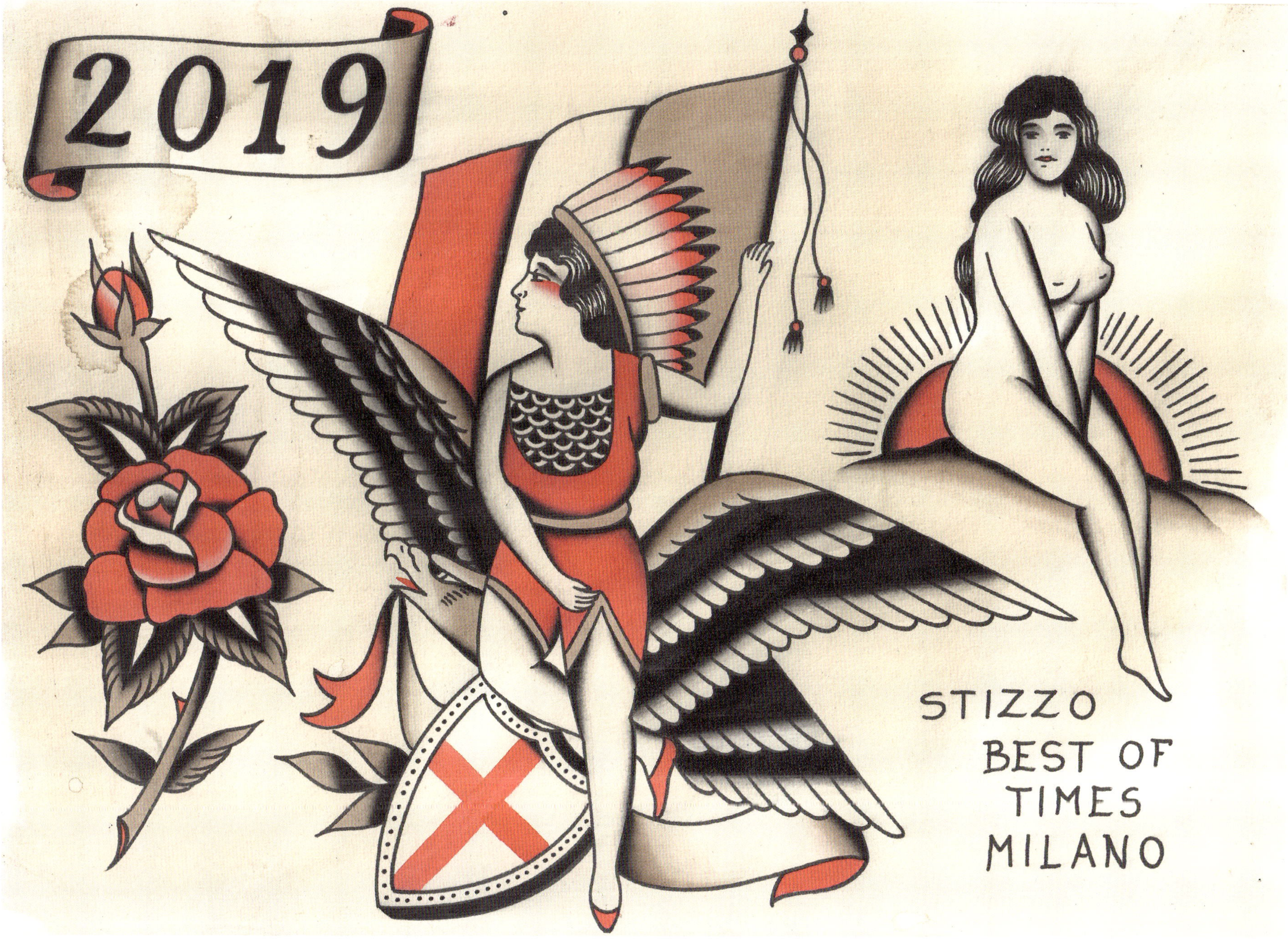

2019

STIZZO
BEST OF
TIMES
MILANO

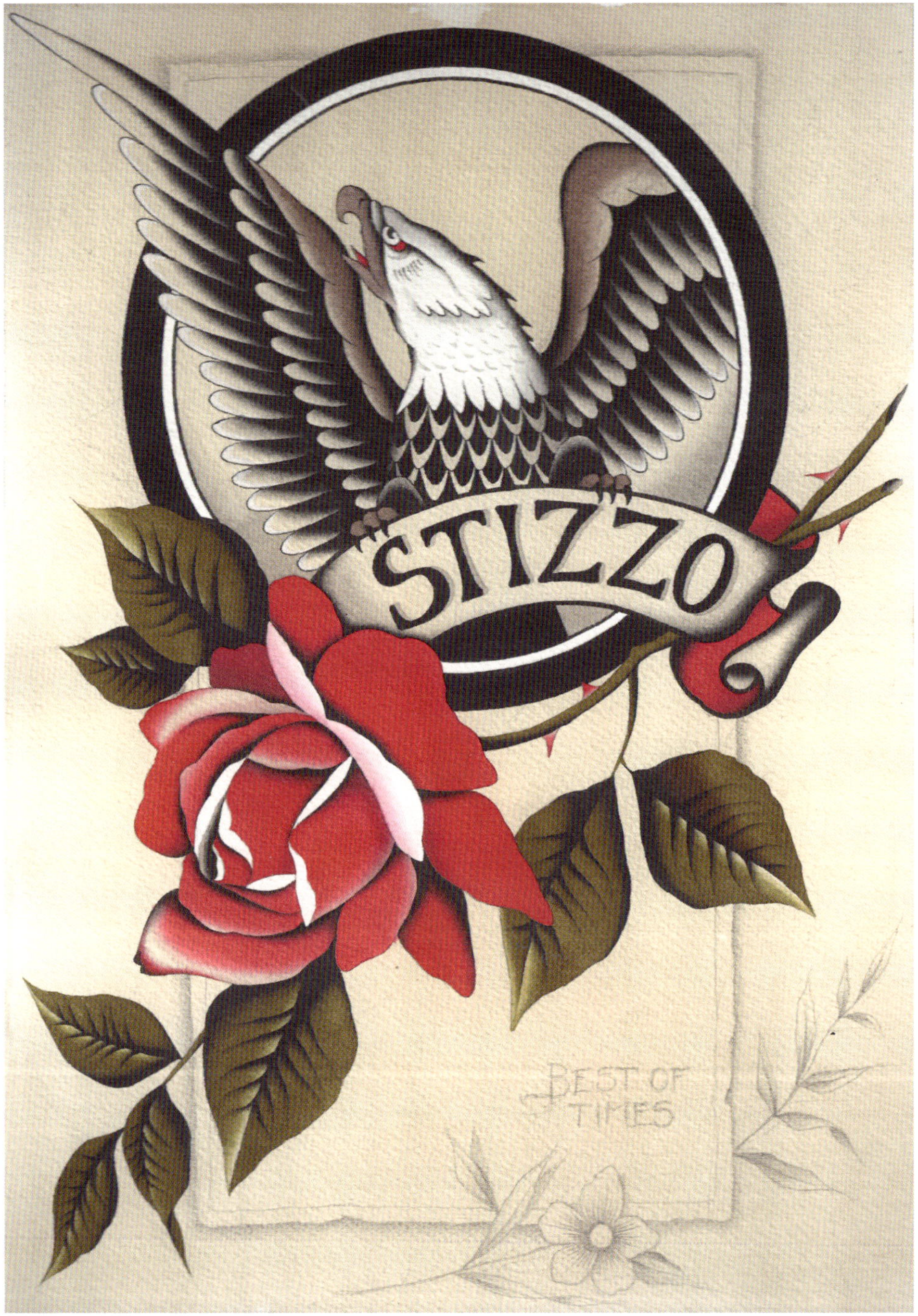

STIZZO

BEST OF TIMES

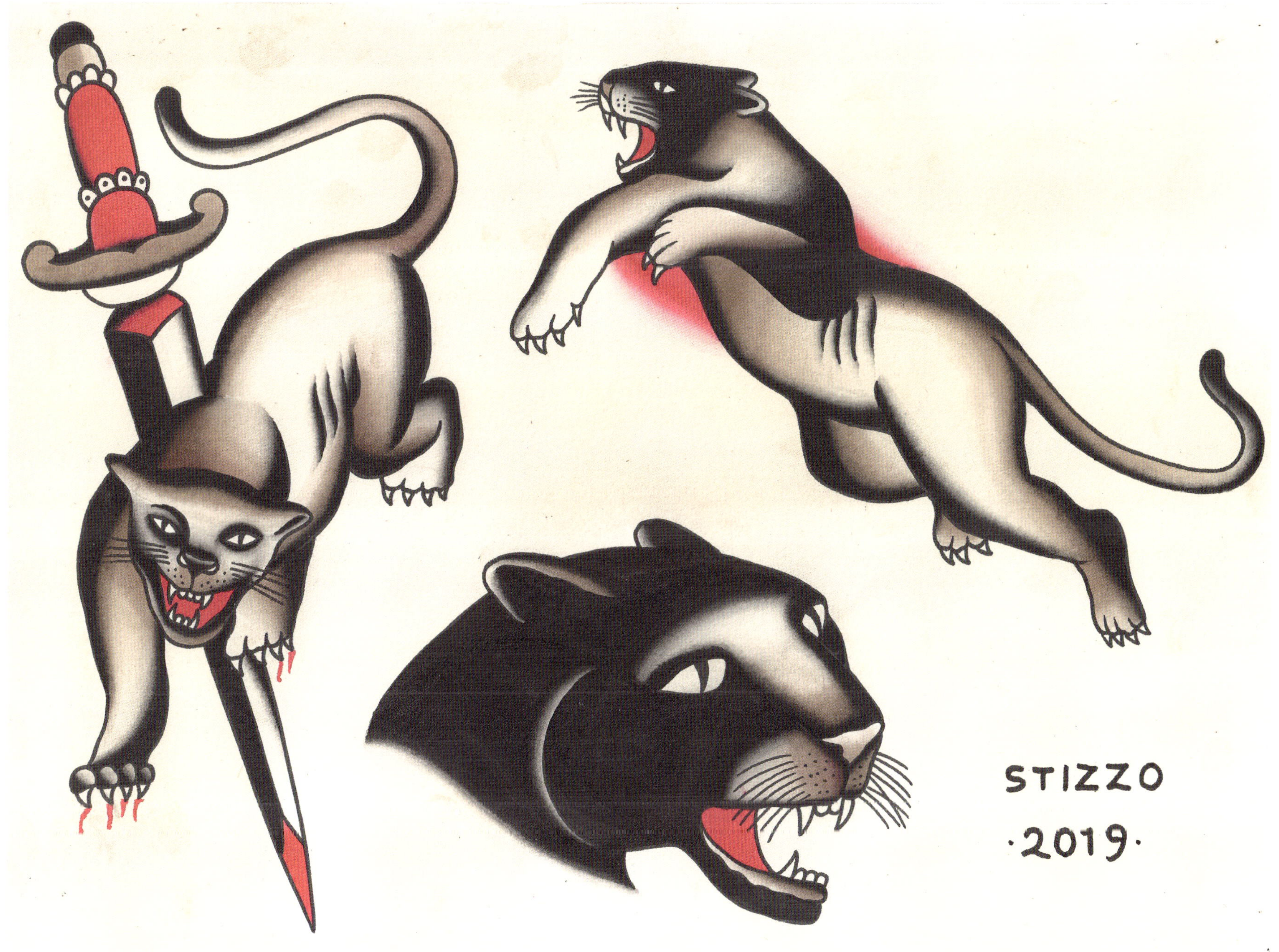
STIZZO
·2019·

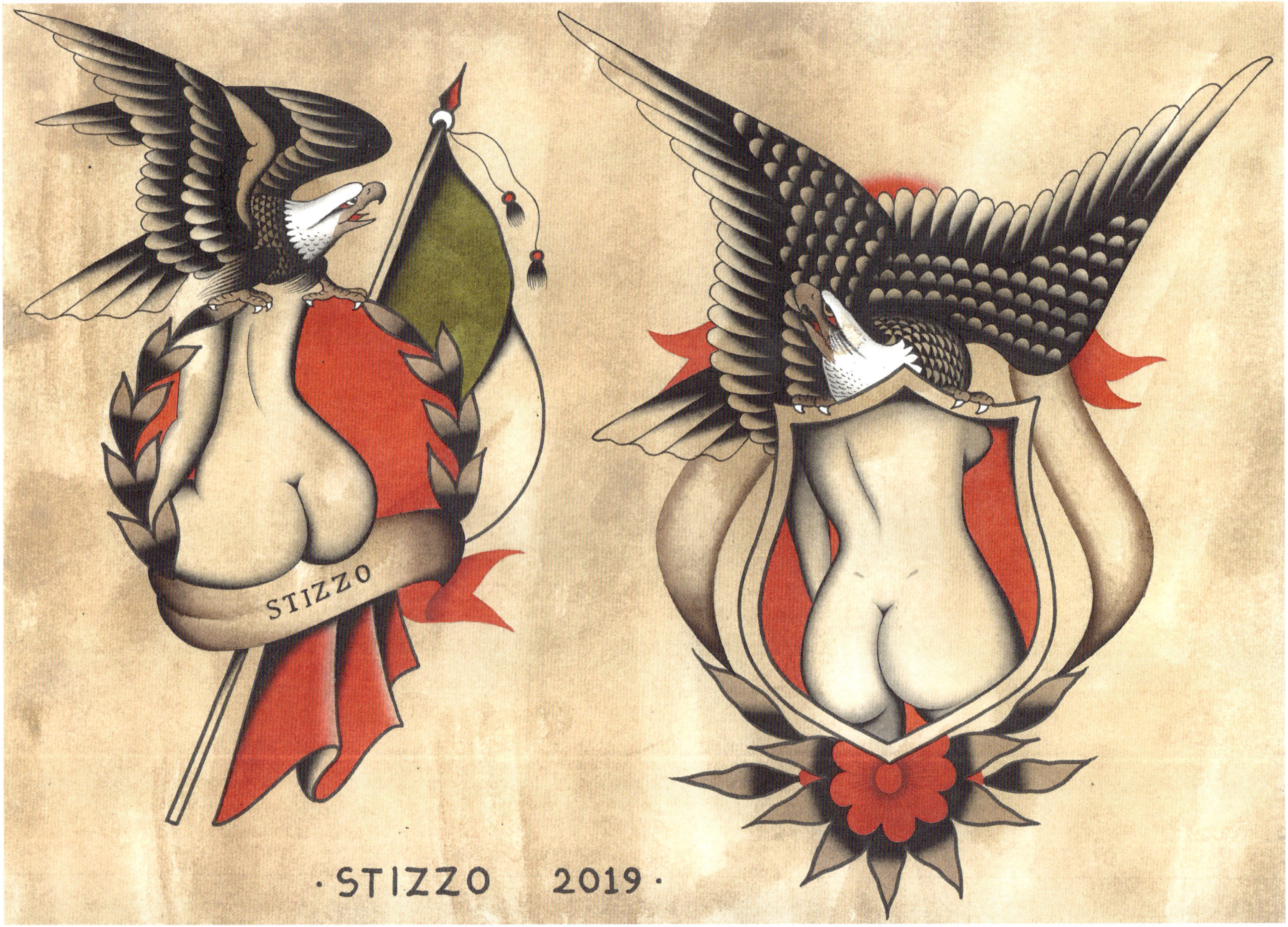

STIZZO

·STIZZO 2019·

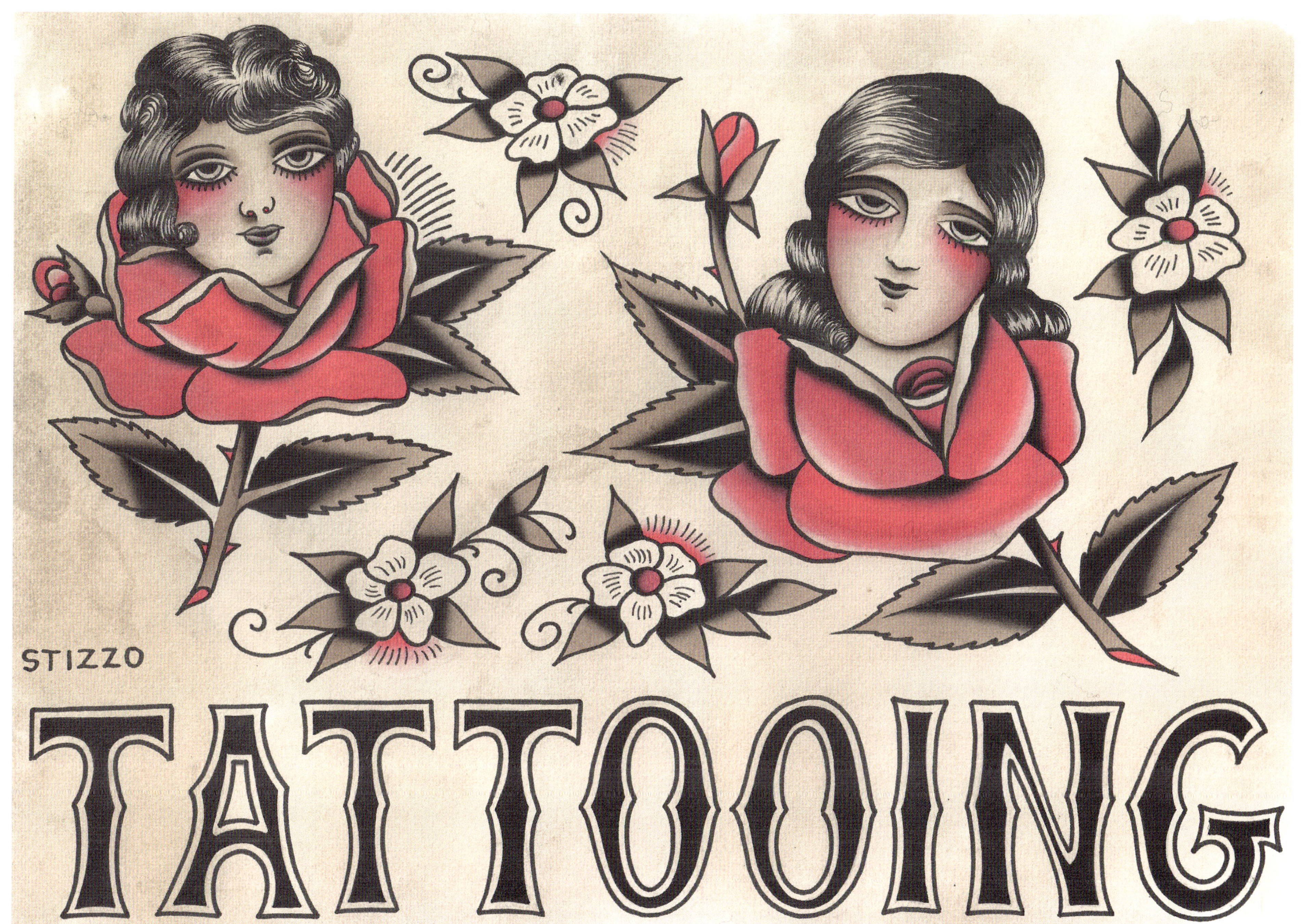
STIZZO
TATTOOING

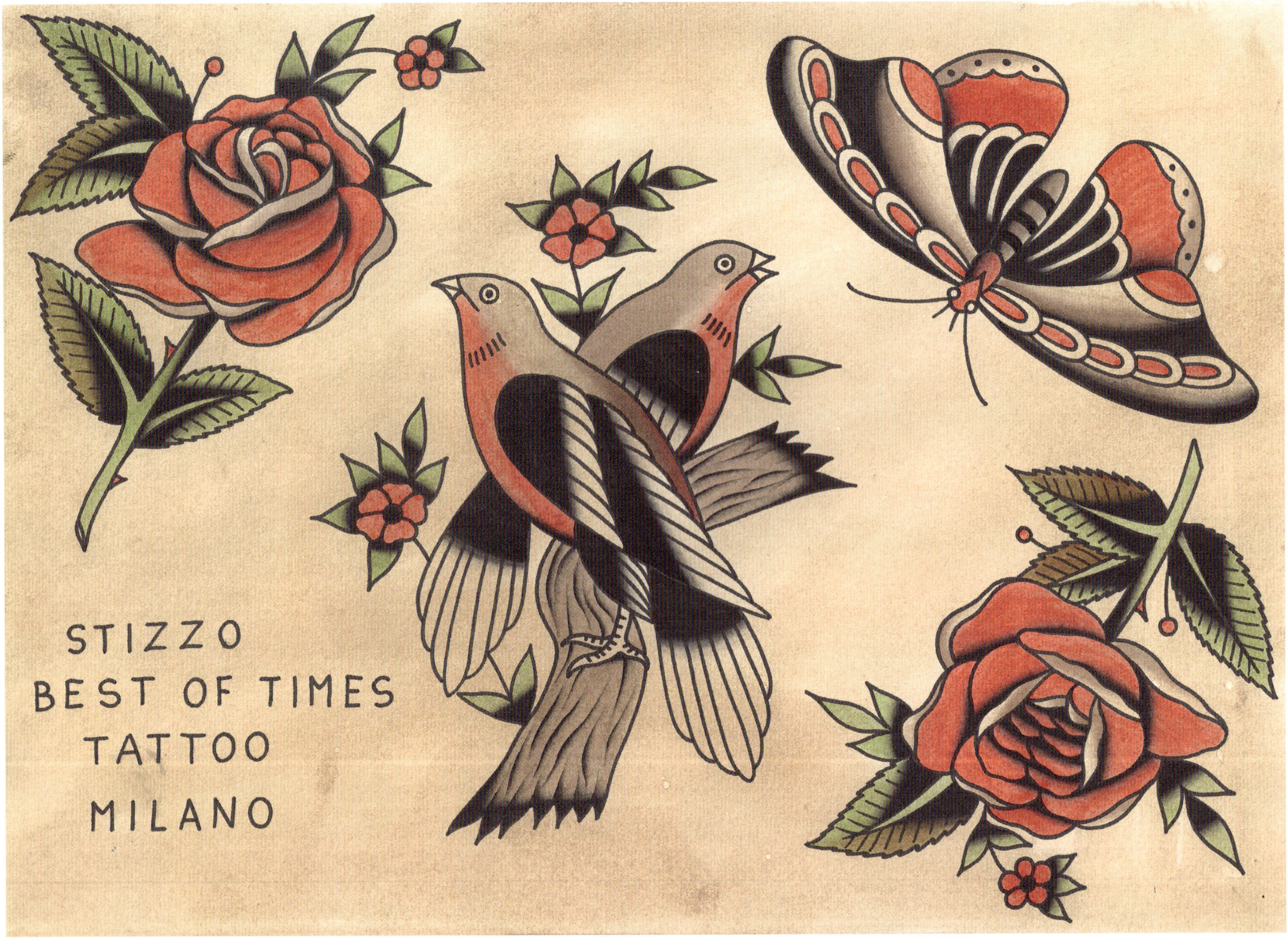

STIZZO
BEST OF TIMES
TATTOO
MILANO

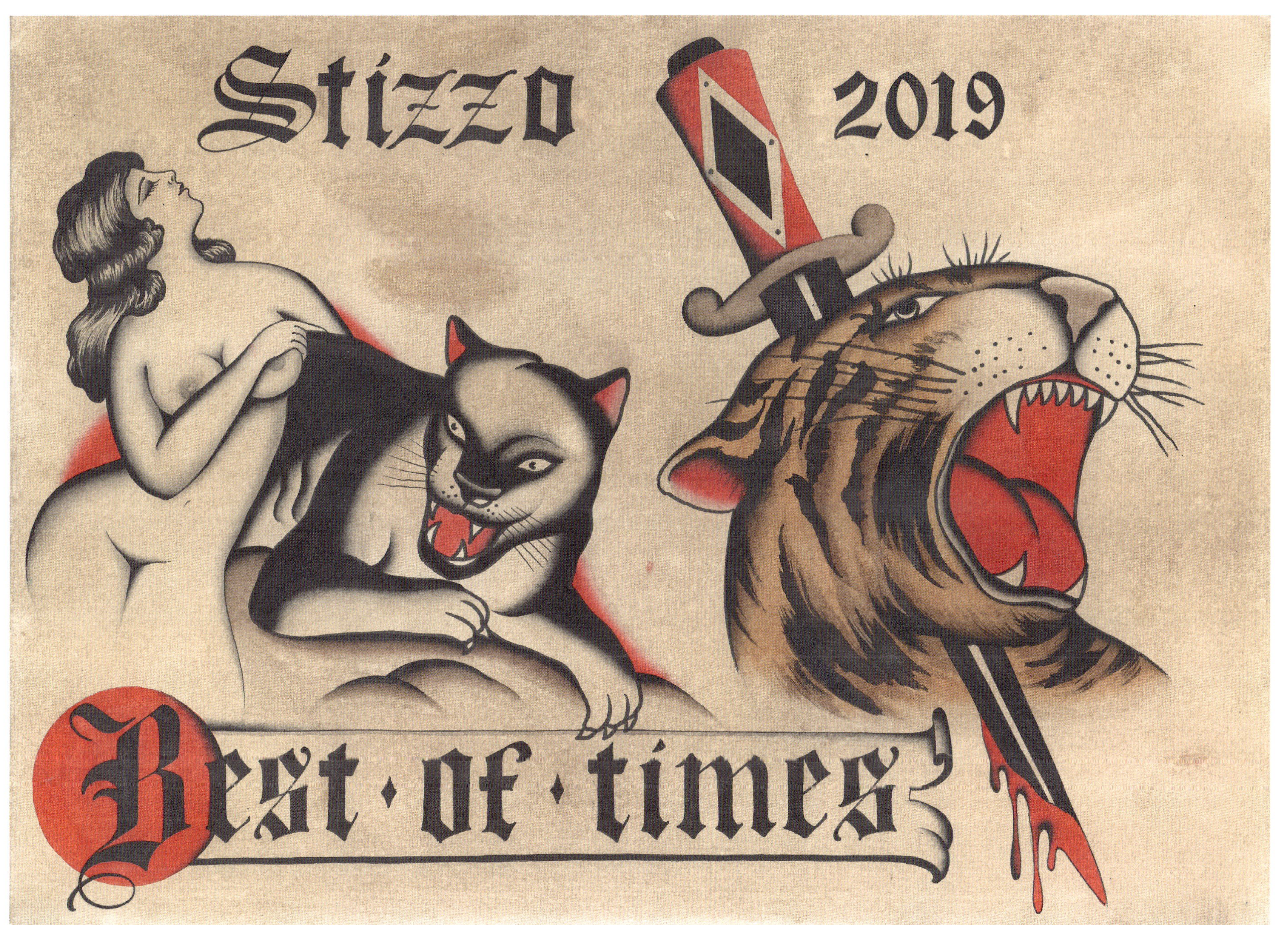
Stizzo
2019
Best · of · times

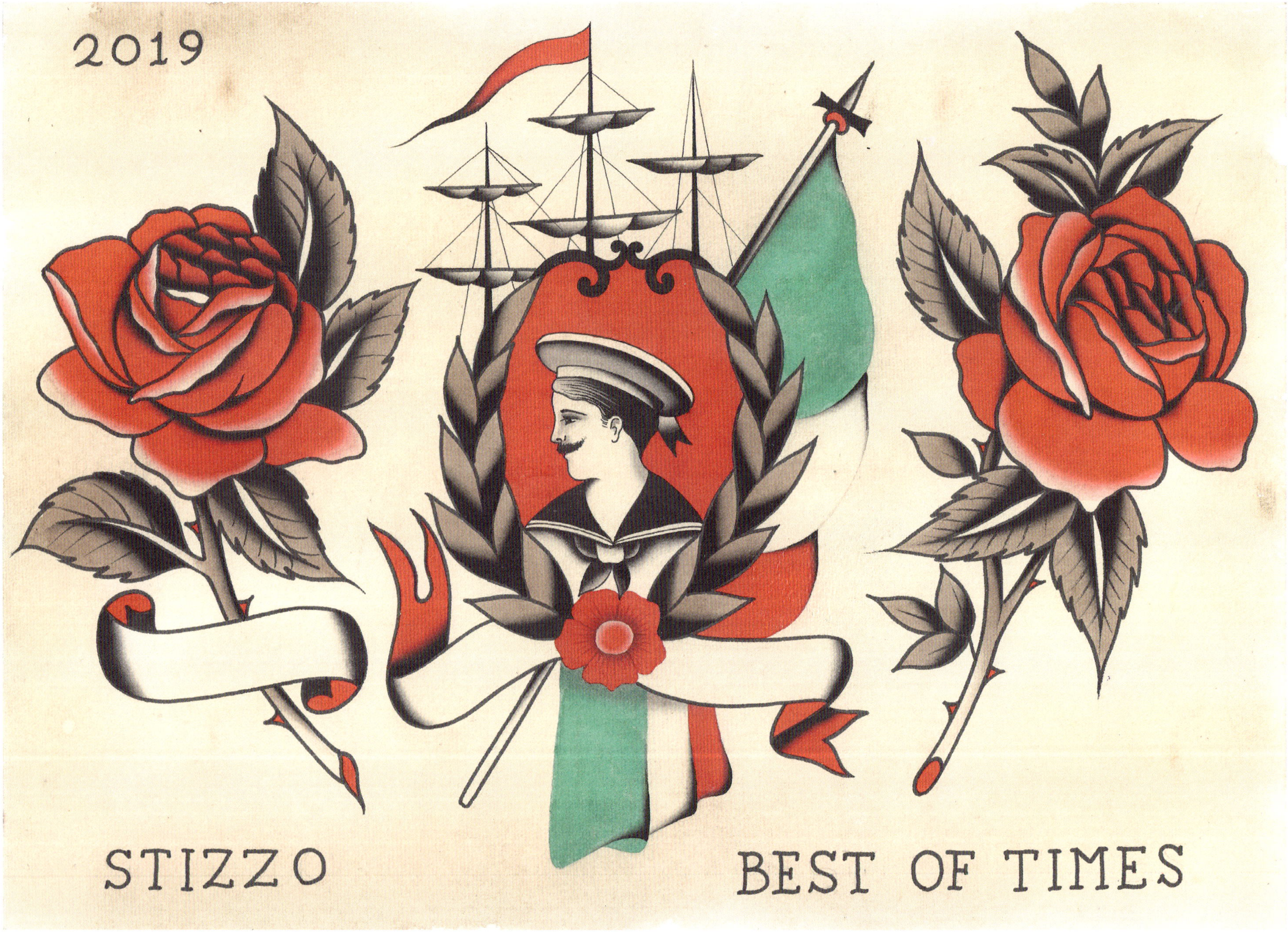

2019

STIZZO

BEST OF TIMES

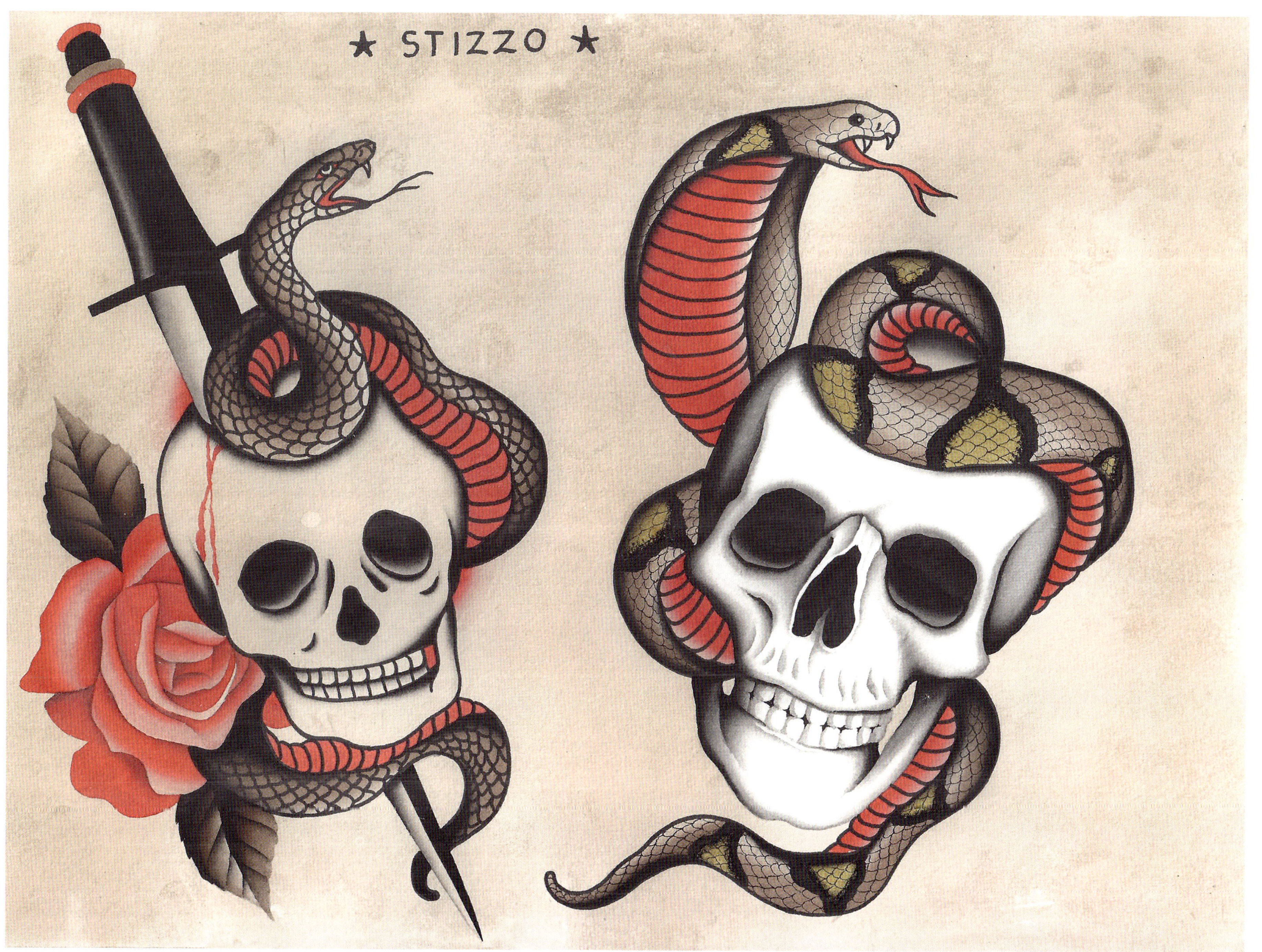
★ STIZZO ★

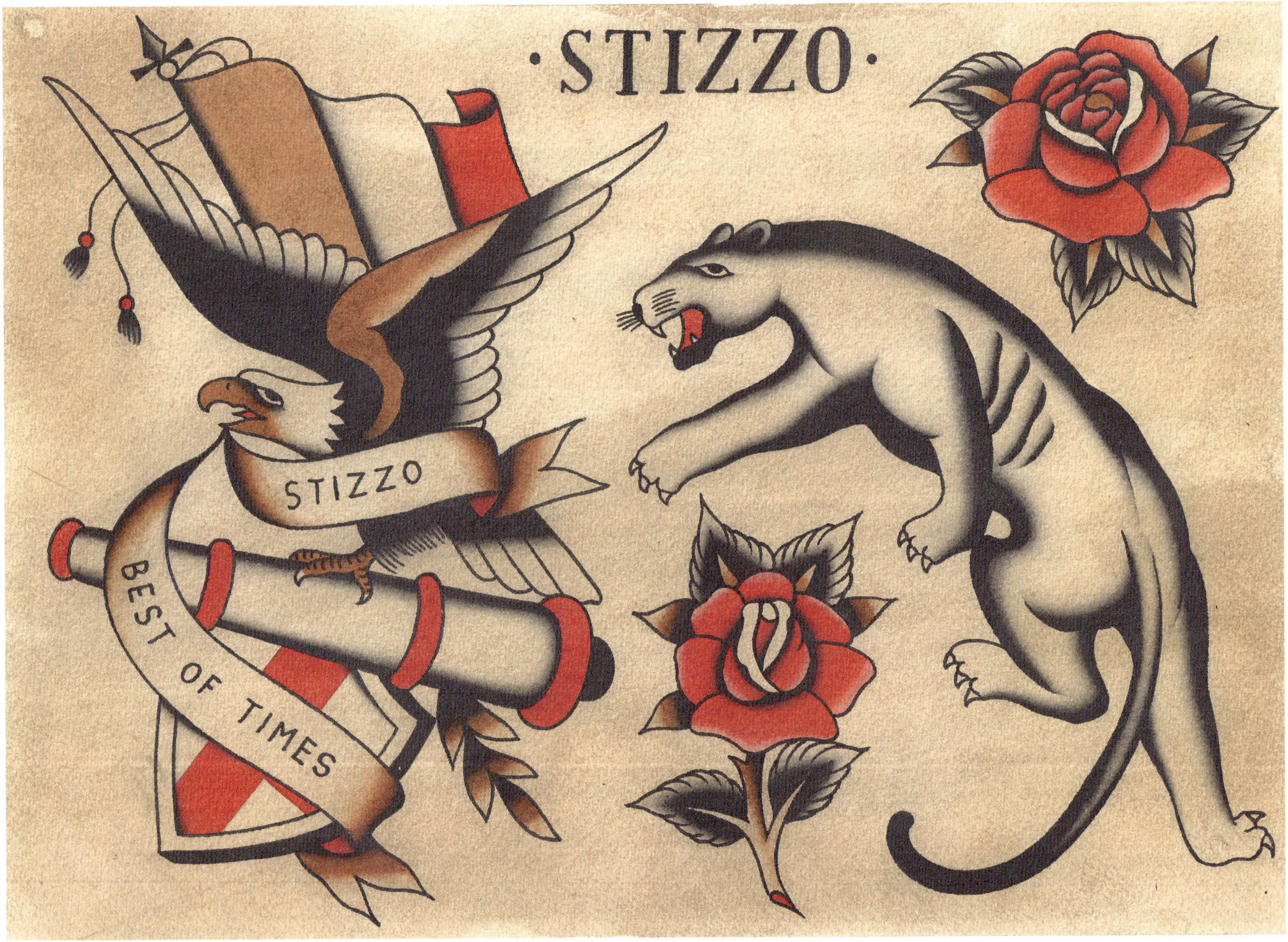

·STIZZO·

STIZZO

BEST OF TIMES

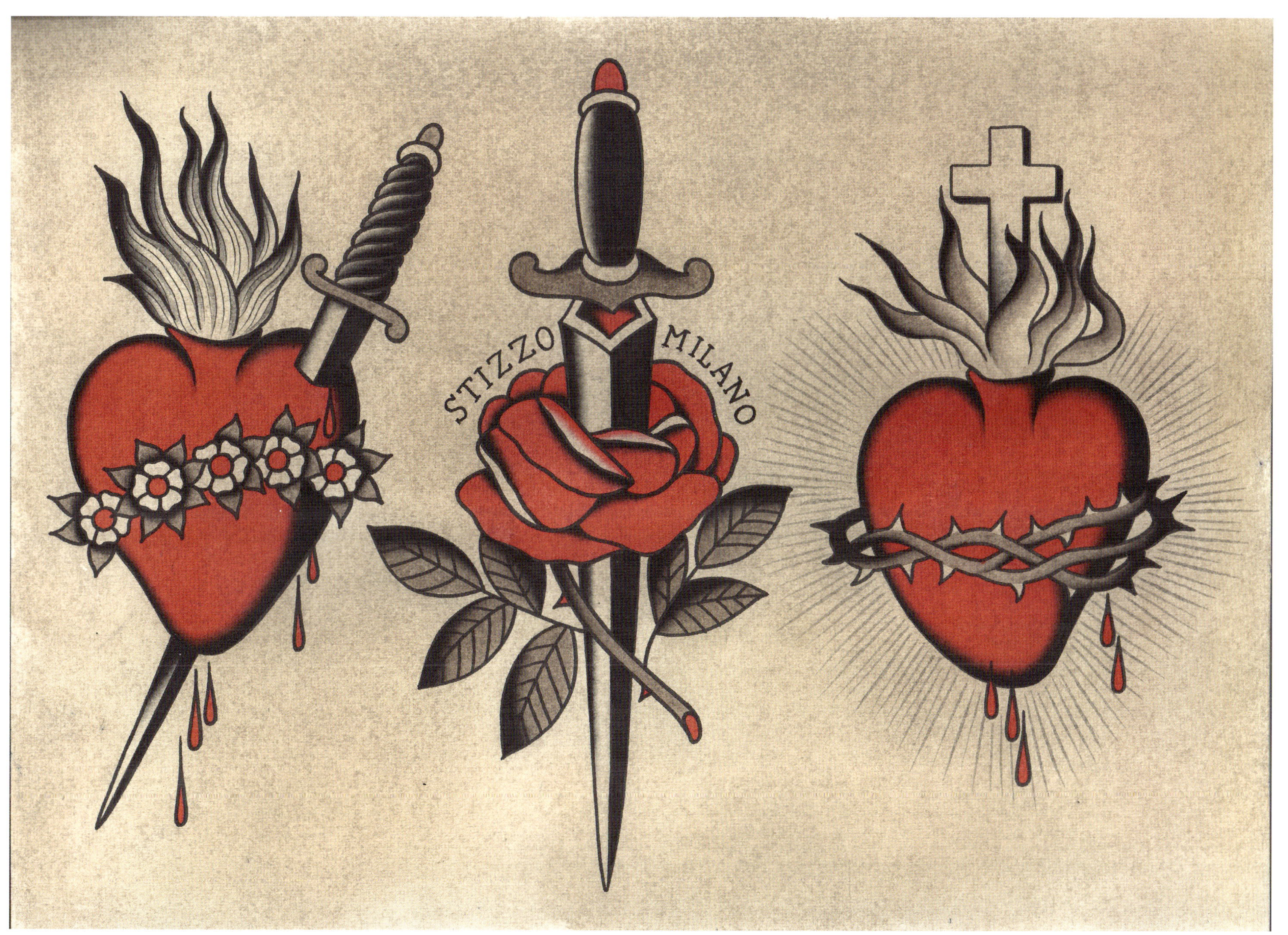
STIZZO MILANO

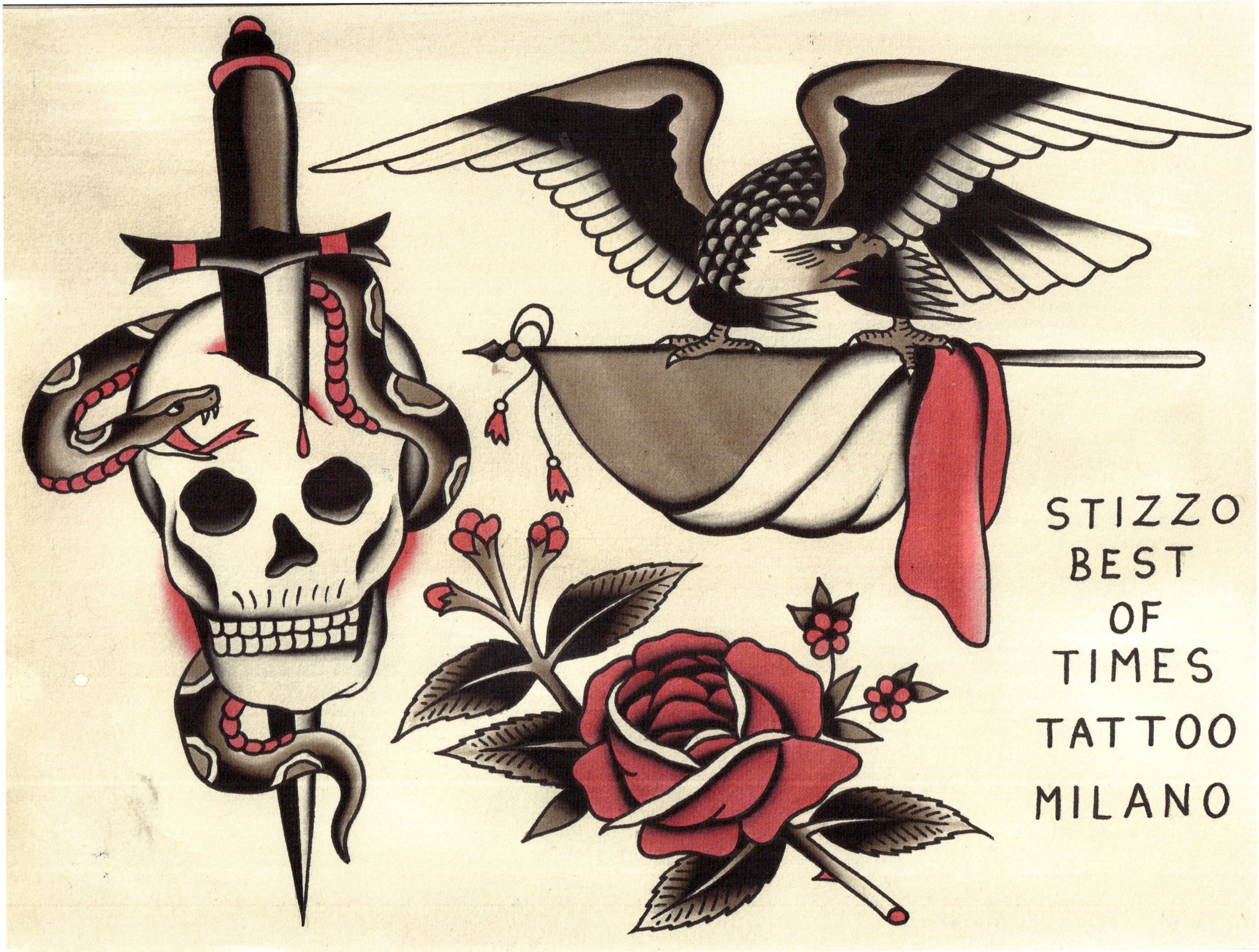

STIZZO
BEST
OF
TIMES
TATTOO
MILANO

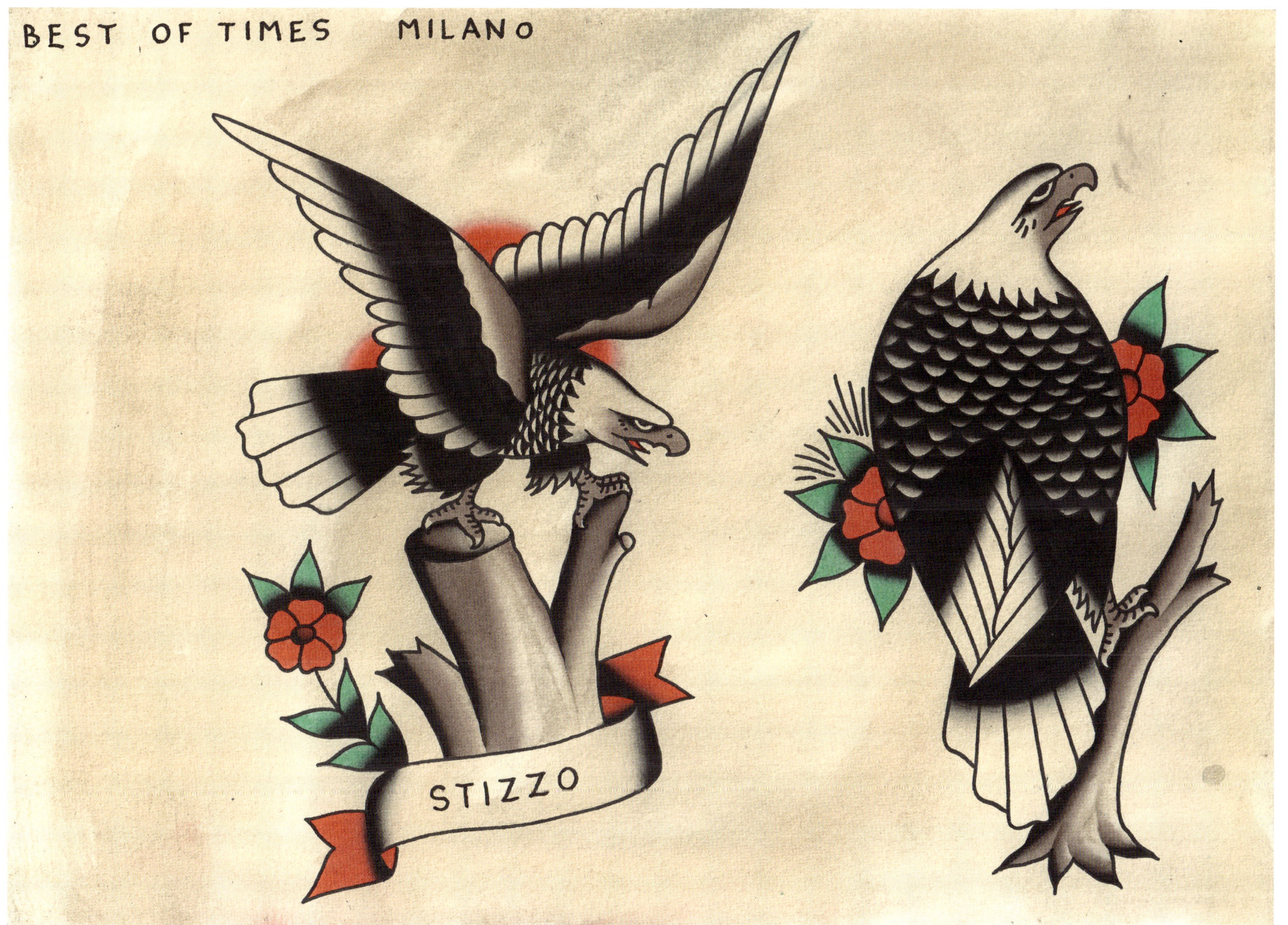
BEST OF TIMES MILANO
STIZZO

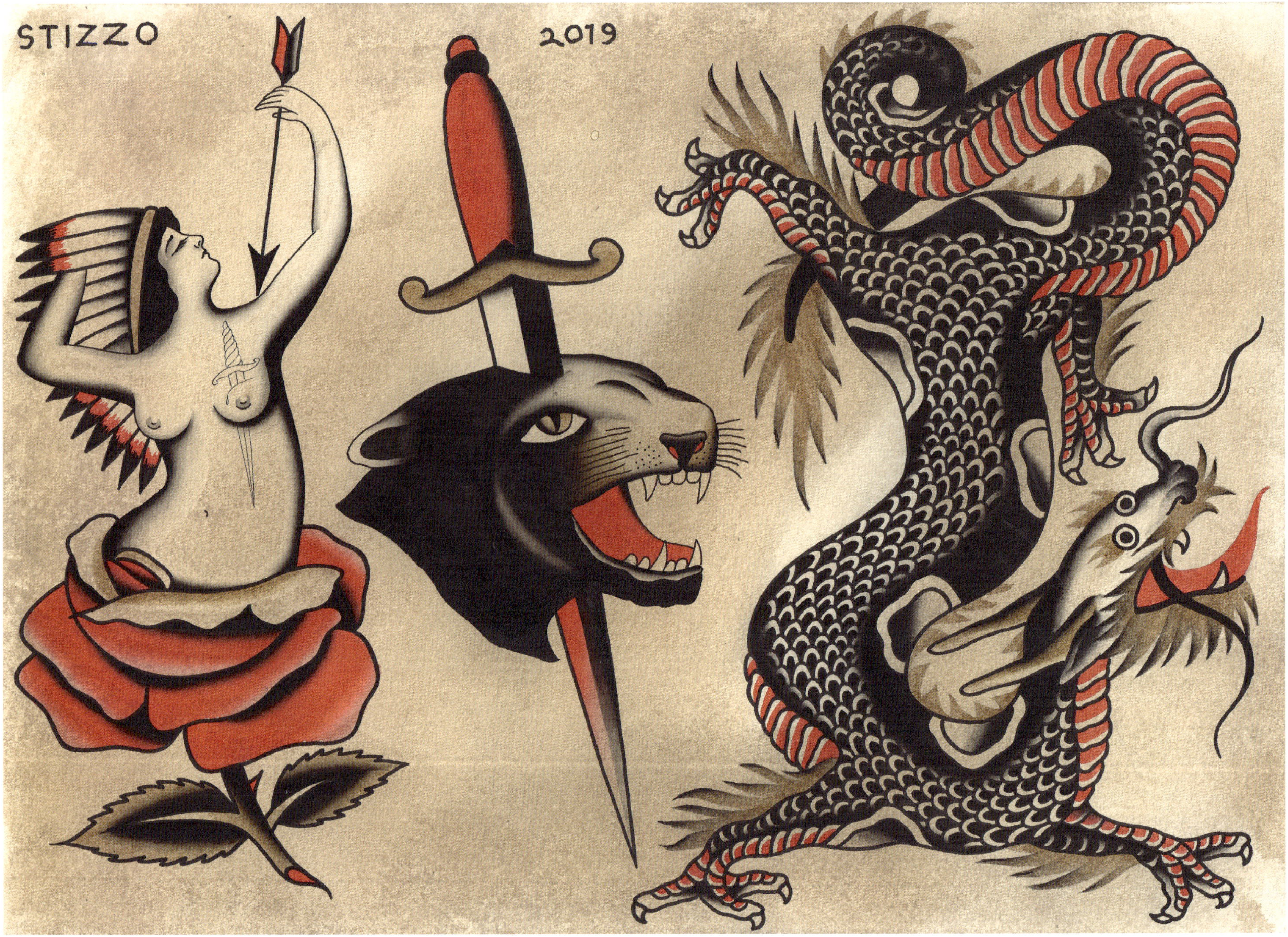

STIZZO 2019

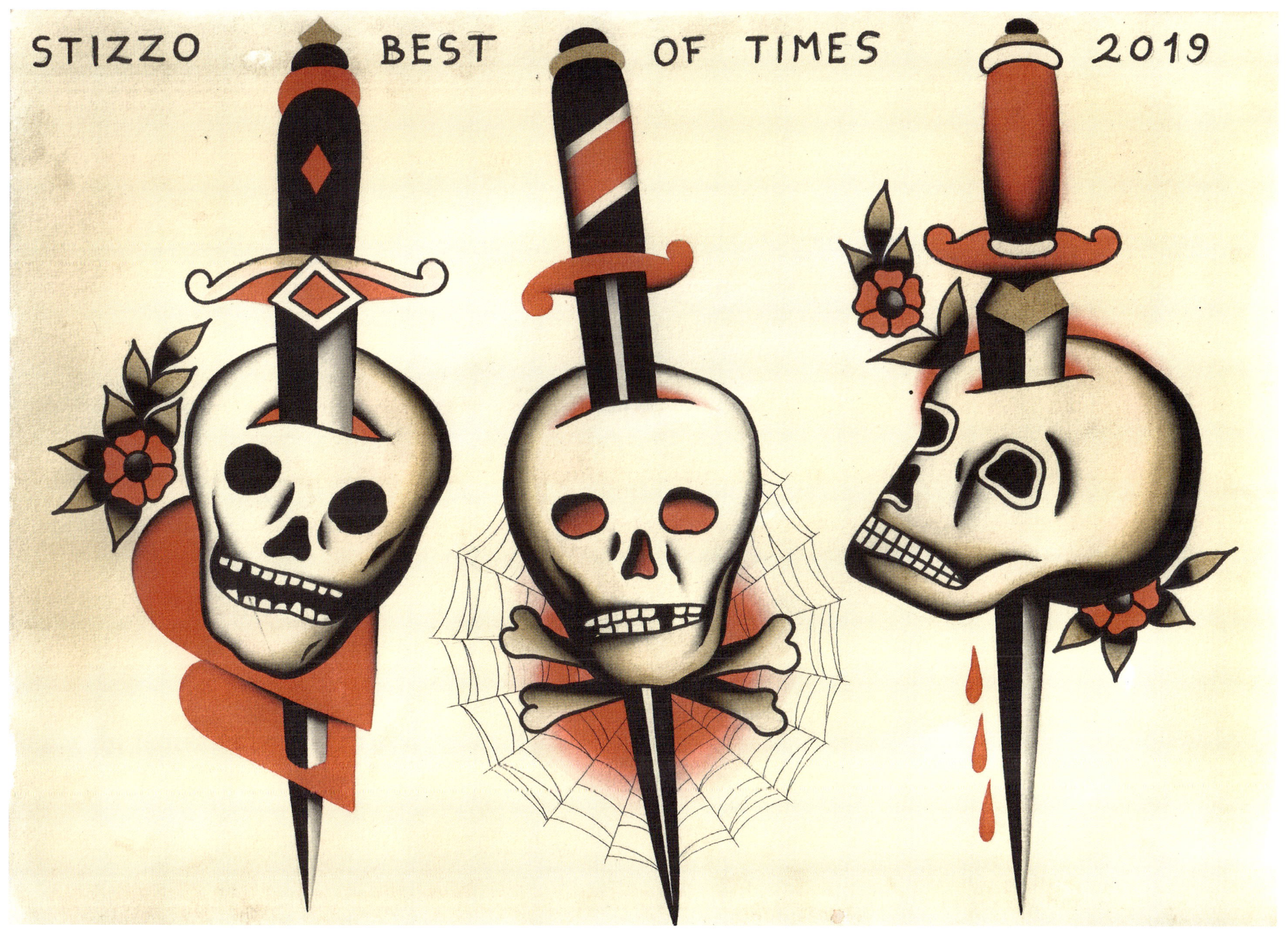
STIZZO
BEST
OF TIMES
2019

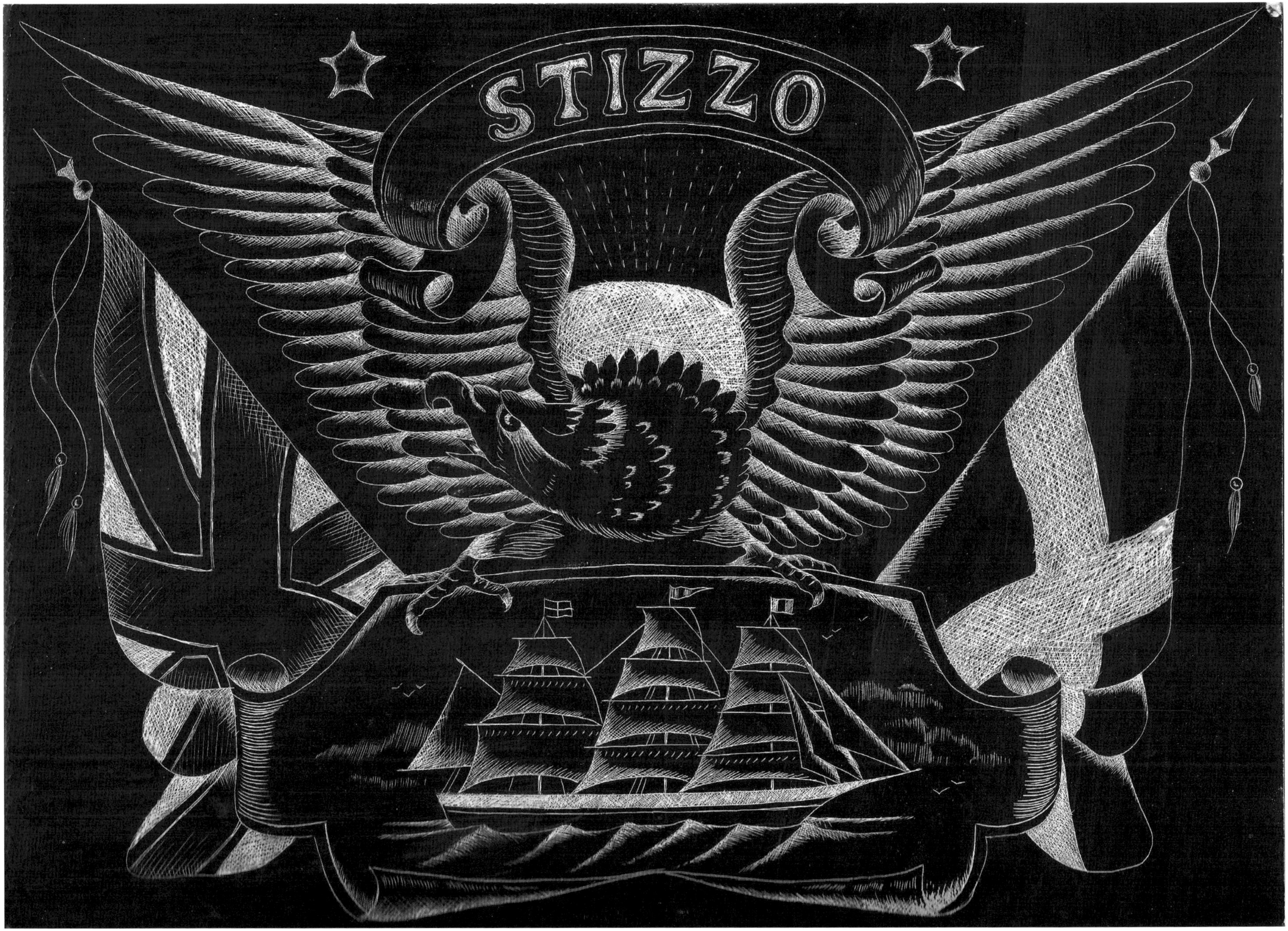

STIZZO

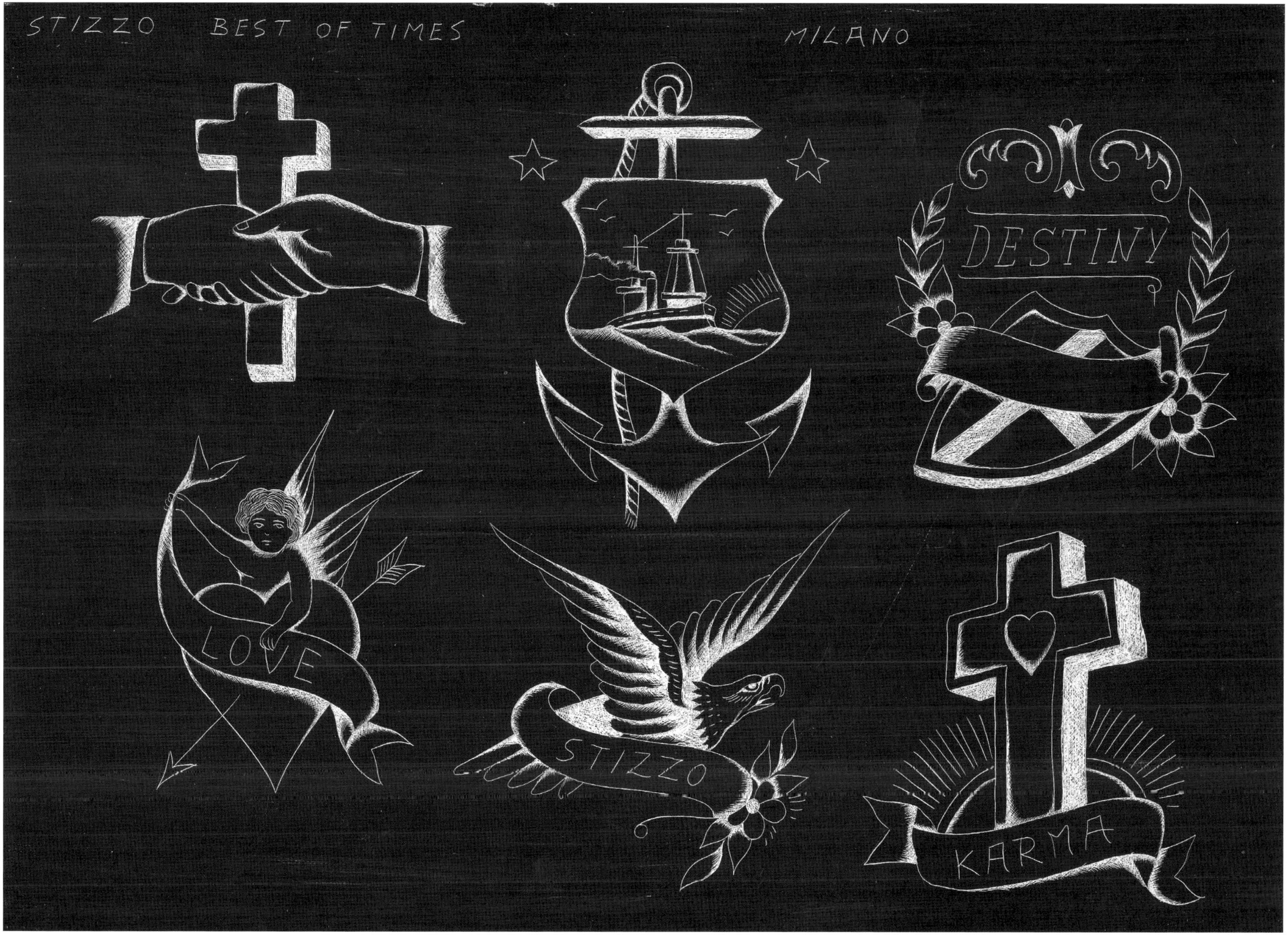

STIZZO BEST OF TIMES MILANO

DESTINY

LOVE

STIZZO

KARMA

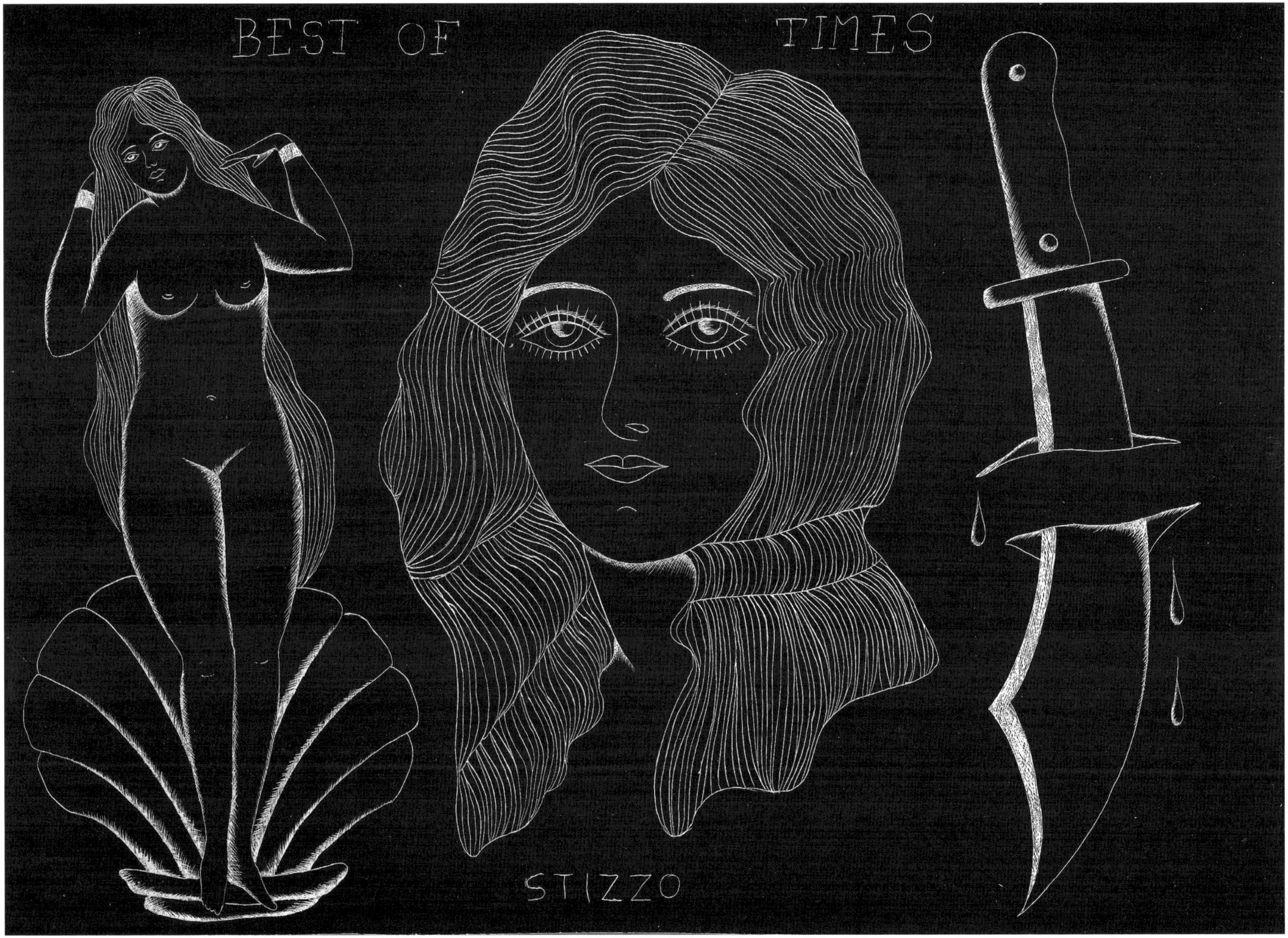

BEST OF TIMES

STIZZO

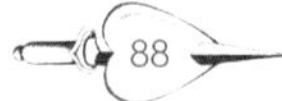

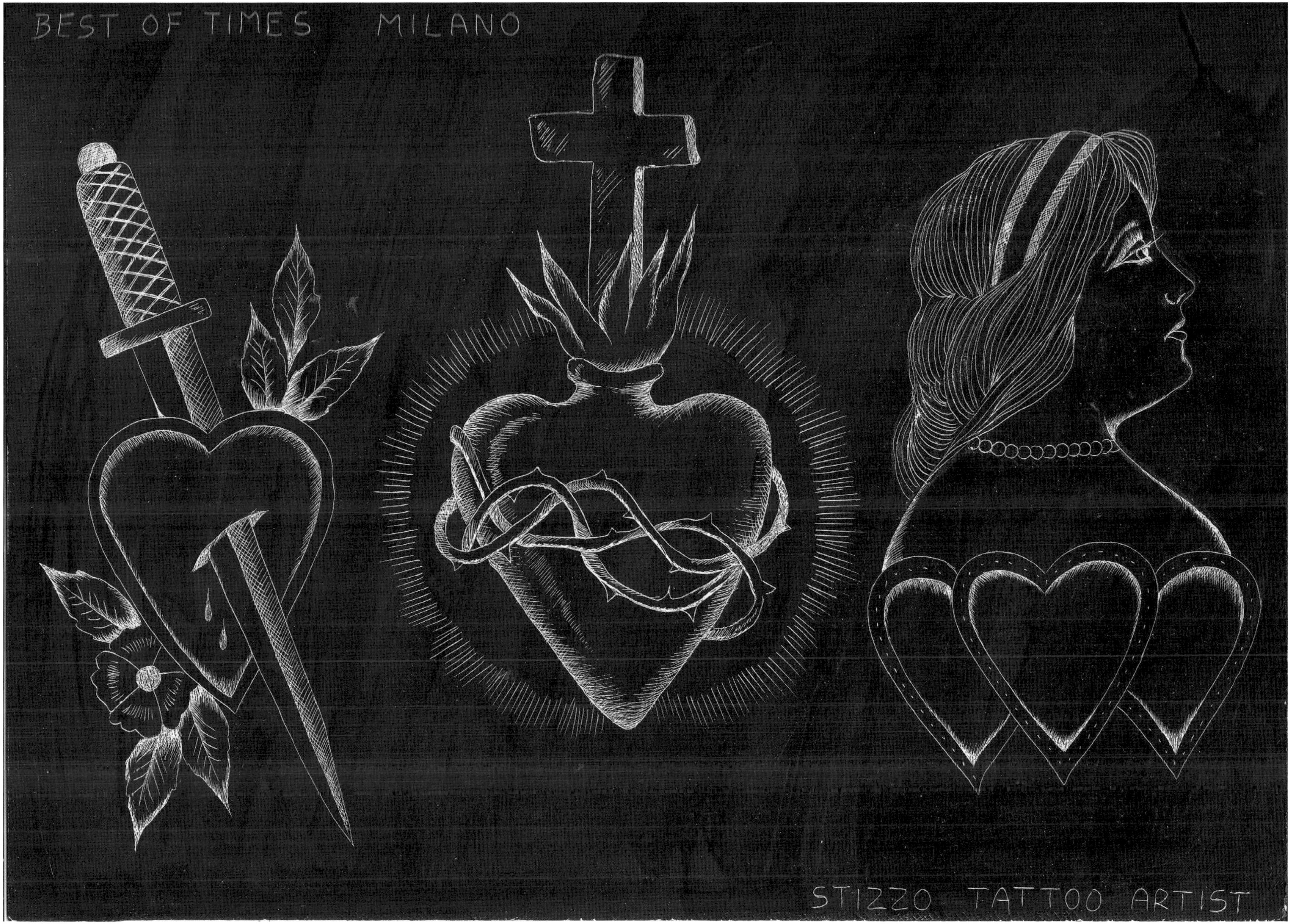

BEST OF TIMES MILANO

STIZZO TATTOO ARTIST

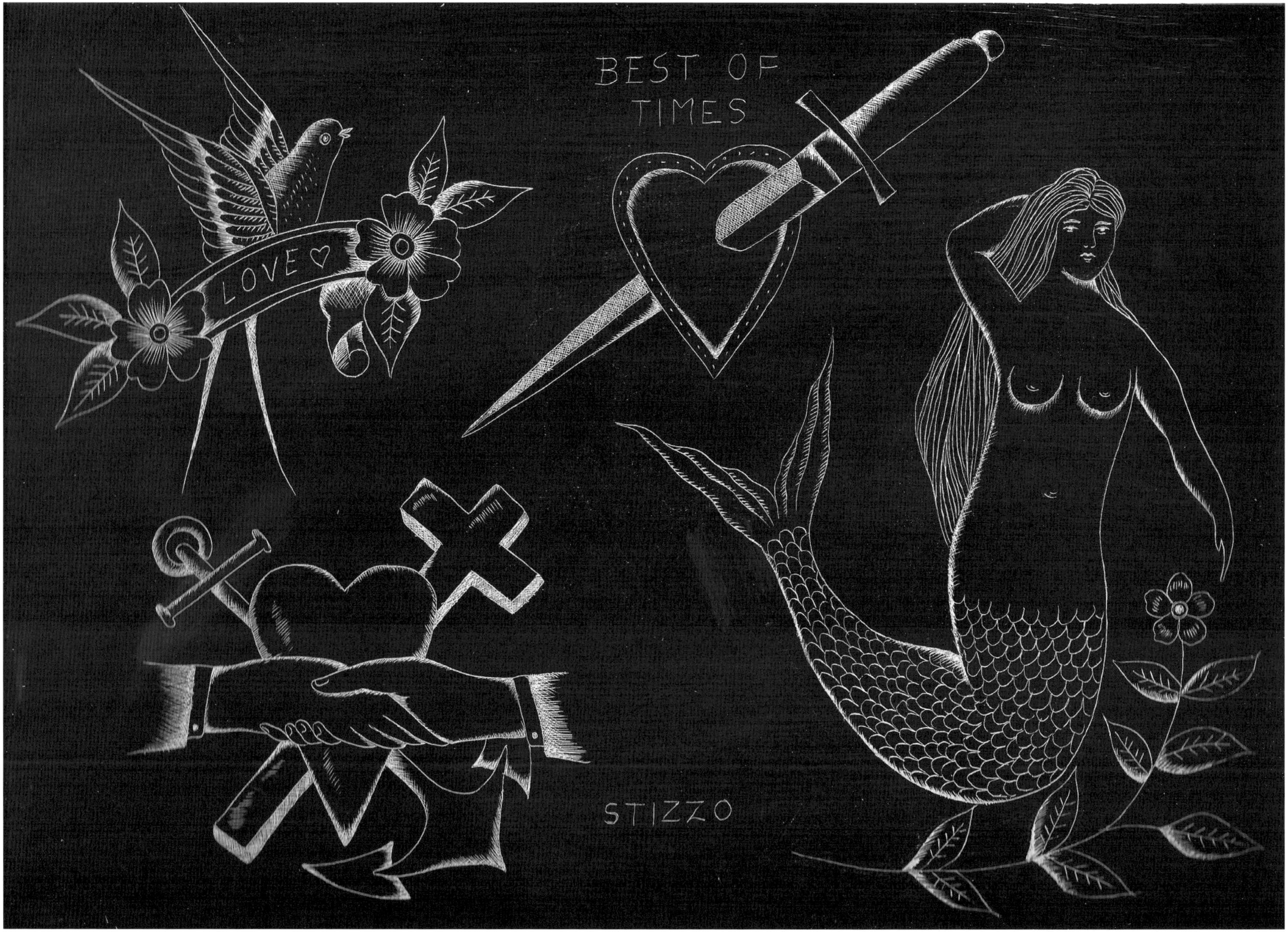

BEST OF
TIMES

LOVE

STIZZO

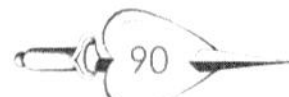

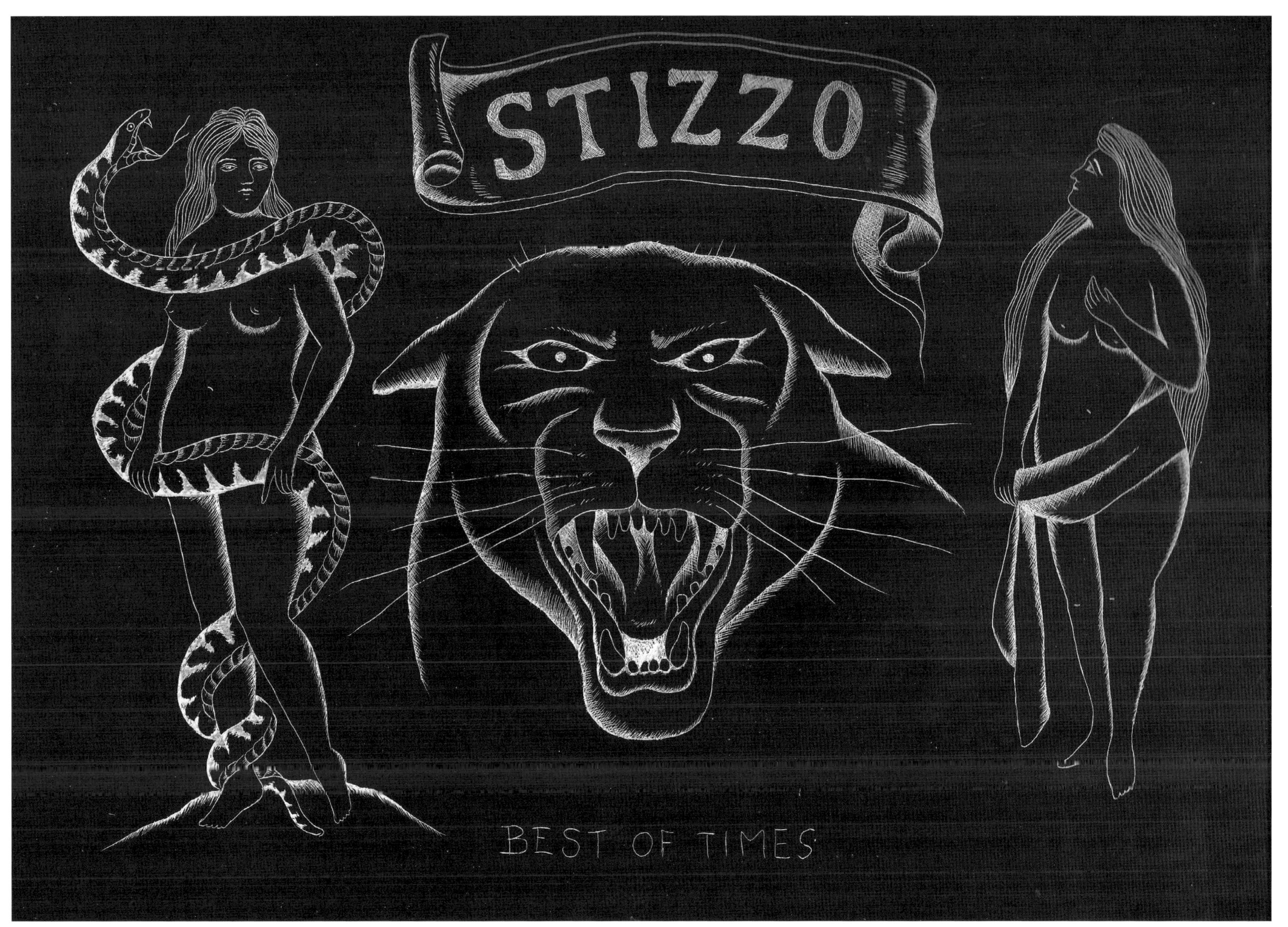
STIZZO
BEST OF TIMES

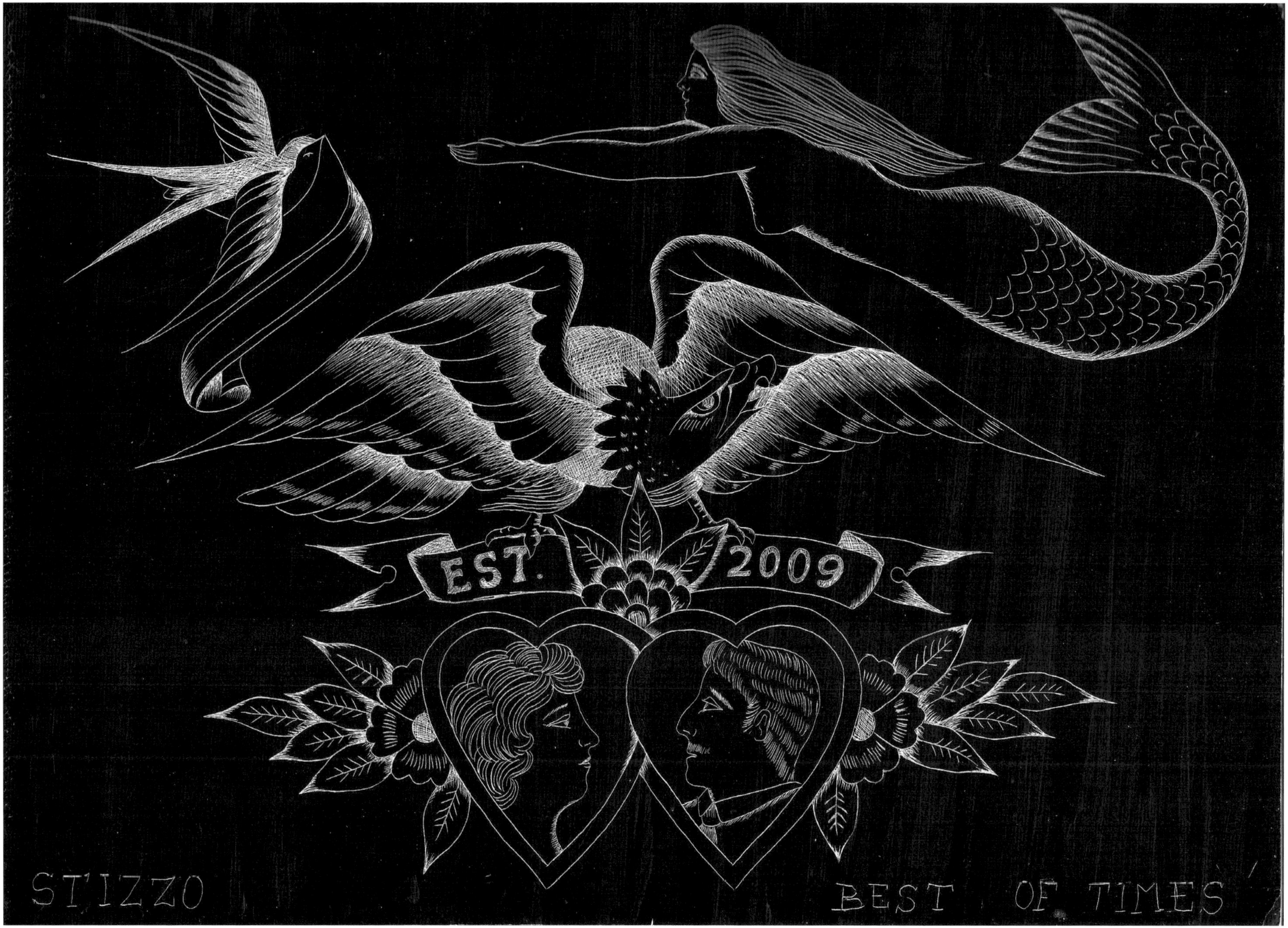

EST. 2009

STIZZO

BEST OF TIMES

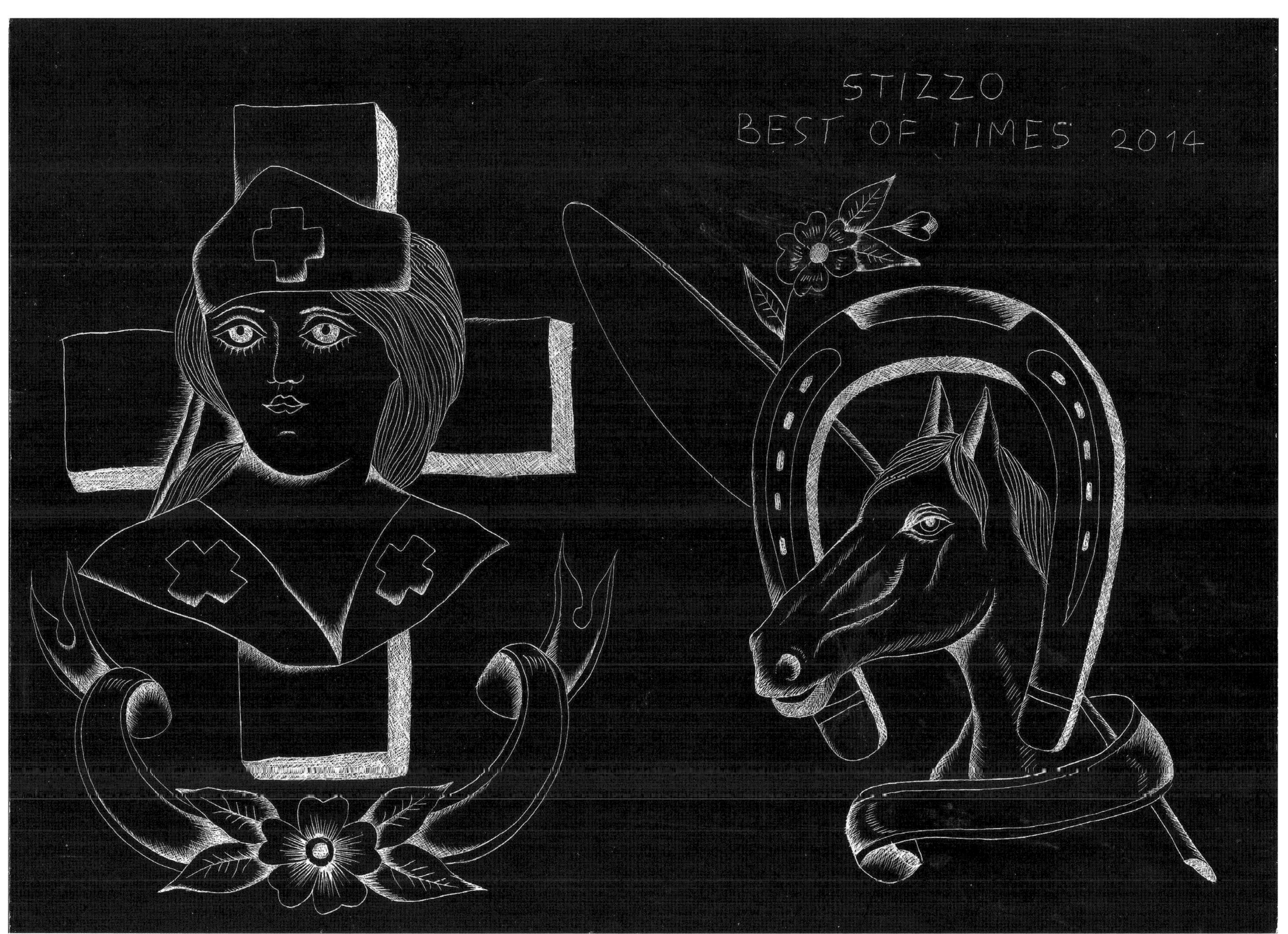
STIZZO
BEST OF TIMES 2014

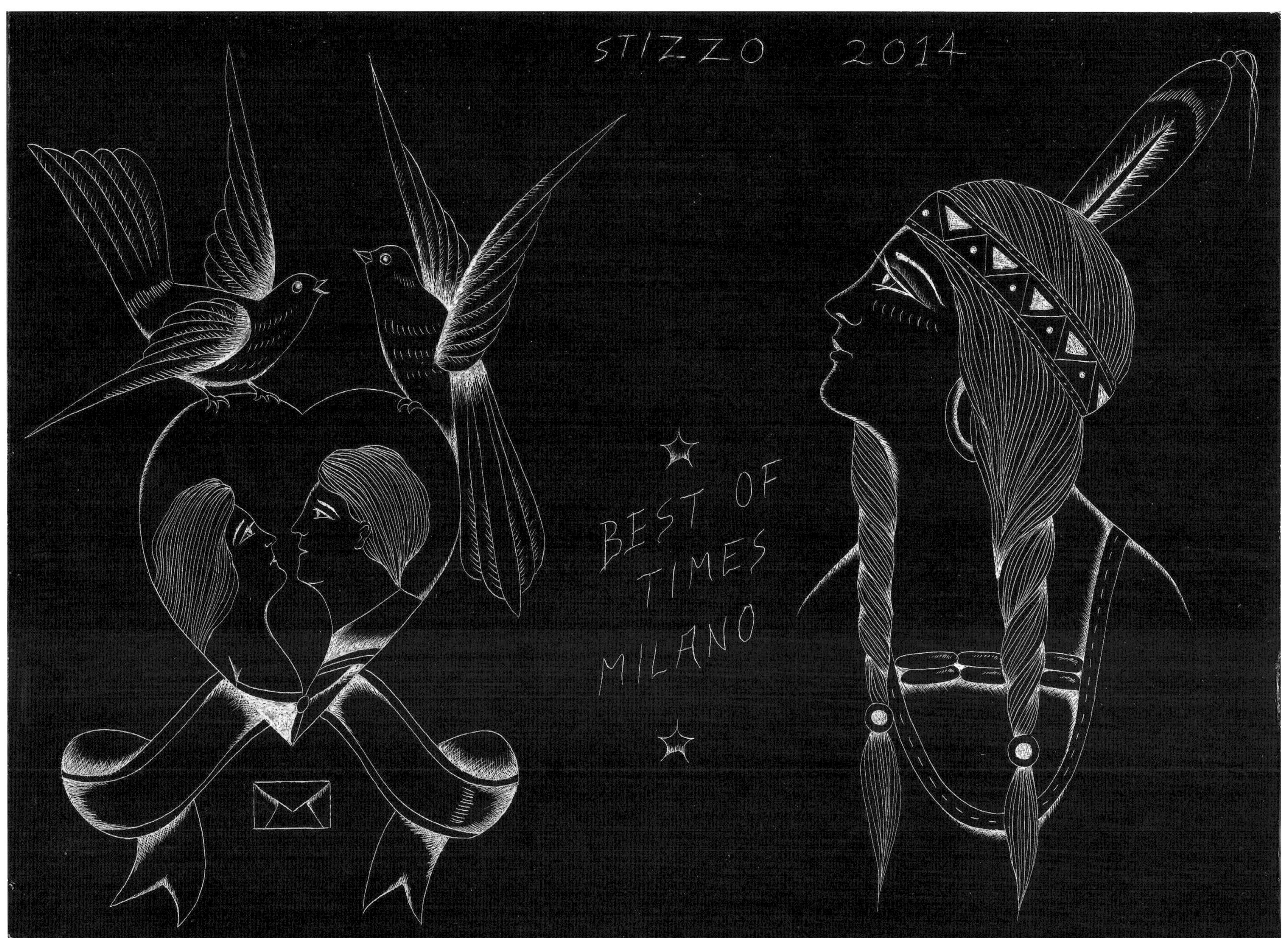
STIZZO 2014
BEST OF TIMES MILANO

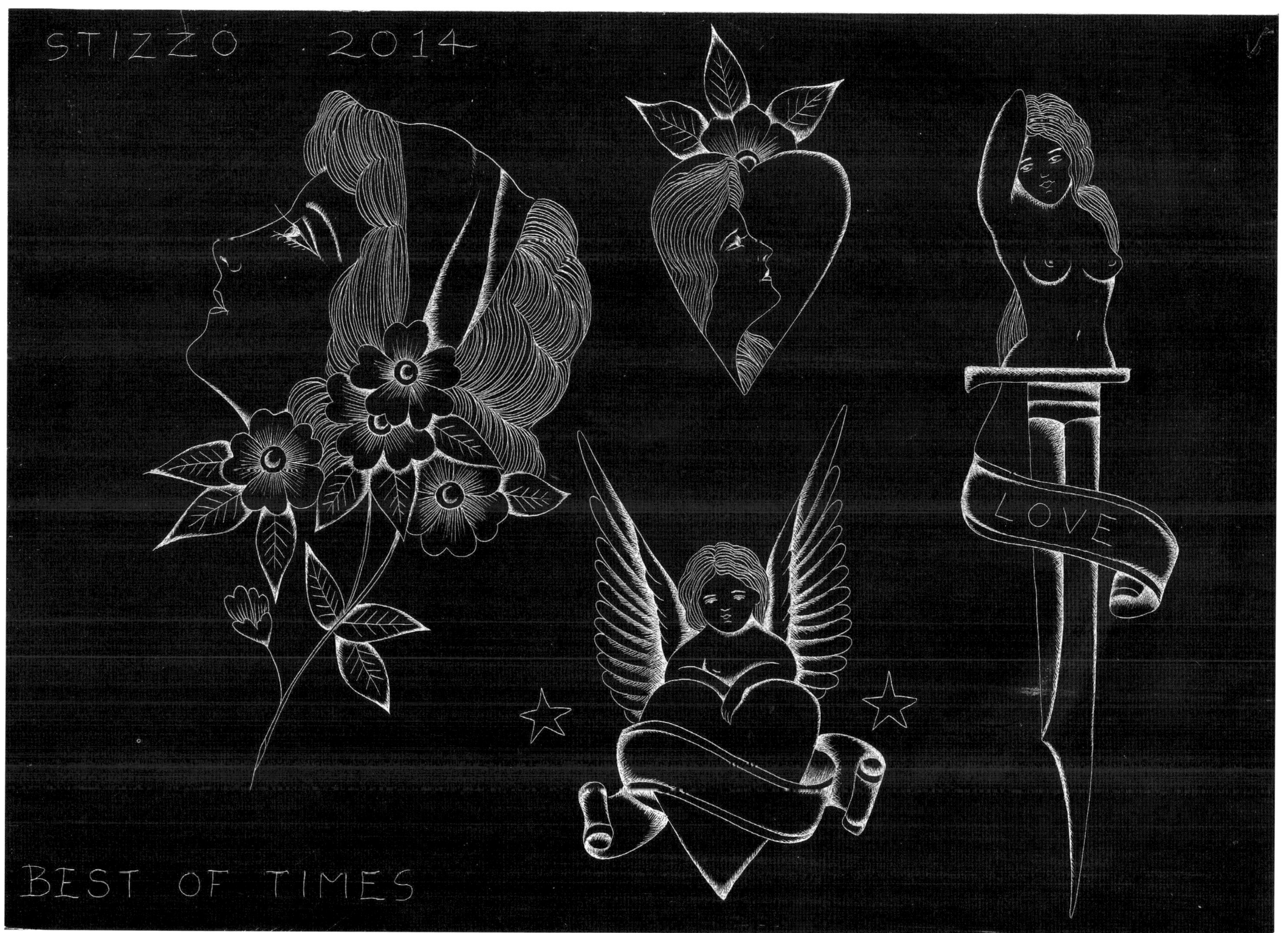
STIZZO 2014
LOVE
BEST OF TIMES

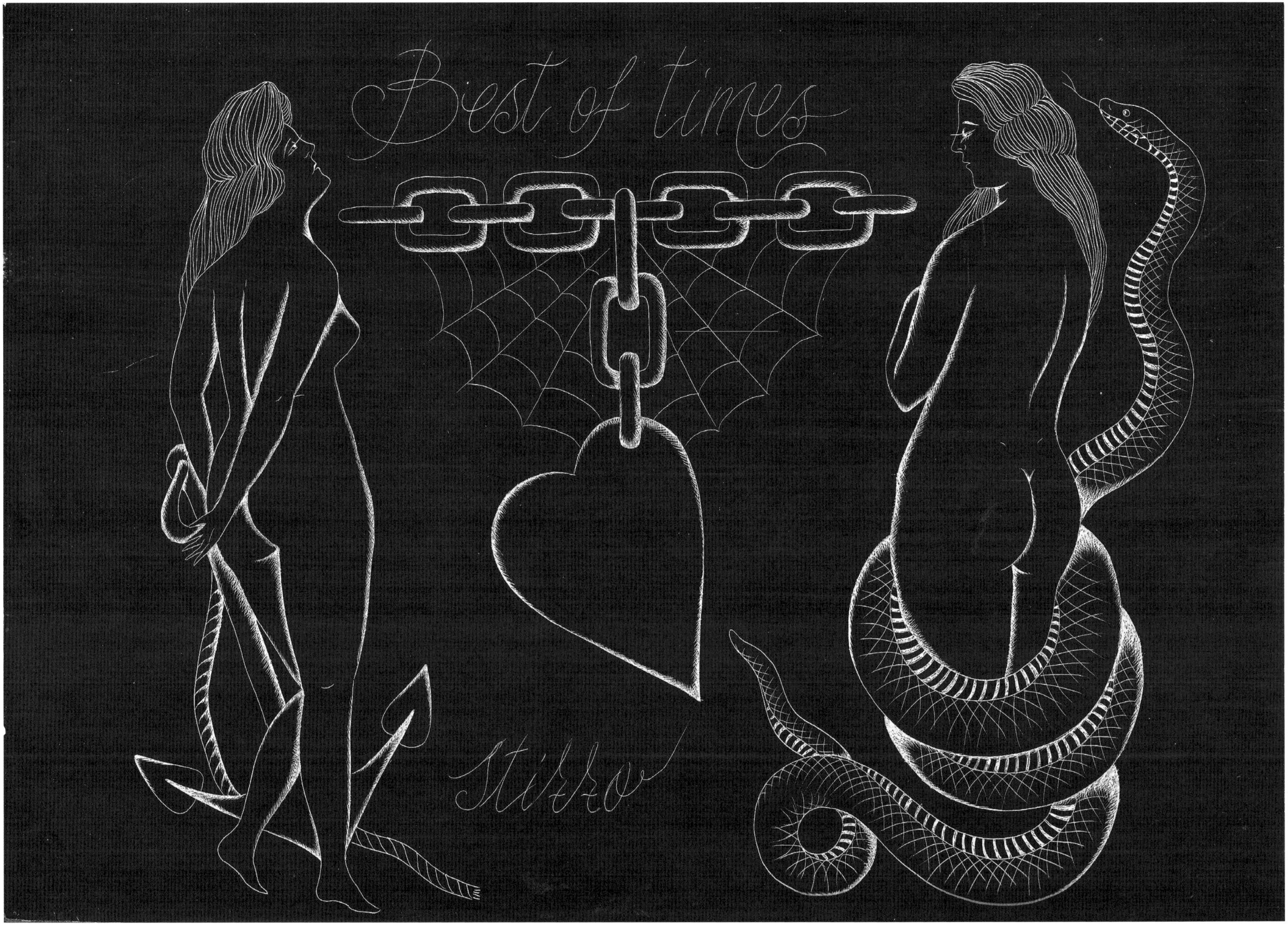

Best of times

Stitko

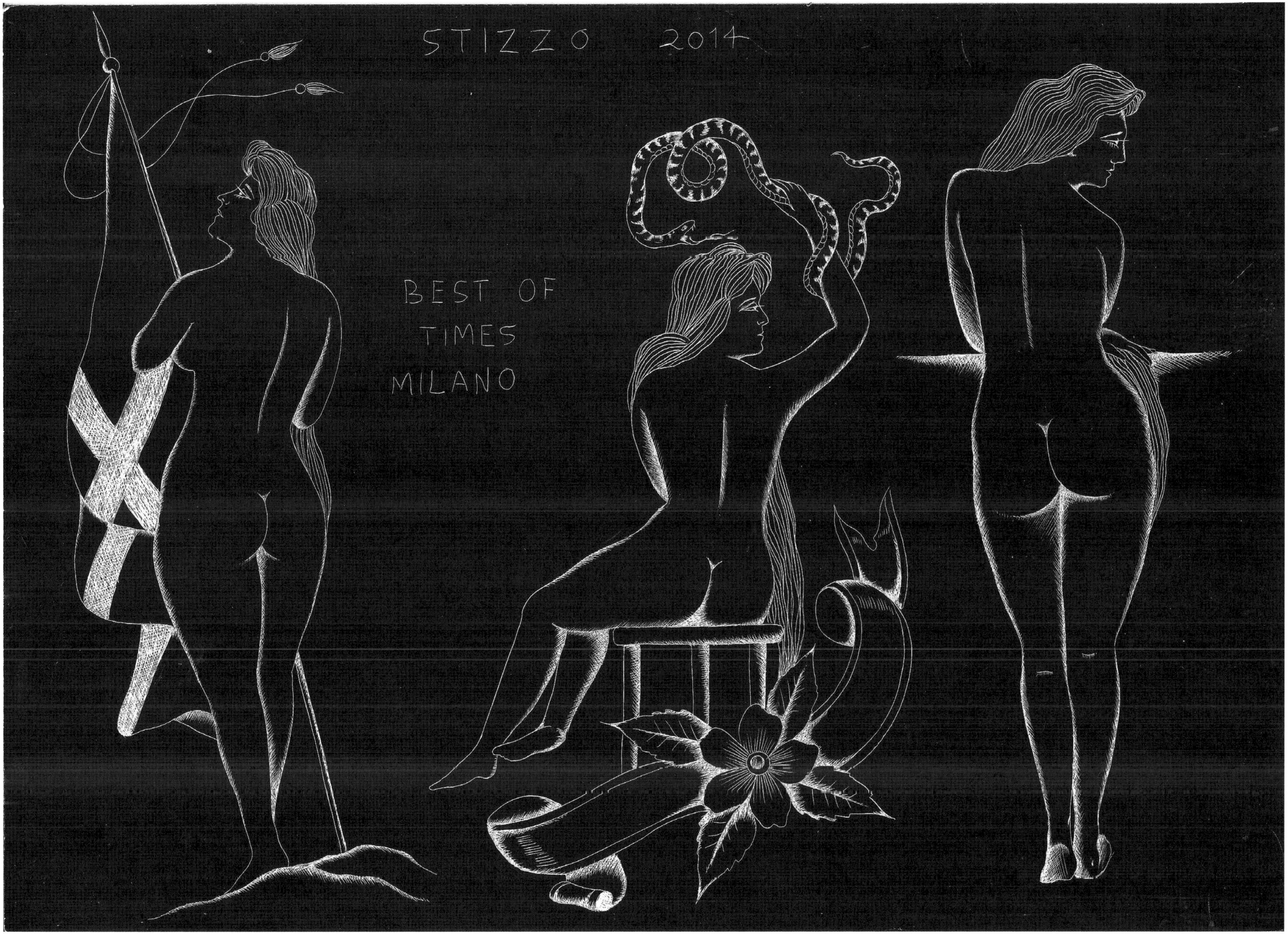

STIZZO 2014

BEST OF
TIMES
MILANO

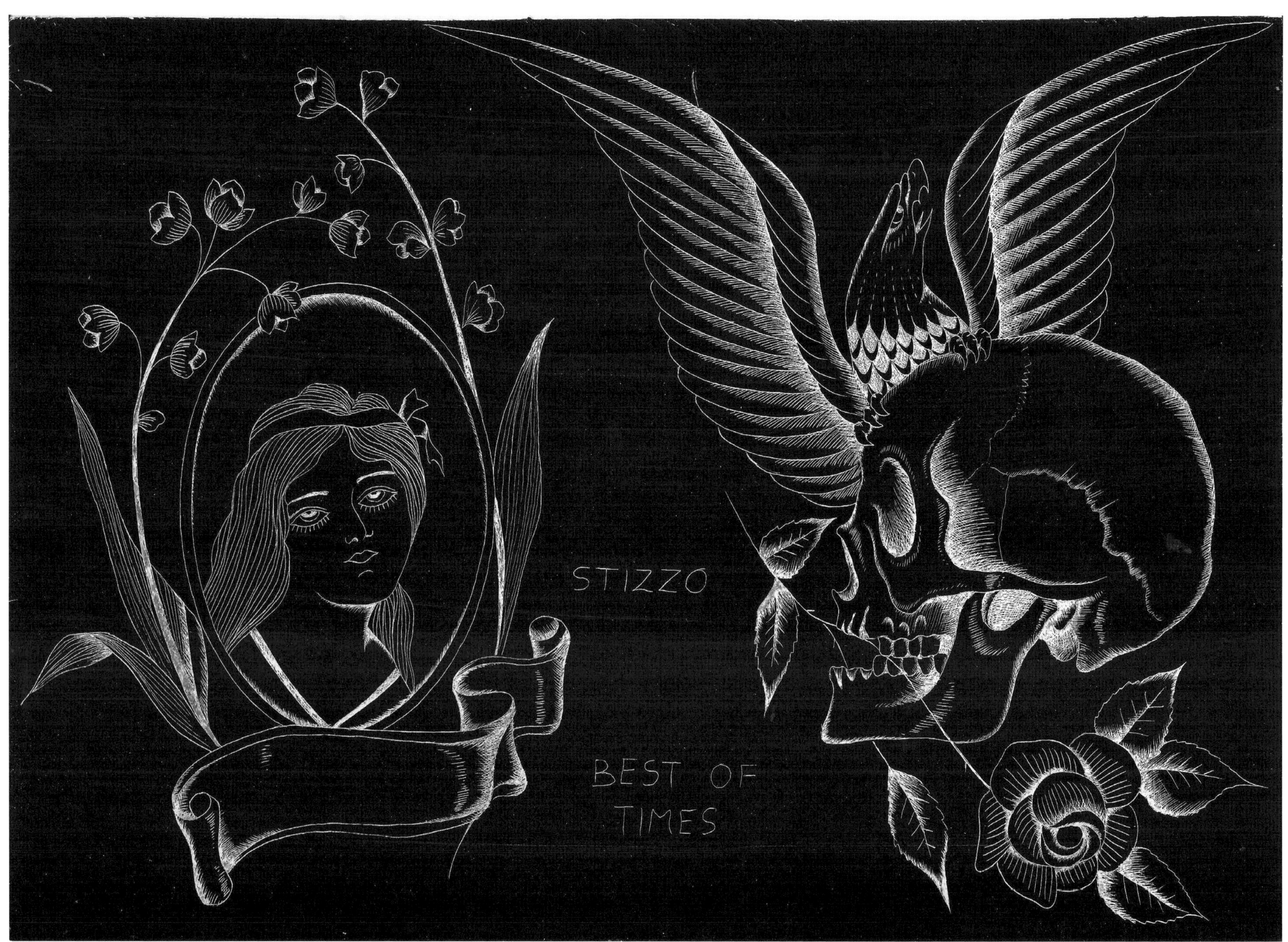
STIZZO
BEST OF
TIMES

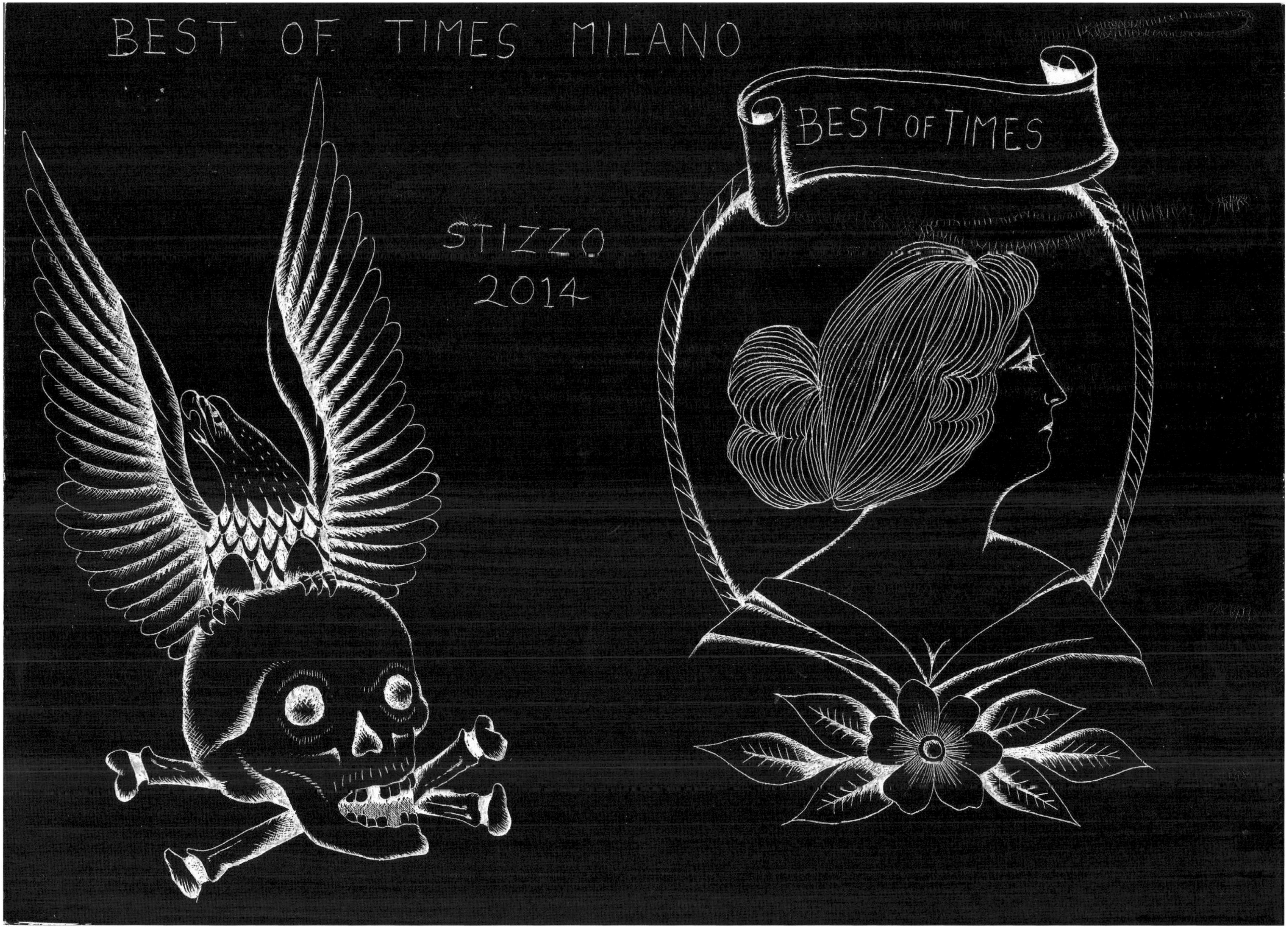

BEST OF TIMES MILANO

STIZZO
2014

BEST OF TIMES

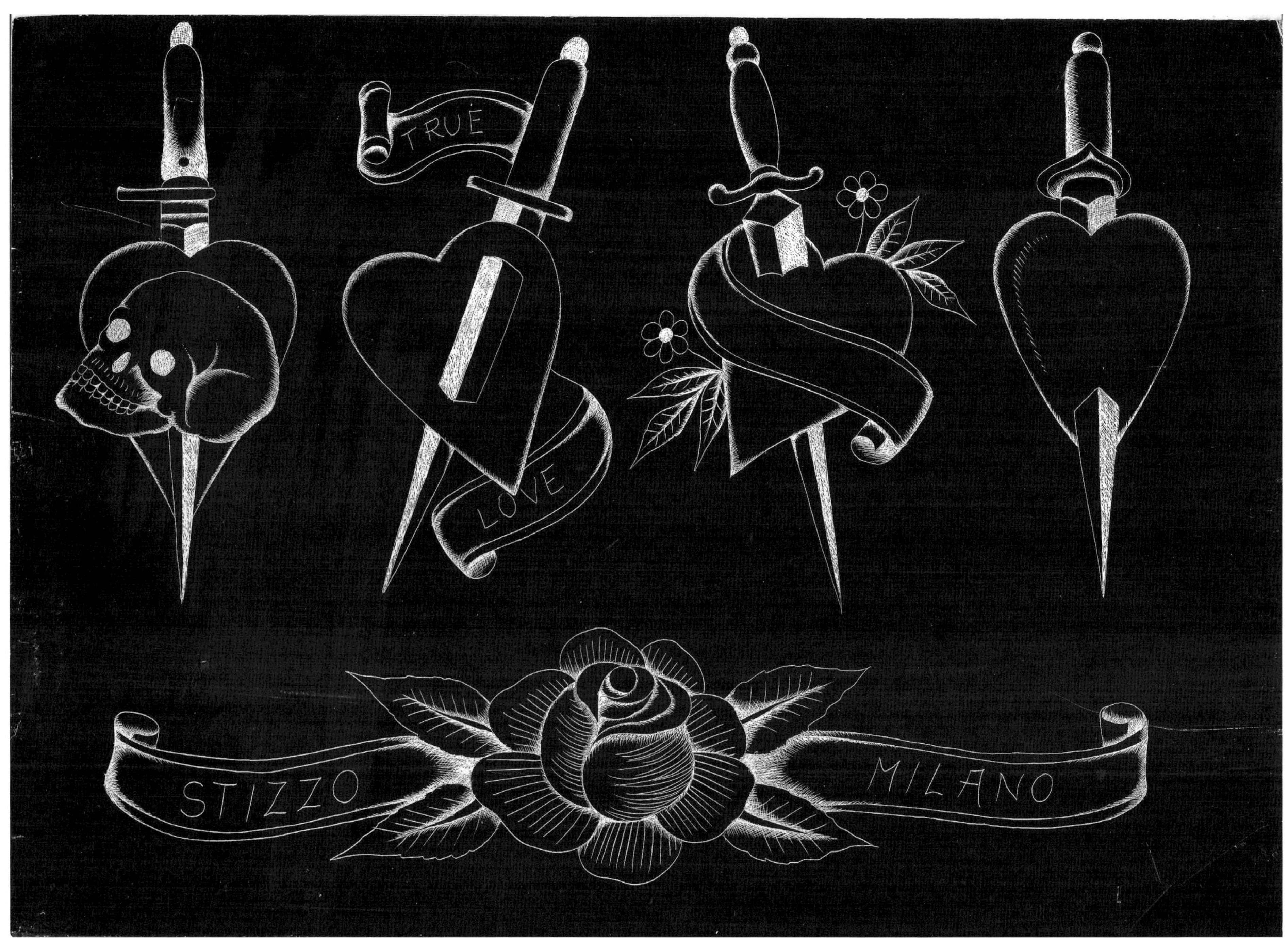
TRUE
LOVE
STIZZO
MILANO

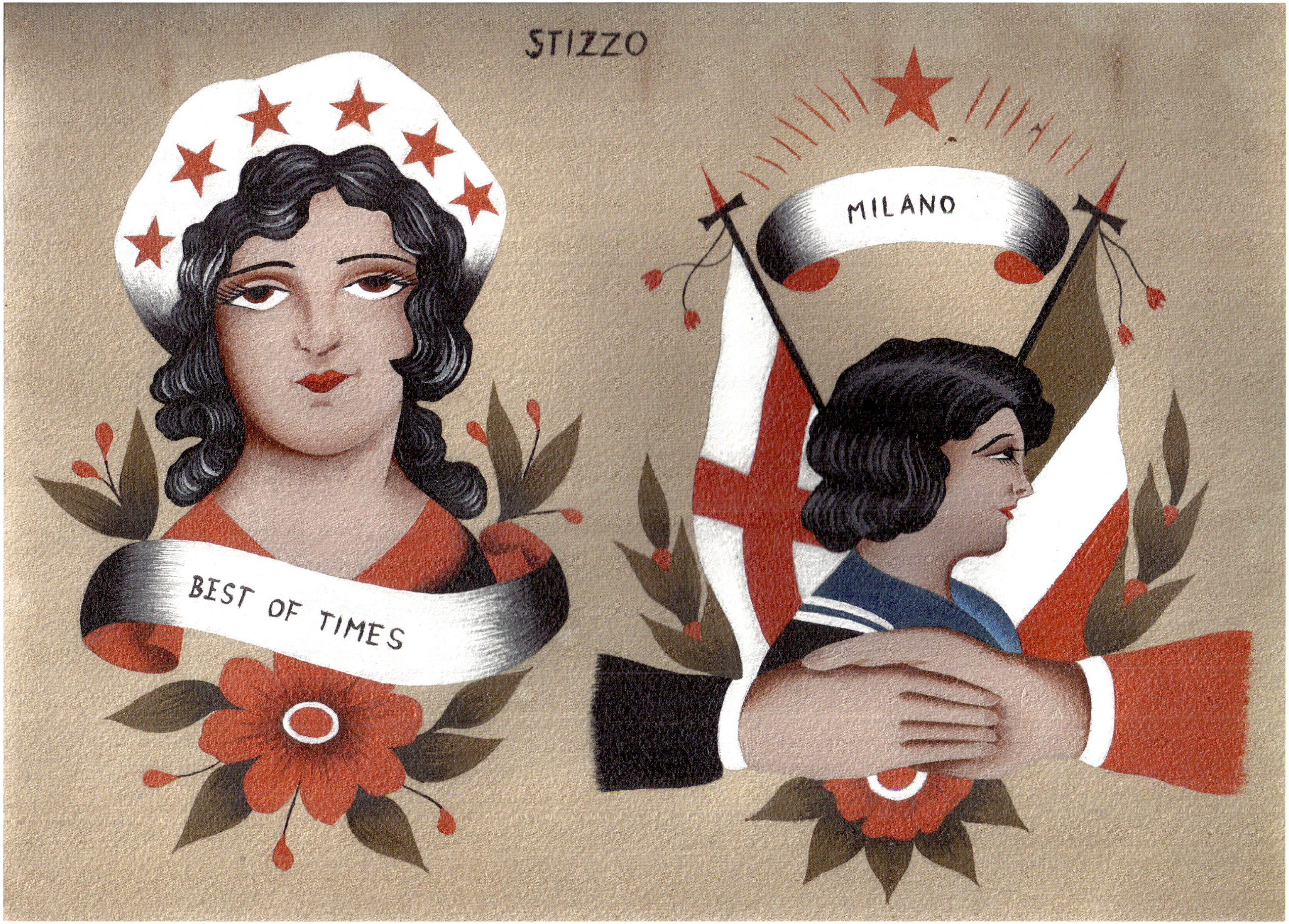

STIZZO

BEST OF TIMES

MILANO

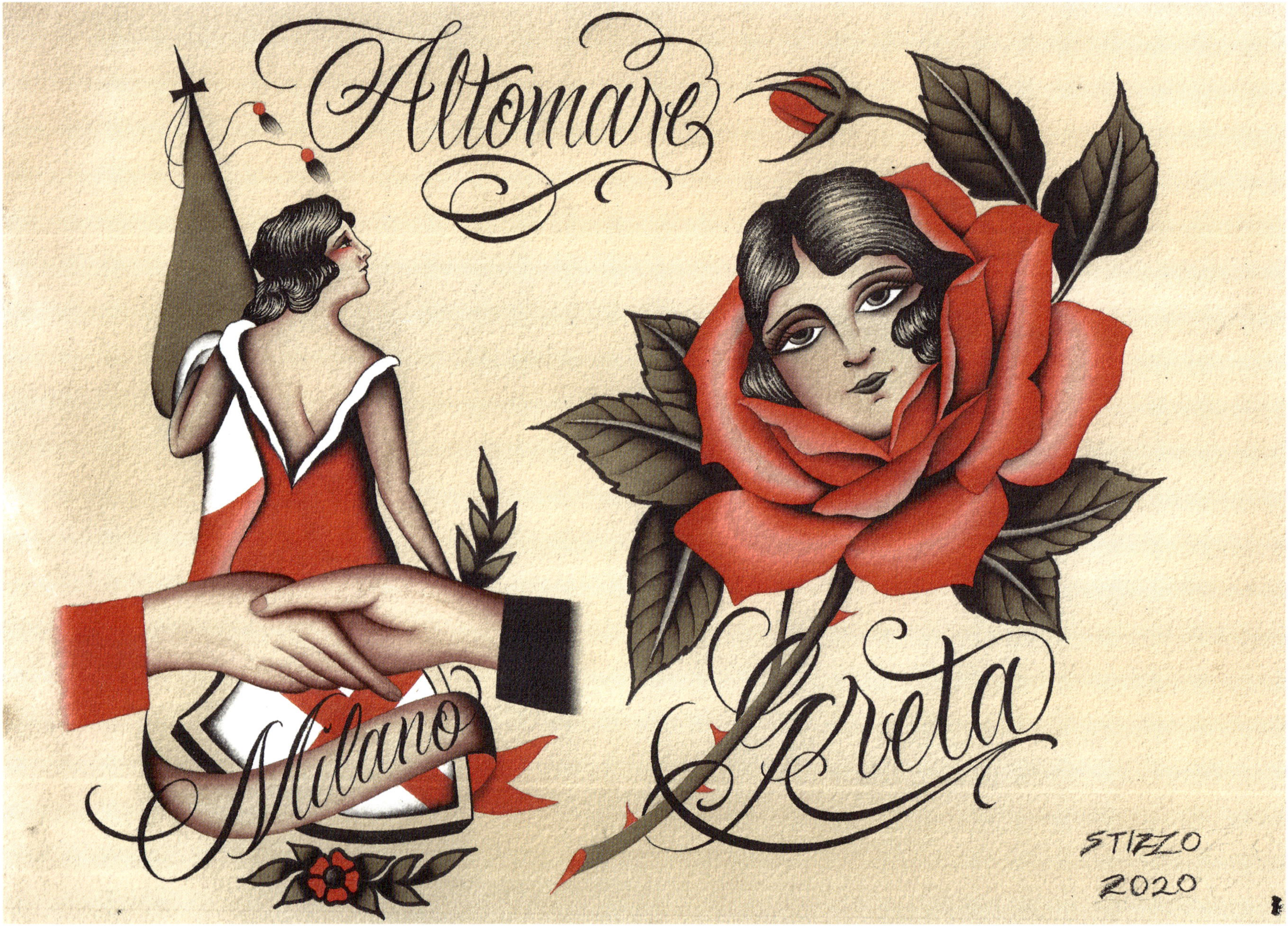

Altomare

Milano

Greta

STIZZO
2020

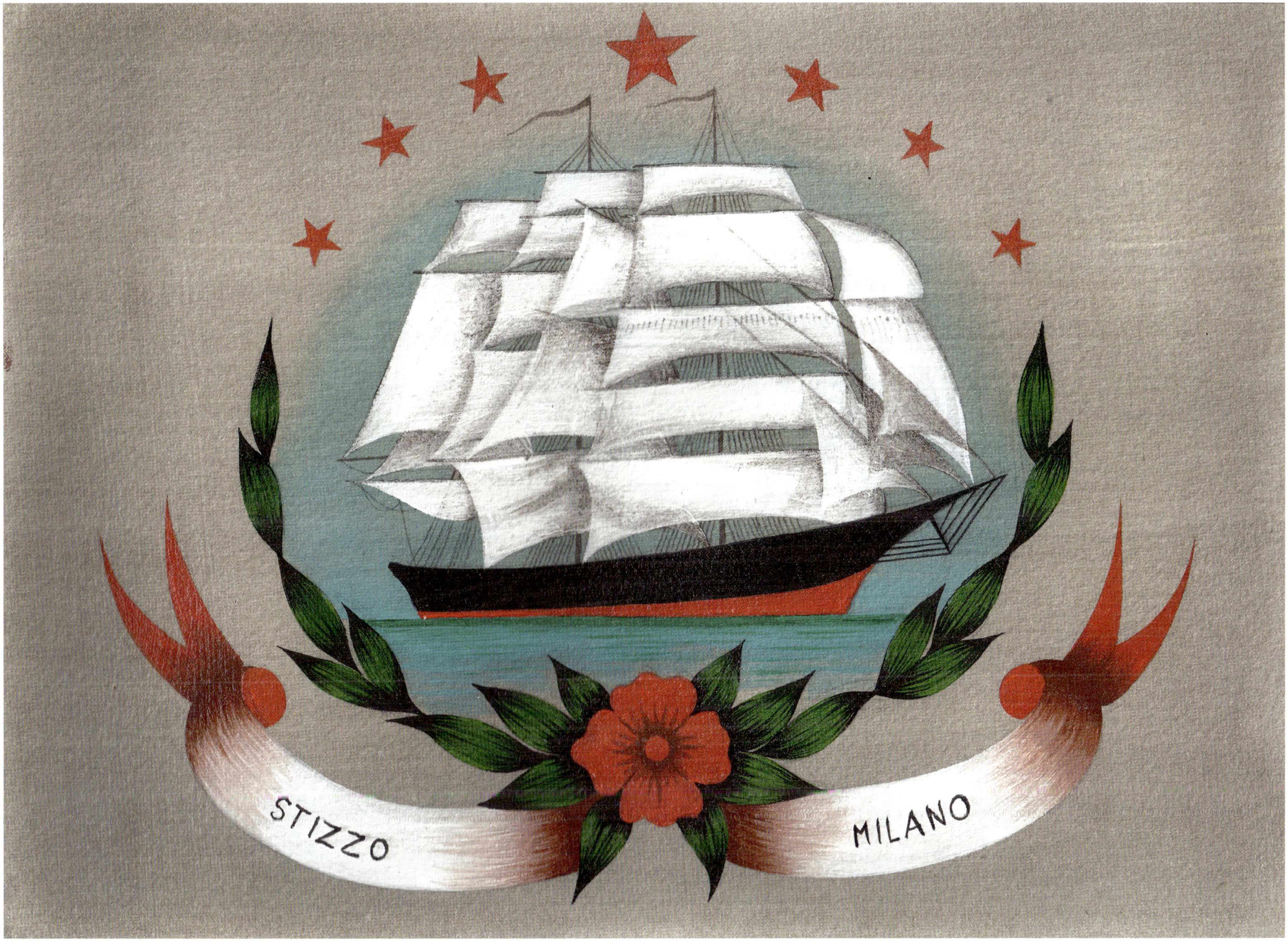

STIZZO MILANO

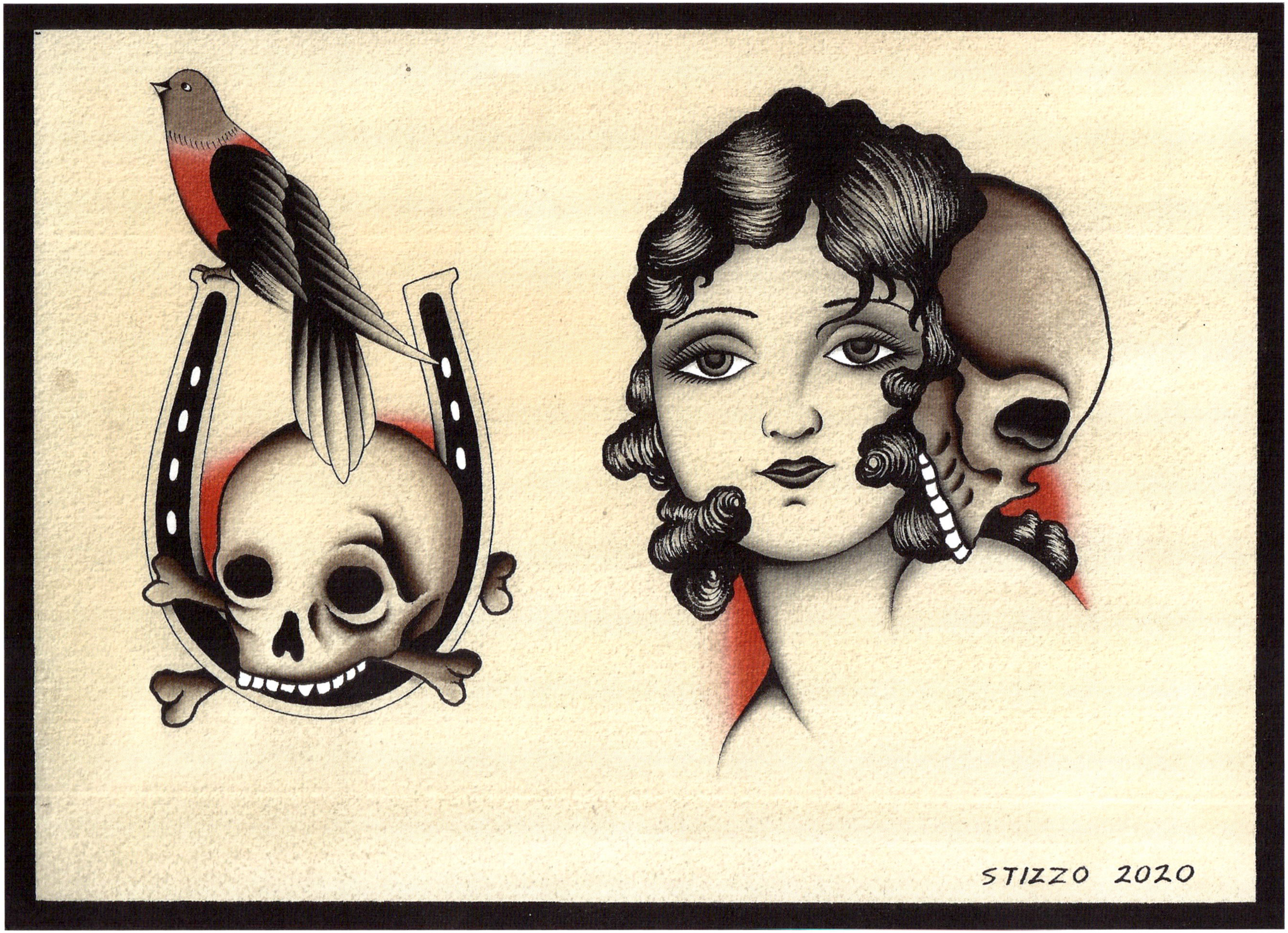

STIZZO 2020

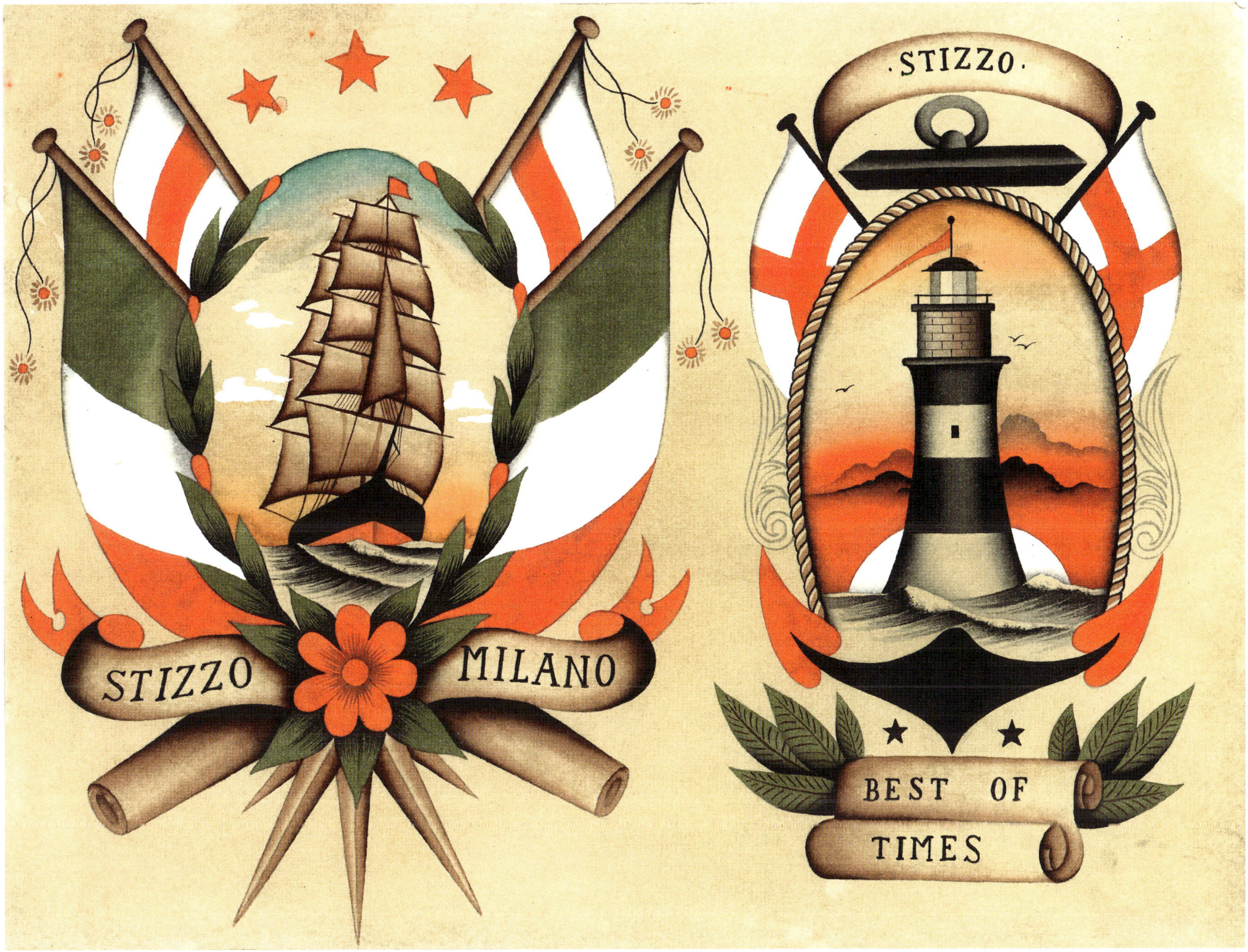

STIZZO
MILANO
STIZZO
BEST OF
TIMES

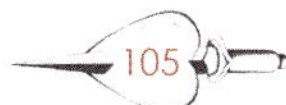

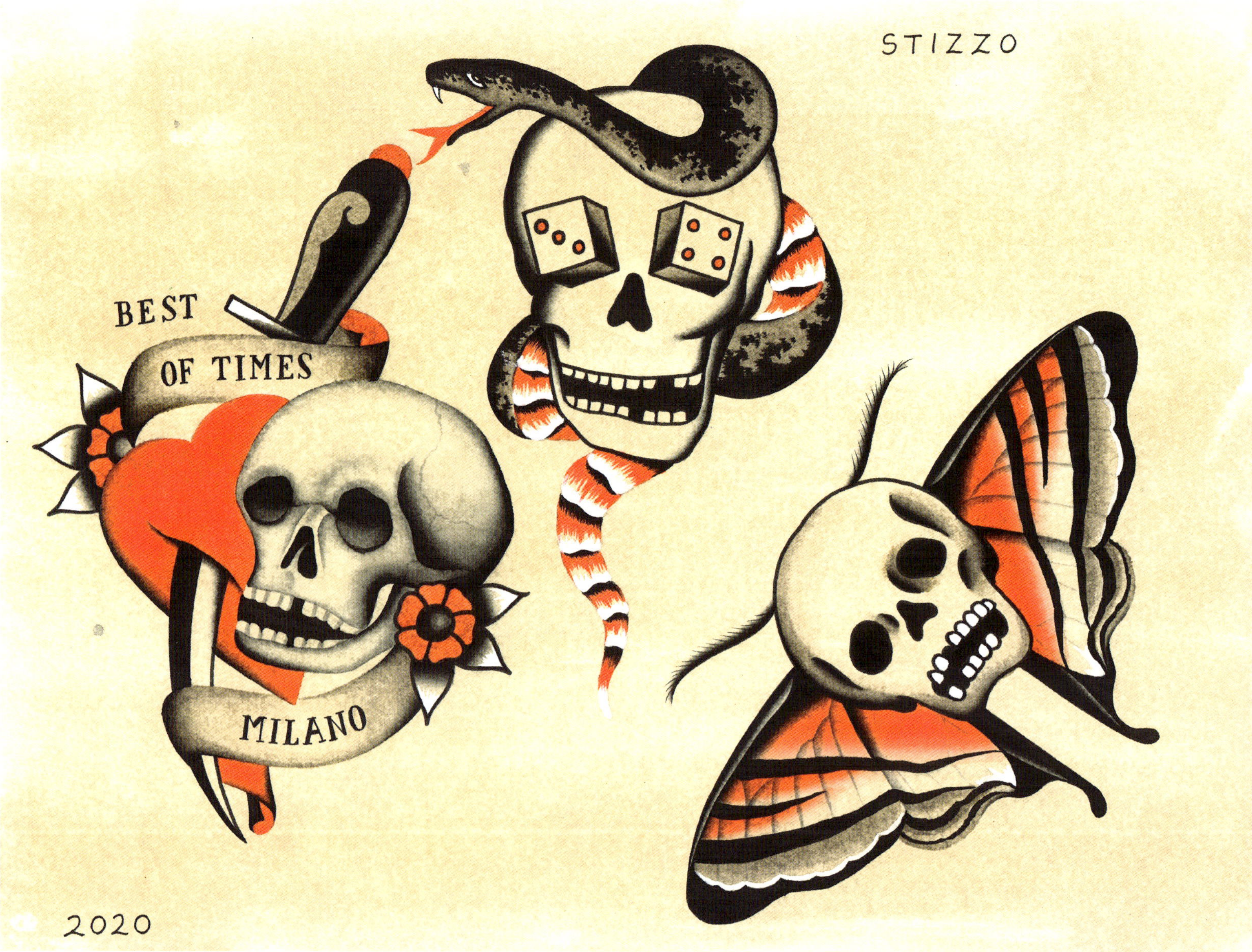

STIZZO

BEST OF TIMES

MILANO

2020

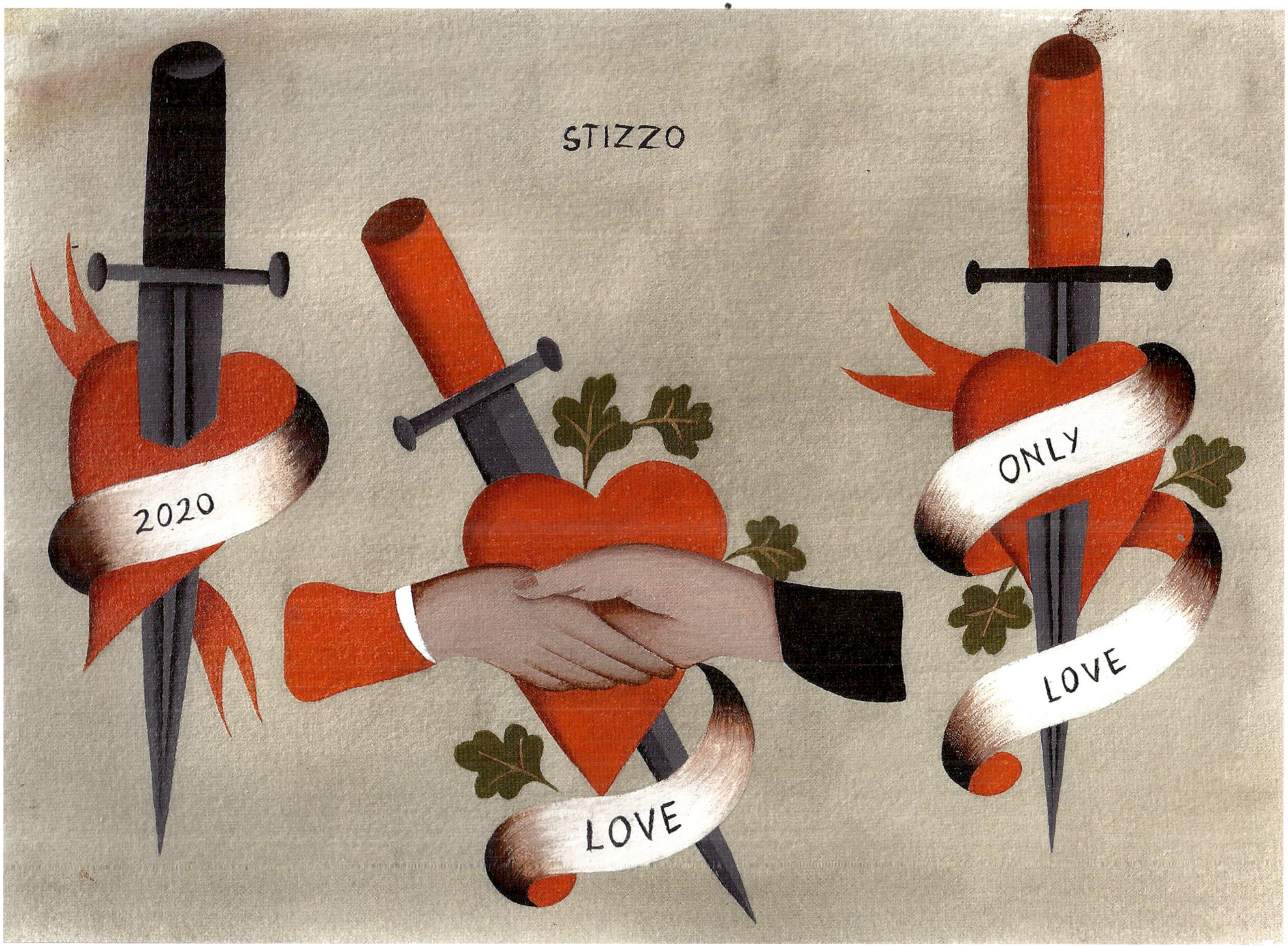

STIZZO

2020

LOVE

ONLY

LOVE

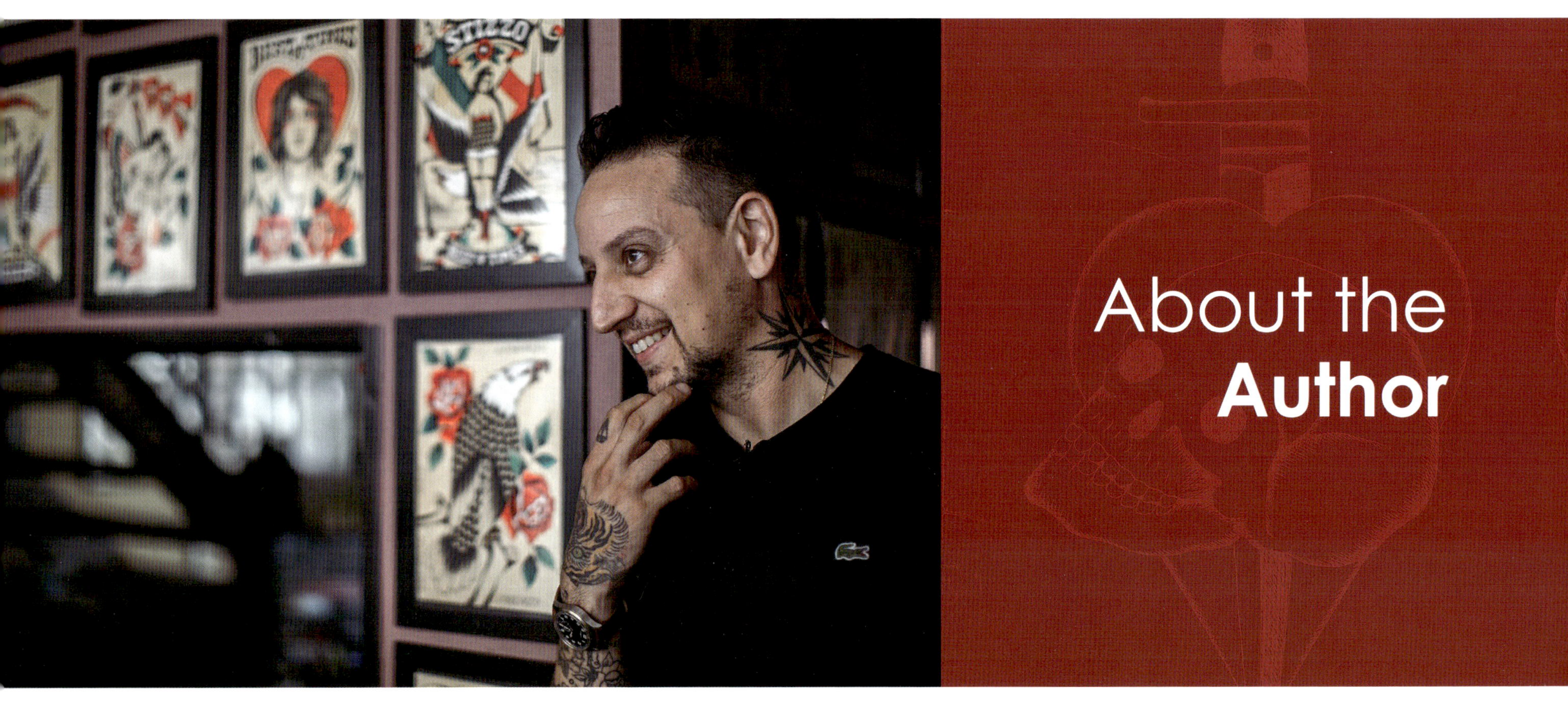

About the **Author**

Born in Milan in the spring of 1978, Stizzo entered the world of tattoos at the end of the 1990s. After learning tattoo techniques and secrets from a master who specialized in tribal and Marquesian tattoos, Stizzo improved his skills, applying all that he learned to the traditional style. After working for many tattoo shops in Milan, Stizzo decided in 2009 to open his own shop, Best of Times Tattoo, known for classic, traditional tattoos.

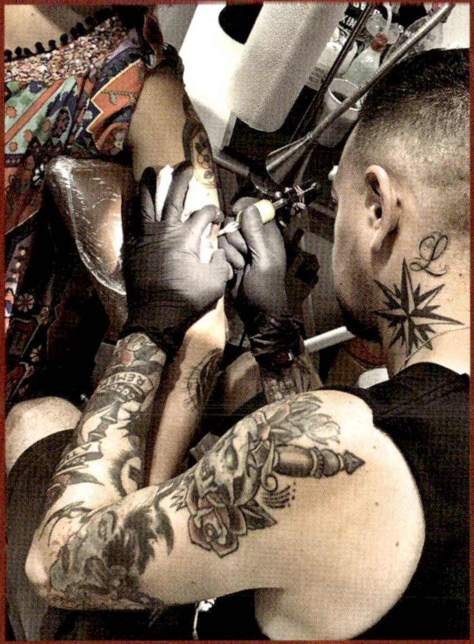

Also by the **Author**

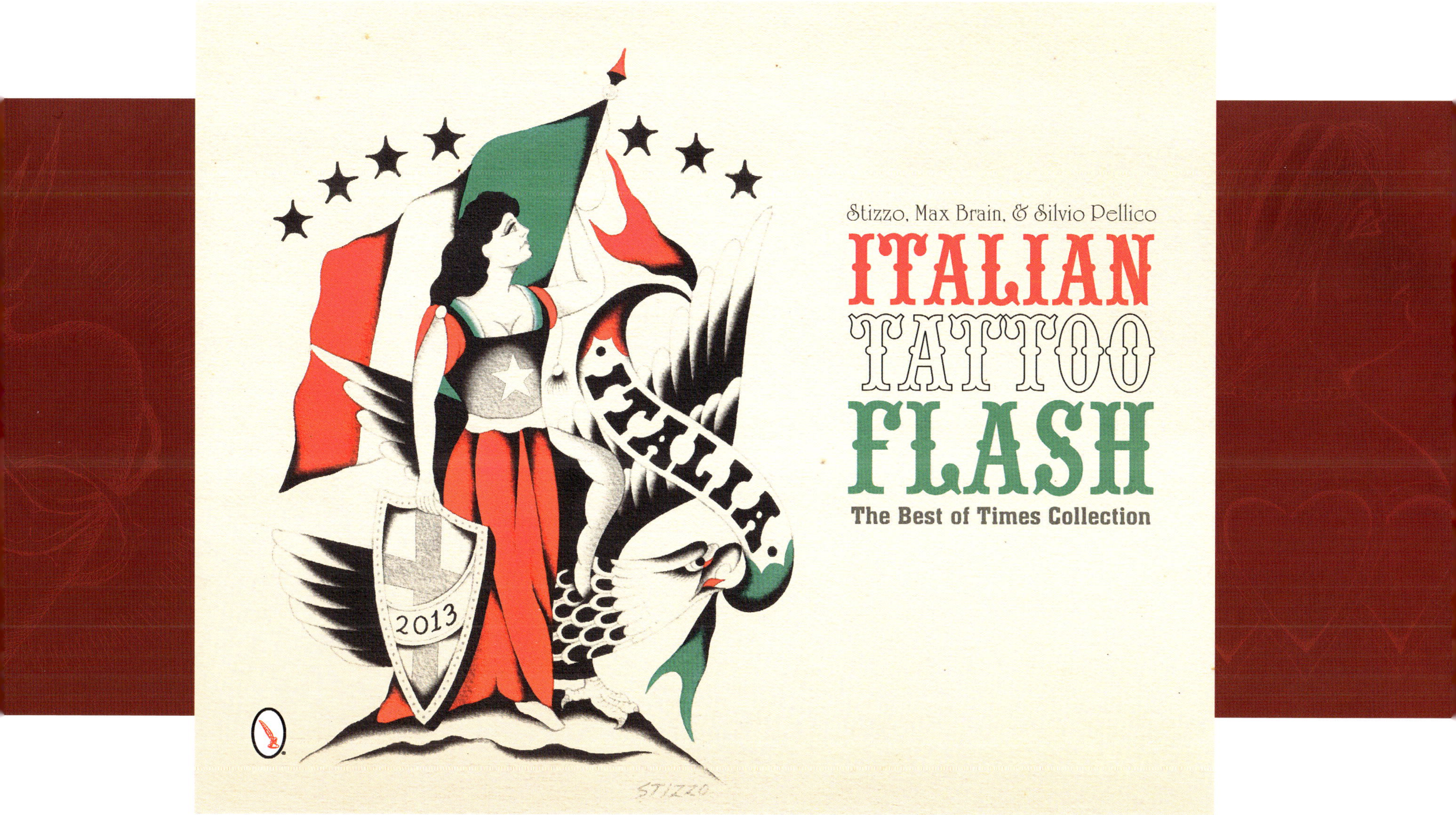

Stizzo, Max Brain, & Silvio Pellico

ITALIAN TATTOO FLASH

The Best of Times Collection

ITALIA.

2013

STIZZO

Italian Tattoo Flash: The Best of Times Collection

Authors: Stizzo, Max Brain & Silvio Pellico

ISBN 978-0-7643-4626-2

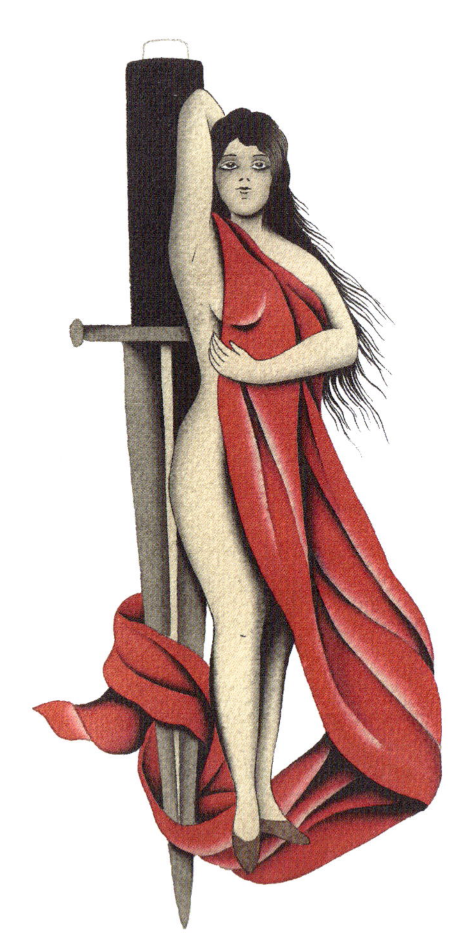

STIZZO